Winchmore Hill People an
Contents

Part 1: A New Set of Accounts from Ordinary People

Part 2: The Great and the Good

List of Illustrations

Plates between Parts 1 and 2

Ordinary Peoples' Accounts

Page

Accounts of 'The Great and The Good'

Previous 'Lives' Books revisited — Page

20th Century

Introduction

In the late 1970s, I started to read local history books, and then I attended Geoffrey Heney's local history classes on one evening a week. In 1983 I read a then recent reprint of *Recollections of Old Enfield* originally published early that century. It occurred to me that someone should collect a similar set of reminiscences of Winchmore Hill whilst there were still inhabitants who remembered the old village. Regency Press published the accounts that I collected in 1991 as *Winchmore Hill Lives (A Collection of Recollections).*

I thought that would be the end of any further oral history, as it were, of Winchmore Hill. It seemed unlikely I would meet many, if any, more 'old timers' given the amount of searching I had done to locate the contributors to the book. I was proved quite wrong, and in 2004 I self published *More Winchmore Hill Lives (A Further Collection of Recollections)*, which is still available for purchase at the time of writing. Again I thought, well that's it, now for sure there can't be any old timers left, or any other people with an interesting local tale to tell, and again I have been proved wrong.

I don't know if the public still has an appetite for these local memories, but I thought that as so many more people had taken the trouble to give me detailed accounts and old photographs, it would be a dereliction of duty not to publish them. It goes without saying that I am extremely grateful to everyone who has contributed their memories and old photographs for publication since the 1980s. Nobody has ever asked me for a penny for their time and effort. Let me here clear up a possible misconception. Most of the accounts in all my books were given by interview, with follow up correspondence, but even where they have been given entirely by letter, or succession of letters, I have often met the contributor at a later date.

What has continued to surprise me is the way in which people I had never met previously have allowed me into their house for a 'cosy chat', and perhaps a cup of tea, in an age where violent crime is far worse than when they or I were young, and people are generally more wary of each other. It has been very gratifying, although I confess that I have a bad conscience with regard to one account I took that should be in this book, but isn't. Brian Cook put me in touch with Nesta Gibbs, nee Rowe, and she expended a considerable amount of effort in not only giving me an account, but reconstructing the housing layout, and subsequent damage, following the V1 attack on Carpenter Gardens of 7th July 1944. She also loaned me a photo' of her friend Iris Chamberlain for publication. I seem to have lost these – easily my worst lapse in nearly 30 years of doing all this. My public apologies to Mrs. Gibbs, and also my readership, who have been deprived of a very informative contribution.

When I started on all this I assumed that the East End and central London were heavily bombed, but otherwise suburban London was not much affected by the two World Wars. As you read through the accounts in my 'oral history' books you realize that the local community was strongly affected. For example, older contributors had vivid memories of seeing the Zeppelin shot down over Cuffley in the summer of 1916, whilst the V1 attack on Carpenter Gardens in the summer of 1944 is etched on many peoples' minds.

The Kelly's Directory for Wades Grove for 1935 makes interesting reading. There are seven homes listed on each side of the street. On the south side at No. 1 the occupant is shown as John Wackett, at No. 7 is Leonard Pettifer (husband of Lucy), next door at No. 9 is Richard Walter Simpson, and at No.13 is Mrs. Cormell (Bob Hill's Great

Aunt). On the north side at No.2 is Jean Bilton's father Joseph Whitworth. Mrs. Irene Wood says she moved to No. 3 in 1945. I don't suppose in 1935, or 1945, anyone would have suspected that well over half a century later that all these families would have featured in either this book, or the two previous *Lives*!

I have now been browsing in London libraries and bookshops for many years and it occurs to me that my collections of accounts might be unique to the capital in recent times. They would certainly seem to be rare, at the very least. These accounts will be there for as long as there are bookshelves, and I hope that they will be of interest to future generations, long after my contributors and I have passed away.

Whilst publishing the accounts I thought it an idea to also research and present details of some of the people who have been associated with Winchmore Hill who have achieved national, or even international, fame. That section does *not* include an account of every one of the area's 'great and good'. For example, I have omitted a detailed look at the Taylor Walker family because I made a start on them in my **Winchmore Hill Village 1780 – 1830** book, and hope to write more on them in a subsequent volume. Then, apart from considerations of space, there are others who I have been unable to unearth much on. I would, for example, have been keen to include an account on Ted Ray, who I remember for the *Ray's a Laugh* radio programme of my childhood. I was very impressed when recently that grand old man of stage and screen, Ken Dodd, said that Ted was the best stand up comedian he had seen.

As usual I am grateful for the help I have received from *The Gazette*, for letting me reproduce their archive material, and John Clark and Kate Godfrey of Enfield Libraries Local Studies Unit, in Thomas Hardy House, for their assistance and use of the Unit's material. With those sources, photographs given to me by various people over the years, and my own collection of postcards, I have been able to publish a significant number of visuals in this large volume, which hopefully help to make it good value for money. They say that a picture is worth a thousand words, and I know they are popular with the public. You must remember that for the early photographs going back to Edwardian times, this is the world that various contributors over the years were born into.

There are two old maps at Figures 1 and 2 which I would refer the reader to, as I think they are a great help in following the accounts, and show at a glance how the area changed in the first half of the last century. You should remember when reading the accounts in the first part of this book that you are reading of peoples' memories, many of which will no doubt be in accord with reality. But you should bear in mind that all humans are fallible, so you mustn't take everything as cast iron historical fact until verified against other information. Nevertheless, I hope you derive as much pleasure from reading these accounts as I had in compiling them.

Stuart Delvin, 11th March 2011

P.S. I have been invited by Hugh Humphrey, who runs N21.net, to script the film he intends to bring out to mark the centenary of the first publication of Henrietta Creswell's classic book, *Winchmore Hill: Memories of a Lost Village.* Look out for this new DVD in the second half of 2012!

Part 1

The first part of this book is a collection of accounts of ordinary people, mainly secured since the publication of More Winchmore Hill Lives in 2004.

Robert 'Old Bob' Cook. At Page 108 of his 'Old' Southgate Herbert Newby identifies the site of this photograph as being the former style to the Bourne Hill entrance to Winchmore Hill Wood, marked today, approximately, by the southern start of Broad Walk. "Old Bob" came to Winchmore Hill from Suffolk. When he died in 1924 he had lived for over 50 years at No.4, Salisbury Cottages, Hoppers Road, which were also home to the Teer and Hemington families.

Jean Bilton, nee Whitworth - Interview 11th March 2005

I believe that my father was born in the old village. He was named Joseph Henry Whitworth, as opposed to his own father Joseph Edward - shown as living at 3, North Row, Vicars Moor Lane, in the 1899 – 1900 Kelly's Directory. Grandpa was cowman for Paulin on the Broadfields estate. Dad is the taller boy in the photograph at Plate 1, which also shows his brother Horace and their mother, who looked after Udall's Chapel in Vicars Moor Lane. It was presumably taken outside the family home in the 1890s. (North Row cottages are still there today, and are pictured at Plate 2.)

My mother, Mildred May Waller, was born in Saffron Walden in November 1889. She married dad on 25th December 1914 at the Baptist Church at the foot of Compton Road at a time when my mother was living at 4,Myrtle Cottage, Highfield Road. I was born in 1922 at 2, Wades Grove, which was the biggest house in that road. It is because Colin (Wackett) was a neighbour in Wades Grove that I became friendly with his family and he is sitting here chatting with us both now. (Note 1.)

When I was young Wades Grove was home to less well off families in the area, and at one time had a reputation for attracting 'undesirables', though I suggest that was undeserved. Certainly the worst poverty of those far off days can't be imagined in this age of comparative affluence and the welfare state. To supplement our income my mother took in washing, and I can remember that she put me in a pram when she used to go off to houses in Winchmore Hill Road. Nanny Haynes, who lived at No. 27, apparently came from Deptford in 1912 by wheeling her possessions in a handcart and carrying her son in her arms.

As a youngster I remember playing on The Green. Phillips the butcher in nearby Devon House used to slaughter his own sheep. Occasionally a few of these escaped onto The Green and he would have to round them up. At that time horses were still using the trough opposite *The King's Head.* I can also remember Mum giving me 2d to go round the back of the pub to get some Piccalilli. At this time Tancock ran his florist business from the shop at 5, Wades Hill, near Wades Mews, but I used to take a jug to fetch a pint of milk from the rear of his house – which was the first one north in the Georgian row nearby. I have never understood why Mum got her milk from him rather than Nix's dairy!

At this time the mansion on the corner of Broad Walk and The Green, called The Limes, was still there. It had a colonial look to it, with shutters and a veranda. Like Colin I remember it being taken over by the Red Cross in the 1950s, not long before it was pulled down.

I can remember there being plenty of snow when I was young. Once we made a giant snowball, which we wheeled into the doorway of Tidey's at the corner of Hoppers Road and The Green, and prevented him getting out, as he was only a small man.

I remember the Muffin Man coming round on a Sunday. There was also a winkle man, whilst knife grinders travelled the streets touting for business. Chalkley's delivered hot bread on a Friday evening. At the rear of the main premises to Chalkley's bakery was another shop, also run by a Chalkley, the premises remaining today. It sold a variety of things, from broken biscuits to corn. I was told it was an old farmhouse. Downes on The Green was also a corn merchant then, of course, before he turned to coal.

At the base of Church Hill was Regnart's Stone Hall Estate. I found Mr. Regnart a little frightening for some inexplicable reason, but the estate was lovely. When it became vacant in the early 1930s I went there to explore and play with other children. Beautiful rhododendrons formed a walk and there was a variety of vegetable beds, including asparagus. There was also an array of fruit trees, including peaches. There were stables, but not any horses that I can remember, though there obviously must have been in Mr. Regnart's time there.

Incidentally another adult who scared me at this time was a Scotsman who went around The Green playing the bagpipes. He and they so scared me that I used to run home and, to this day, I cannot stand the sound of pipes!

I used to go to the Rialto in Enfield for Saturday morning pictures, where they usually showed cowboy pictures. If we were scared we hid under the seats! There was sometimes a sing-a-long. Admission was 6d.

Also on The Green was a man who was a Black Shirt at the start of the War. Strangely enough he even looked like Hitler! His family was actually quite nice and his wife was a good cook. Anyway, when the locals found out about his sympathies, as they did in due course, he had to leave the area.

When I was 14 I started work at Mummery's, which was the first shop down from the railway bridge on the south side of Station Road. I was an apprentice on the top floor in the curtain and upholstery department, earning 7/6d per week. Of this I gave Mum 5/- and kept 2/6d. Of that half a crown I would spend, say, 1/- on something like stockings, 9d on the cinema, leaving me with 9d in hand. Mrs. Knowles, wife of 'Ossie', who owned the business premises at the southern corner of Wades Hill and Wades Grove, was manageress at the shop and, to be honest, she was a bit of a tartar. Through her I left in a huff, about the time that war broke out, and I joined Chalkley's bakeries. Unfortunately I fell out with them too and ended up at the telephone company STC, which was then based at Bowes Park. I did piece work on making coils until the end of the war.

My late husband Peter had been a reconnaissance Spitfire pilot in the RAF, once having bailed out over Italy. Most of the training was carried out in Canada. He was discharged late in the War and we married in 1946, the reception being at St. Paul's Institute, where my Aunt Lucy and Uncle Art (Price) were caretakers. (See Plates 57 & 58.) I became a housewife and Peter started as a cashier in North Met House, Wood Green, for £4 a week. He left for Hoovers and worked as a salesman for them for many years.

We began married life in the Hadley Hall flats just off Hoppers Road, behind the *Salisbury Arms*. Then we moved to Drayton Gardens, then Grange Park Avenue, then to my current address, in Vicars Moor Lane, in 1988. My daughter Denise, who still lives in the area, was born in 1949, and my son Adrian in 1958.

You ask me when money seemed to go furthest. Now I think. As to when the area was at its most pleasant to live in? I tend to agree with Colin that the area was probably in its prime in the late 1950s. By then people were comparatively comfortable, there was still a family atmosphere, and there was very little crime.

Author's Notes

1. *The listing for Wades Grove in the 1932 Kelly's Directory is as follows –*
   South Side: Knowles, Oscar S. motor engineer at 10, Wades Hill (i.e. the corner), then 1 Wackett, John; 3 Briggs, Mrs. C.H. cost. mr.; 5 Roberts, Geo; 7 Pettifer, Leonard; 9 Simpson, Rd. Wltr.; 11 Cornelius, John; 13 Cormell, Mrs.

   North Side: 2 Whitworth, Joseph Hy; 4 Easton, William Arthur; 6 Kelsey, William Charles; 8 Slade, Alfd. Ernest; 10 Dee, Mrs.; 12 Englefield, Albt. Victor; 14 Boniface, Mrs.

2. *I would like to thank Jean for not only talking to me, but also supplying a pleasant light lunch for Colin and myself.*

Eddie Bolton (1930 - 2008)

Although I have never been a member of any political Party I have often attended UKIP meetings, and it was there that I met Eddie, though I was never friendly with him in the way that I was with John Lyon. Eddie's quiet unglamorous life probably paralleled that of many other Winchmore Hill residents over the years.

In July 2004 Eddie told me that he was the nephew of Bolton, the former Chemist on the Green. His family once had a greengrocer's shop on the corner of Westbury Avenue by Turnpike Lane. He told me that he came to live in Winchmore Hill in 1936 and spent five years in the RAF before moving to Canada. He returned here in 1968, but he regretted this.

The Southgate District Civic Trust Newsletter of January 2009 carried Peter Hodge's brief obituary of Eddie, who had been an enthusiastic member for some years, being particularly passionate about tree preservation. He was heavily involved in the fight against Dutch Elm Disease in the early 1970s and had been distressed at the more recent loss of trees in the local railway cutting. One of his contributions to the work of the Trust was as a distributor of its Newsletters.

All Eddie's years in Winchmore Hill had been spent at the same house in Roseneath Avenue. He had been a cabinet maker by trade, and had undertaken work for many local organisations, including St. Paul's School and Winchmore Hill Baptist Church. Eddie belonged to the League against Cruel Sports and the Royal Society for the Protection of Birds in addition to, as previously noted, the United Kingdom Independence Party (UKIP).

Peter concluded his piece by saying, 'He was a kind and modest man – trustworthy and well informed – but a man of strong views and unafraid to express them. Eddie was a familiar figure in the locality – he walked everywhere – and will be missed by all who knew him.' In a sense Eddie was a 'Mr. Everyman' of Winchmore Hill.

Sergeant Walter C. Burch

The front page of *The Recorder for Palmers Green, Winchmore Hill and Southgate* of 9th September 1915 bore the headline, '120 Degrees in the Shade. Warmer than "Dear Old Winchmore Hill"'. It ran, 'We have received another welcome letter from

Sergeant Burch, of the Herts. Yeomanry, who, with other Winchmore Hill men, is helping to keep open our "short cut" to India and the Far East, via the Suez Canal. Incidentally, they have been qualifying as salamanders, for, in the course of his letter, Sergeant Burch refers to a temperature of 120 degrees in the shade. This, no doubt, throws some light on the interesting photo he sends and on his statement that it illustrates "a fairly common occurrence".

There is a touch of pathos in his reference to "dear old Winchmore Hill". When the war is over the sight of its verdant beauties should indeed be welcome after the arid sands of Egypt, and we are sure the reception which will be given to our local heroes will gladden their hearts. Britishers are not emotional, and seldom wear their hearts on their sleeves, but underneath a reserved demeanour there is much sincere feeling. The letters from our local men who are manfully shouldering the burden of Empire abroad are read with deep interest by many outside the circle of their own acquaintances, for, while we value the services of all our brave soldiers, we take a special pride in those who represent our own district, and have in many cases left those they love to watch and wait for the safe return which we wish them. Sergeant Burch writes:

'"D" Squadron, 1st Herts. Yeomanry, British Forces, Egypt. Dear Sir, In the words of the song, "Here We Go Again", still going strong. Since my last letter we have been swimming horses over the Nile at the Barrage. Perhaps a description of the Brigade Competition would interest your readers.

The squadron was drawn up in squadron column about 50 yards from the bank, each man knowing exactly what he had to do. The Brigadier started us. Certain men took the "built up ropes" (ropes four feet long, having a loop at one end and a toggle at the other, so that a long rope is easily made up), rushed to the water's edge, and made an endless rope. Other men removed saddles and put them in lines by the water, while eight men launched the raft made of a tarpaulin filled with straw.

A boat had meanwhile gone over to the other side, taking a line with it, in the centre of which the raft is fixed. The raft then goes to and fro, taking first the endless rope, then men and saddles. The endless rope being across the river with the necessary men at each end, i.e. pullers, tiers, untiers, and cutters (in case the knot jams), the horses are led in single file, tied on to the rope , the rope goes round, they are untied, taken away by men, saddled up; finally the built up rope is pulled over, taken to pieces, and we are off. "D" Squadron made the record for our Brigade by swimming 92 horses in 42 minutes.

Just recently a detachment from the squadron have been to Abu Zabal guarding the wireless station there. It is quite an outpost of our Empire, and I regret that I am unable to give you any details, as there may still be some spies about.

I enclose a photo of a fairly common occurrence in the camp. From left to right the photo shows Lance Corporal Schultz, Corporal Dykes, Lance Corporal Carroll, Lance – Sergeant Carroll, Sergeant Burch, and Corporal Eastwell. (See Plate 3.)

I understand that you have had fairly hot weather in June. We had to put up with 120 degrees in the shade for three or four days in June. Trusting all is well with dear old Winchmore Hill. I remain, Sir, Yours very sincerely Walter C. Burch, Sergeant No. 2 Troop.'

The Recorder of 10th February 1916 featured a further letter from Sergeant

Burch of B Squadron, Herts. Yeomanry, from Matruh, Egypt to the Editor of *The Recorder* dated 2nd January 1916. It read as follows,

'Dear Sir, I spent a Christmas Day that will live in my memory for a long time. When we were supposed to be celebrating Peace on Earth we were on several occasions in the midst of bullets. The Sennussi tribe had a camp about seven miles away, and a strong force from here left camp at 5 a.m. – i.e. before dawn – the infantry marching direct at the enemy and the cavalry making a detour, No. 2 (Enfield Troop) being escort to two guns of those we have here. We got right round the back of the enemy before they noticed us, when we heard our advance cavalry in action, and one or two bullets came over towards us. Then the guns were ordered into action, so over the brow of the hill we dashed and halted 100 yards from the top. The bullets started to hum round us a bit; then one section was ordered to dismount in a gully close to the guns, and I took the remainder of the troop back as guard over the limbers; it all took a very short time.

As we went over the hill a terrific bang went off. I thought it was a shell, but it was our first gun fired with grand effect into the middle of the enemy. They soon retired, followed by shrapnel, so we took the horses back, and went on soon after. We came to a bit of a dip where we waited for a time while the cavalry advance went on, dismounted action. Then we went on again; more bullets over us, and then drove the enemy away with more shrapnel. All becoming quiet, we fed the horses and ourselves. We then turned left, and made a sweeping movement and tried to drive the enemy on to our infantry, which we succeeded in doing.

Turning right again, we made towards the sea. We were on the left flank of the guns in extended order, halted, when the enemy about 1,000 yards away started a devilish fire, and there was nothing else to do but to dismount for action. So away the boys went to the left. I had to take the led horses to the right into a gulley 300 yards away, and I can tell you that – the horses being a good mark – they sent plenty of lead round our ears; several came jolly close to us, and the ground was continually being knocked up by bullets. However, I got all the men and horses safely away, and a whole regiment of Australians dismounted and let off at the enemy with the result that it was all over in ten minutes.

We got a signal to return to camp then, so off we went, and arrived back at 7 p.m., all of us feeling dead beat. Major – says that it is only due to Providence there were no casualties in our regiment at all and only one horse slightly wounded. Well, we are the first squadron of ours to go into action as cavalry and we have come out of it with flying colours, so we were more or less told.

On December 28th we suddenly got an order at 11.30 a.m. that we were to move off at 1.15, so we had to work and get ready, but we did it, and a good mixed force went off at 2 p.m. We were right flank guard. Marched to ---, arrived there without any incident, shackled down our ponies, wrapped our saddle blanket round us, stuck our heads in the insides of our saddles, our feet in our horses' nosebags, munched a biscuit and went to sleep.

December 29th – Up at 4.15 a.m., marched off at 5.30, and found that the enemy must have learnt of our presence and had gone off in haste, although infantry, who had gone the other way round so as to get them in a circle, came on their camps, which they burnt up; they found the chief's cave, with carpets, tables, chairs, papers relating to Germans, & c. Well, before long there were fires all over the place. We got all their sheep and camels, and two prisoners, so you see we have inflicted a great loss on them. I think after their Christmas present they have bunked off.

I hope before very long that I shall once again see the green fields of Winchmore Hill, and it will be a treat not to have the glare of the sun. I don't suppose the old village will have altered much; anyhow I shall be truly thankful to see dear old Winchmore Hill again after eighteen months' absence. With kindest regards. Believe me, Yours very sincerely, (Sergeant) Walter C. Burch.'

The Chalkleys (and the Old Bakery)

Station Road Preamble

Horace Regnart was born in 1875, and moved to the village, aged 3, in 1878. At P80 of his book *Memories of Winchmore Hill* he tells us that Holly Cottage was the home of the bakers and confectioners, Mr. and Mrs. Binstead. At his P79 is an old photo' for which the caption reads, 'Holly Cottage and the Shop, once Chalkley's, in Middle Lane'. (Station Road was called Middle Lane in Victorian times.)

At P7 of *More Winchmore Hill Lives* Mrs. Claire Dougal, nee Hollingsworth, says, 'Until at least 1916 an old man by the name of Waters had a little house and shop opposite *The Queen's Head* in Station Road. He sold home made jam and pickles as well as brown china tea pots. My grandmother was a regular customer there. Miss Cresswell makes mention of Waters in her *Memories of a Lost Village*, when Station Road was sometimes referred to as "Waterses Lane". I presume this was the same family that had, over the years, moved over the road from a site adjoining the Inn.'

As a footnote to Mrs. Dougal's account I reproduced a *Palmers Green and Southgate Gazette* obituary by Arthur Willis ('Memorabilia') for James Waters, upon his death aged 95 in November 1939. It started, 'Sadly and wistfully I have to record the passing of my old friend, James Waters, who was born on September 19th 1844, at his parents' grocer's shop and residence, Middle Lane, Winchmore Hill; later the little building became No. 41 Station Road until it was demolished and the eastern end of the *Queen's Head Hotel* was erected on the site....'

At Page 9 of *More Winchmore Hill Lives*, accompanying Mrs. Dougal's account, is an old photo' from an undated *Gazette* which the newspaper had titled, 'Mr. James Water's grocer's shop, Station Road, from a photograph, period 1870-5.' The paper's caption tells us that the wording on the shop window was 'Baker', and that, 'the shop was occupied by one Richens, the predecessor of the late Mr. Chalkley (senior) at that shop. Mrs. Binstead (nee Udall) is seen standing at the gate of her cottage garden ....'. Mrs. Binstead was in the foreground.

At P44 of her *Memories of a Lost Village* Henrietta Cresswell, who was born in 1855, talks glowingly of the Waters' little shop adjoining *The Queen's Head.* In his books on the Borough's pubs Gary Boudier tells us that the inn was rebuilt only in the mid 1930s, so in my notes accompanying *The Gazette* photo' at P9 of *More Winchmore Hill Lives* I wrote, 'The near premises are obviously the shop and the white building behind it is therefore, surely, *The Queen's Head* in its previous guise.' This is wrong.

The photo' at P9 of *More Winchmore Hill Lives* is in fact identical to the one on P79 of Regnart's book, and I now (belatedly) realise that the nearest building is therefore what for years was known as Holly Cottage, the Bakers building past it being what was later Chalkleys. My apologies for not realising all this in 2004! I now also see the photograph's similarity to the one at P44 of my 2001 *A Look at Old Winchmore Hill.* That photo' was taken in about 1930, looking down Station Road, with the station on the left. The first building past the station (still on the left), bears a strong resemblance to Holly Cottage at P9 of *More Winchmore Hill Lives* of 2004. At this book's Plate 4 is another view of Holly Cottage, and the reader will immediately see the resemblance to the snaps in the previous publications.

At P42 of her *Memories of a Lost Village,* Miss Cresswell tells us quite a bit about a shop belonging to the Binste(a)ds in about 1860. She says that, '....On the north side of the pond on the green was a pathway known as the 'Trap Gates', or sometimes as the 'Clappers'.....First there was a high, quickset hedge, then a few cottages standing back in long gardens where cabbages and potatoes received more attention than floriculture, and at the end of the row the shop of Mr. and Mrs. Binsted, Bakers and Confectioners .... On the counter in the shop, among the sweet smelling loaves of new bread, stood a squirrel's cage with a wheel, which he spun rapidly with much apparent enjoyment ...'.

For some while I thought that this must be one of the premises in the afore mentioned photographs, but early in 2011 I came across an article in the Local Studies Unit's many scrapbooks which has stopped me from falling into that trap. I'm not sure what local title the following snippet is from, but it is dated 10th August 1928:- ' "W. Binstead, Genuine Bread and Biscuit Maker, Corn Dealer, etc. Winchmore Hill" has its interest. His shop stood on the site of the Winchmore Hill railway station, frontage in Middle Lane (Station Road), and it was his own property; he had no personal practical knowledge of the baking trade, being a draper's assistant, and he worked for Udall and Childs, and married Mrs. Child's sister (nee Udall). When they were out together his wife habitually walked about three yards ahead of him. The shop was demolished in 1869 to make the railway cutting, the compensation being sufficiently ample to enable him to build Binsted's cottages at the rear of Carter Page's conservatory (next the station), in addition to which he sold the goodwill of his business to Mr. Richens, who occupied the premises of the present veteran, Mr. James Waters. Years afterwards Mr. Richens removed into London, and was later killed in a road accident, when the late Mr. Chalkley succeeded to the business, ultimately removing it to the centuries old wooden farmhouse in Hoppers Road.'

Binsted's Cottages were a terrace of three, set back from the roadway and at right angles to it (i.e. parallel to the railway), immediately east of the railway station. They were captured in the 1895 O.S. Survey, and logged in the 1899 – 1900 Kelly's Street Directory. The late builder, Ewan Lewis, gave me a photograph of the cottages as they were when he was about to demolish them. (See Plate 5.)

Given this latest 1928 press clipping I now feel inclined to suggest that the facing pictures at pages 43 and 44 of my *A Look at Old Winchmore Hill* both show Holly Cottage to the viewer's left. In the case of the 20th century picture (P44) Winchmore Hill Station comes before it, whereas in the 1850-60 likeness (P43) I believe we are looking at the row of cottages containing the *old* Binstead shop that Miss Cresswell describes, before we come to Holly Cottage.

At P170 of **Winchmore Hill Village 1780 – 1830** is a map of the area between what are now Station Road and Vicars Moor Lane at the time the common fields and marshes were enclosed under an 1800 Act of Parliament. The map was made in 1801-2, and the field system where the railway line now runs can still be recognised in the 1895 O.S. Map. The railway station was built on Jacob Harvey's 1801/2 one acre Green Man Field, which soon fell into the possession of Joseph Osborn(e), who already owned tenements at the SE corner of the field.

It would seem that what for some years was known as Holly Cottage, rested on the site of Osborn(e)'s tenements, suggesting that the shop and cottage there may well have once been Osborn(e)'s property. In the David Hicks Archives lodged with the Local Studies Unit at Thomas Hardy House is a paper by David which says these properties, 'were situated whereon formerly stood the *Green Man* Public House. They survived the coming of the railway, which sliced through Green Man Field ...' *The Green Man* was known as late as 1773. I don't know where David got his information from.

At P83 of his *Fond Memories of Winchmore Hill* Alan Dumayne says that the premises we are talking of were demolished in 1963, but for once I am not sure that Alan got it right. In the Hicks Archives is a photograph of the Binstead/Waters shop (hiding Holly Cottage) in October 1972. I moved to nearby Radcliffe Road in November 1972, and I can remember Milton Lodge being constructed on the site in the Spring of 1973, encountering a hedgehog on the building site one night when returning from the pub!

Having (hopefully) sorted out my previous confusion, let us move onto an account of the Chalkley family, who have been mentioned by so many contributors to my 'oral history' series.

The Chalkley family

In his 1952 book Regnart says, 'Stern (probably Richens) sold the business to Mr. Chalkley's grandfather about 1880 or soon after. He used a pony and trap for delivering the bread, and many a time I saw Mr. Chalkley's father, then a boy of nine or ten, helping with the delivery. Now Chalkley's have a smart motor van. The other day I shook hands with Mr. Chalkley's small daughter, so I have now known four generations of the family. Another baker, Goldsworthy, had the old wooden shop in Hoppers Road. He was also a corn merchant. We used to go there with our governess to buy the food for our fowls. Goldsworthy had a long red beard. When he died, Chalkley bought his business and gave up the shop in Middle Lane which was taken by Press as a newsagent's ....'

It seems Press was followed by Waters sometime before the 1899-1900 Kelly's Directory was prepared, because it lists Mrs. Binsted as being the occupant of Holly Cottage, whilst James Water, grocer, is listed as the next occupant going east. Meanwhile at the top of Hoppers Road we have 'Chalkley Thos. & Son, bkrs.'.

The following is information that the Chalkley family has kindly supplied in letters to me, along with some very welcome old photographs. (See Plates 6-10 inc.) I am particularly indebted to Margaret Johnson, nee Chalkley, although she herself was not raised in the area. Margaret says that it was her Great Grandfather Thomas (1844 – 1921), with his wife Eliza (1845 – 1914), who started the business in Middle Lane, probably in about 1880, as Regnart suggests. Thomas was the fourth youngest of nine children born to James Chalkley (b. 1815) and Ann Watson (b. 1811). (After Ann died James married Ruth Bunyan, a widow with no children of her own, who took on the nine children!) Thomas married Eliza Fletcher on 15th January 1872, his occupation on the marriage certificate being shown as 'baker', as was his father's. The photograph of

Chalkley's in Hoppers Road at P140 of my Winchmore Hill Village 1780 – 1830 bears a shop front inscription suggesting that the business was started in 1801 (though outside our village), so presumably James's father was a baker too.

Thomas and Eliza had nine children – Wilfred Fletcher (1872 – 1941), Florence (1874 – 1934), Lillie (1876 – 1933), Gertrude (1878 – 1955), Doris (aka Ethel; 1880 – 1938, born in Barking), Percival (1882 – 1919, born in Winchmore Hill), Archibald (1884 – 1952), Reginald (1885 – 1934), and Ralph (1888 – 1918). Margaret sent me a copy of the Commonwealth War Graves Commission entry for Ralph's death in battle on 5th January 1918, though his age is erroneously given as only 25. It is clear from the birthplaces given for Doris and Percival, that the Chalkley's move from Barking to our village took place in the period 1880 – 1882.

The first born, Wilfred Fletcher, who was Margaret's Grandfather, married Emily Morris in September 1905 (see Plate 6), with his and his fathers' occupations both being listed as 'baker'. Emily had no occupational status, but her father William Morris was listed as a baker. They were married at Ninfield in Sussex and had five children – Wilfred b 1906, Harold b. 1907, Gordon b. 1909 (Margaret's father), Ruth b. 1915, and Winifred b. 1916. (See Plate 7.) It was Harold who took on the business from Wilfred Fletcher and Emily, and he married Doris Stockton, daughter of the nearby butcher's. Harold's son, John Harold, has, at cousin Margaret's prompting, also supplied me with information.

Margaret's father Gordon was born at 11, Compton Terrace, but by the 1911 Census Wilfred and Emily had moved to 63, Hoppers Road, with Wilfred's occupation listed as Manager. They had a servant girl of 17 it seems. Margaret thinks they moved to live in the farmhouse and bakery in the 1920s, after Great Grandfather Thomas died. Margaret's brother Allan, who was born in the village in 1928, remembered his parents living there in the 1930s, so Harold and his family were presumably still there at the time. Margaret's parents left the area in 1939, Margaret being born in Worcester in 1940. Margaret's mother died in 2008, at the remarkable age of 100 years and six months.

The Palmers Green and Southgate Gazette of 13th August 1921 reported, 'Death of Mr. Chalkley. By the death of Mr. Thomas Chalkley, which took place on Monday afternoon after a long illness, the district loses one of its most respected inhabitants. Mr. Chalkley came to Winchmore Hill over 40 years since to succeed Mr. Binstead, who for many years carried on the business of baker and confectioner at the premises now occupied by Mr. James Waters, grocer and provision merchant, Station-road. After a few years he acquired the business of Mr. Goldsworthy at Hoppers – road, where he had since carried on a prosperous and increasing trade aided by his sons.

For the past few years he had been in failing health, which was brought about by the grief which he suffered by the death of one of his sons who was killed in the great war. He was amongst the oldest tradesmen in the village. A man of unobtrusive, kindly manner, he was greatly respected by his neighbours.'

I covered the history of the bakery in Winchmore Hill Village 1780 – 1830. (See Plates 10 & 11.) I reported in there that *The Southgate District Council Guide* for 1922 carried an advert placed by W.F. Chalkley at Page 68 headed, 'Ye Olde Village Bakerie', which claimed the building was then reputed to be about eight hundred years old, the heavy hewn, irregular oaken beams of the frame - work being fastened together with stout oak pins, the oak being so hard that it resisted all nails.

At P151 of his 1996, *Enfield - Portrait of a London Borough,* Matthew Eccleston told us that the bakery once had a garden facing onto The Green, but this disappeared when the present shops, Nos. 17-21, were built sometime between 1881 and 1891, the corner one being occupied for some years by the Chalkleys. This parade has sometimes been called Devonshire Place. In the David Hicks Archives, mentioned earlier, is a paper by David saying of Compton Terrace, 'In 1885 John James Butson took a 99 year lease on a piece of ground facing the Green and bordering Hoppers Road, the railway and Roseville. It included the farmhouse and the barn yard, but not the big barn. He built the terrace on the barn yard.' (Butson had bought Woodside House, now on Broad Walk, in 1883.)

Allan Chalkley has said that he can remember his Grandmother, Emily Chalkley, pumping water up from the well in the cellar, to the kitchen. Alan Dumayne later saw the well and wrote that it was of pure water, with the level rarely deviating more than a few inches below the basement floor. Margaret's brother also remembered there being a separate room where the cakes and pastries were made. He recalled sitting with David, his younger brother (by 3 ½ years), at the loft doors in the mornings, watching the horses pulling the bread delivery vans out of the stable yard. Apparently there were four horses. Margaret's brother said that their Grandmother ran a small teashop in the farmhouse for a short while, but it was principally a grocery shop. It was eventually closed, and used as a store room, with the groceries moving to the corner shop.

Incidentally, with regard to the corner shop, this was not part of the Chalkley holding when the family first moved to the old bakery. The London Joint Stock is shown as being on the corner of The Green in the 1903-4 Kelly's Street Directory, managed by A.H. Cox. It was still there at the time of the 1909-10 Kelly's Directory, and I am not sure when the Chalkley clan took the building over as their corner shop.

When Wilfred Fletcher died in 1941, Harold and Doris, later on aided by their son John, took on the running of the business up until the early 1960s, but they stopped baking before then. Alan Dumayne tells us that the family's corner shop continued to operate throughout the wartime years, 'with an ever cheerful Mrs. Chalkley coping with our demands for bread and cakes'. Alan says that the bakehouse ceased to operate from about 1945, and for some years served as an antiques shop.

Harold's son John writes, 'I can remember helping in the bakery as a child. At one time we had four horses stabled there, and we delivered bread and cakes over a very large area, extending, for example, as far as Grange Park and Southgate. I can recall a number of other traders associated with The Green, which other contributors have no doubt mentioned, such as Grouts the drapers, Bolton's the chemist, Westoby's the Estate Agent, Tidey's the Newsagent, and the two butchers, Davis and Stockton. George Nix the milkman had several horse rounds, whilst near Wades Hill was Paterson and Young's General Store and Post Office. This had a small sorting office attached, and several telegram boys used to deliver from here on their bikes. I continued in the business until 1960, a couple of years before it was closed down, upon my father's retirement. The reason we had to cease being a baker was the advent of sliced bread, which undercut us on price.'

The loft doors, where flour used to be pulled up, were still there in a visit Margaret made to the old farmhouse in 2010. Margaret saw the old bread oven, presumably the more recent of the two Alan Dumayne described in his book. Alan saw evidence of the old original oven, with its curved and domed walls, and observed that there is a more recent oven bearing the clear inscription of 'J.C. 1822'. At the rear Alan saw the old stables and straw house.

The 'J.C. of 1822' was probably John Catchpool, baker & corn dealer, nephew of John Decka, who, when the Edmonton Enclosure Map was drawn up in 1801/2, owned the plot of land containing the old mansion of *Roseville* and the nearby bakehouse. Both men were Quakers, as was Lydia, wife of John the baker. John was a major beneficiary of Decka's Will, and presumably he inherited both *Roseville* and the bakehouse at Decka's death in 1820.

At P34 of my 1991 *Winchmore Hill Lives* I recorded, with regard to the now disappeared *Roseville*, that, 'However, a part of the old grounds remain in the form of the wall and "shed" on the western boundary to the flats (built on the site of the old mansion). The wall bears a plaque inscribed, "J.R. 1830", the "J.R." presumably denoting John Radford. At the south end of the wall the "shed" bears a plaque inscribed "J.C. B.G. 1831".' One assumes that the J.C. is the same J.C. - John Catchpool - as for the bakery oven in 1822. Could the B.G. be the William Gates listed as a plasterer in the 1826 Pigot's Directory?

We know that in 1830 Radford bought *Roseville* and grounds from Catchpool, or a successor, with Catchpool retaining the bakery and adjoining strip along Hoppers Lane, a wall being erected between the two men's holdings. Henrietta Cresswell (b.1855), tells us that at one time the Quaker couple Mr. and Mrs. Burns had the bakehouse, and that they were preceded by 'the two Miss Catchpoles'. However, it seems likely that the Catchpool family retained at least some of their plot for over a hundred years.

At the London Metropolitan Archives is a set of papers (ACC 1016/224 – 232) concerning, 'Edmonton Manor. 1 -12, Compton Terrace and 1 – 3, Devonshire Place, Winchmore Hill.' Devonshire Place is the small parade of shops on The Green mentioned earlier as having been built between 1881 and 1891. The papers explain that the properties had formed the estate of the late Miss Catchpool, who had died in 1926 at the age of 84, and she had left them to her nieces Grace Mary Young and Francis Maud Young. Although Butson sub leased and built on the land, and the Chalkleys lived on it, the Catchpools seem to have retained the original lease direct from the Lord of the Manor.

Brian Cook - Interviews 29th June, 31st August & letter 24th August 2005

The Gladwins

I am very much a 'local boy' and I have recently been doing much 'digging' in the Palmers Green Local History Unit to uncover more clearly my links with the old village through my 'Gladwin' lineage. I am pleased to tell you that I have unearthed the following little story. I suggest you put my direct line in itaelics for clarity.

The 1841 Census shows Bricklayer *George Gladwin,* 25 (possibly a mis-print for 35), with his wife *Ann* (35) and sons *James* (2) and George (2 months), living in 'Dog and Duck' - presumably Lane. John Dean (15) and Thomas Dean (14) were sons from *Ann's* previous marriage who were living with them, *Ann's* maiden name being Daniels. All but *George Snr.* were born in Middlesex. (Note 1) I have ascertained that he was born at Munden, Hertfordshire, whilst *Ann* was born in Dog and Duck Lane (now Bourne Hill) and must have surely known families traced back in *More Winchmore Hill*

Lives who lived in that part of the old village. *James* was born on 16th August 1838 and died on 3rd December 1889. I now realise that he was my great grandfather. He is pictured at Plate 12 outside the then new St. Paul's Mission in Highfield Row (now Road) in 1887.

Remember that in the 1841 Census adult ages were rounded down to the nearest 0 or 5. Even so, the 1851 return makes interesting reading! *George Senior* is shown as aged 49 in it, whilst, miraculously, his wife *Ann* has only aged to 37. Son *James* is now 12 and George Jnr. is 10. The family is shown living in Dog and Duck Lane, though by now the Dean boys had flown the nest.

The 1861 Census has *George Snr.* regressing to the age of 47 and wrongly indicated as having been born in Hartford (presumably Hertford) in Herts. Wife *Ann* had now aged to 56. George Jnr. was now aged 19 and working as a Day Labourer. These three were living in Green Lanes roughly where Hazelwood Lane now is. *James* (23) had moved to Grove Lane in Winchmore Hill (now Station Road) with his wife *Elizabeth* (24) and daughters Ann (2) and Mary (2 months). On Census night they were host to Charlotte Brand (20), a General Servant visiting from Berkshire.

The 1871 Census has Bricklayer *George* (57) and *Ann* (60) Gladwin living in the same place on the east side of Green Lanes in Palmers Green. Son *James* (33) is also now shown as a Bricklayer and living locally in Tile Kiln Lane with his wife *Elizabeth (33),* indicated as being born in Winchmore Hill. They have four children - Anne (11), Mary (10), James (7) and Caroline (5). I have a copy of James's birth certificate, which shows that he was born on 18th March 1863 in Winchmore Hill. *James's* younger brother George (30) is also now living in Tile Kiln Lane. He is working as a General Labourer and has a wife named Phoebe (30), who was born in Hampstead, and three children - George (7), Sarah (4) and Harry (1).

The 1881 Census has *George Snr.* (72) still working as a Bricklayer (a foreman?). It is not clear where he and *Ann* (67) are living - possibly still in Green Lanes, Palmers Green? Meanwhile Bricklayer *James Gladwin* (43) and wife *Elizabeth* (44) have moved to Highfield Row (now Road). Their children are bachelor Bricklayer James (18), Domestic Servant Caroline (15), Lucy A. (9), *William H.* (6), and Rose H. (3). Only Lucy of the four is shown as being born outside of Winchmore Hill. Her place of birth is given as Tile Kiln Lane, Middlesex. *William* is my grandfather, and I have a copy of his birth certificate, which states that he was born on 12th February 1875 in Winchmore Hill.

The 1881 Census shows *James's* younger brother George as living in Palmers Green, though I'm not sure where. In the Green Lanes family home? He is now 39 and a Mason Foreman. His wife Phoebe (40) and six children are living with him - Farm Labourer George (17), Domestic Servant Sarah (14), Harry (11), Annie (8), Ada (4) and Hannah (1). The offspring are all shown as being born in Southgate, Middlesex.

My Great Great Grandfather *George Snr.* does not figure in the 1891 Census, presumably having died. His son *James,* remember, died on 3rd December 1889, so he too is absent from the return. However, his widow *Elizabeth* (53) was living at Oak Cottage, No. 1, Highfield Row and working as a Charwoman. Living with her were unmarried sons James (27) and my grandfather *William H.* (16). Both are shown as Labourers. Also living at Oak Cottage, as Lodgers, were two Labourers from Somerset by the names of William (22) and John (19) Tancock. I was intrigued when you published this entry for Oak Cottage in *More Winchmore Hill Lives* in relation to Mrs. Christie's family, John probably being her grandfather.

'Young' George Gladwin also features in the 1891 Census. He is shown as a 50-year-old Stonemason living with his wife Phoebe (also 50) at Rose Cottage, Palmers Green. With them are their children, Gardener Harry (21), Domestic Servant Annie (18), Hannah (11) and Frederick (8).

The last Census published was, of course, the 1901 one. This shows Grandpa *William* (24), Labourer and General Worker, living at Oak Cottage as head of household, with his wife *Nellie,* indicated as having been born in Winchmore Hill, Middlesex. However, I have a copy of her birth certificate, which says she was born at New Lane, Baker Street, Enfield! The Census says that living with them is their son Willie (8 months) and *William's* widowed mother *Elizabeth* (63). Both of these two are also portrayed as born at Winchmore Hill, Middlesex, but again there seems to be an error as my Uncle Willie's birth certificate stipulates that he was in fact born at 8, Gordon Road, Enfield! Meanwhile George Gladwin, 2 months old in the 1841 Census you will remember, was now a 61 year old, still living in Palmers Green with wife Phoebe (62) and son Frederick, aged 18 and employed as a Plumber's Labourer.

My father *George Cook* (confusing with so many Georges in the family!) was born on 26th January 1911, but raised in Tottenhall Road, Palmers Green, formerly Tile Kiln Lane, just south of where the North Circular Road now runs. My mother Lucy was born to *William and Nellie Gladwin* on 19th March 1911 and raised in Highfield Road.

In My Lifetime

I was born to *George and Lucy on* 11th September 1935 at 10, Gordon Hill, Enfield. In December 1940 we moved to 7, Cedars Road, opposite my mother's elder sister Eva, who lived at No. 8 with her husband Jack Kemp. (The even numbers back onto the River.) A few months later another sister Nellie, always known as Babe, moved to No. 9 Highfield Road with her husband Bob Kemp, brother of Jack, and their two children Ernest (born April 1934) and Eileen (born August 1938). Meanwhile my maternal grandmother *Nellie* continued to live at No. 31 (re-numbered from No.1).

I knew many of the family names in *More Winchmore Hill Lives* as some were still living in and around Highfield Road during my school days. The V1 bomb which arrived in July 1944 caused a great deal of damage, not least to my grandmother's house, which crumbled around her as she stood holding on to the piano! She survived, but some others did not.

Nellie's eldest daughter Lilian was, at this time, living in Reading with her husband Tom and their three children. Meanwhile her eldest son Willie (aged 8 in the 1901 Census) continued in the Royal Marines, where he had been since World War1. My mother and I were evacuated to Reading, where my brother Michael was born on 18th December 1944. We returned in March 1945 to find many of my friends had moved away, and I have not heard of them since. The Seager family, which lived at No. 37, was one of those to leave, and grandma was able to move into their vacated house, taking the piano with her!

The V1, or doodlebug, attack is covered in *More Winchmore Hill Lives,* with the account by Mrs. Doncaster and the press reports relating to Iris Chamberlain. The photograph of the bombing at Page 54 of that book was taken from Highfield Road looking onto the bombed out properties of Carpenter Gardens. So nearest to the viewer is the property that was actually hit.

I have never been able to work out how the houses in Highfield Road, adjoining *The Orange Tree,* that backed on to those in Carpenter Gardens, survived the blast while those on the 'sheltered' side were damaged and eventually demolished. A few cottages protected by the pub, and the shoe repairers owned by the Tilbury family and lying slightly behind the General Stores owned by the Leighs, were also badly damaged and demolished, whilst *The Orange Tree* and the other shop still stand to this day! Ceilings in our own home in Cedars Road fell. St. Paul's Mission, very near to the site of impact, stayed up, but was redeveloped soon after as fields for the school.

I knew Iris Chamberlain slightly, although she was a little older than I was. She actually lived in Highfield Road, but the story was that she was found in someone else's house, but how that could have happened when her legs had been blown off is a mystery and may have been just a 'story'. Incidentally, Nesta Rowe, who lived in the same little terrace that Iris did by *The Orange Tree,* and now married, still lives nearby, in Farm Road. (Note 2.)

In the 1940s and 50s at the top of Orpington Road was a factory run by Thomas Salter which made jig-saw puzzles. I noticed you admiring my picture of the 1930s Spurs team in the hall, and I am pleased to be able to tell you that in the early 1950s I was taken on in their Youth Team but, unfortunately, like most youngsters, I didn't have that special talent you needed to make it to the top, even in those days before foreign imports. However, I did have the pleasure of meeting Peter Baker. He was a local boy who started off with Enfield FC and ended up as right back in the phenomenally successful Spurs team of the early 1960s. He, like me and some of your other contributors, was a pupil at the local Grammar school, Southgate County in Fox Lane. I help organise the annual re-unions and Peter attended the last one upon his return from about forty years of living in South Africa. Some of the school's other distinguished Old Boys are Warren Mitchell (alias Alf Garnett) and George Mitchell, of Black and White Minstrel Singers fame. (Note 3.)

Despite my disappointment at not being taken on by Spurs I do have happy memories of youthful sporting successes. In 1949, two years after starting at Southgate County, I took up high jumping, and in 1950 became the Middlesex Schools under 15 champion and record holder at the White City, then the main national athletics venue. In 1952 I was Middlesex under 17 national champion and joint record holder and I represented the County in the national championships at Bradford, finishing fourth. However, I didn't let my time on the athletics track and football pitch affect my studies. Anyway, enough of my youth.

The account of the Fentum family by Mrs. Collins in *More Winchmore Hill Lives* was very interesting because my oldest friend is Ray Fentum, who was related to them. He had told me when we were boys that he had relatives in Hoppers Road who owned a sweet shop. Later he also mentioned their connection with theatricals. (See Plates 73 & 74.) I enjoyed Mr. Waring's account too, especially as my Grandfather, *William,* was also employed by Carter Page. However, the most exciting account was the one by Margaret Christie on the Tancocks, given what I found out about my own family's links with them in the 1891 Census outlined above. Even more amazing is the fact that I know Margaret from her working with Alan Stern round the corner from me. Thank you for reacting to the letter I sent you a few months ago and writing to Mrs. Christie about it. She has, in fact, contacted me as a result, and we have enjoyed 'comparing notes'.

Great Uncle James, listed in that 1891 Census, lived in nearby Vicars Moor Lane, until his death in 1939. His widow Lucy, who owned the house, died in

1951, when I was 15, yet I knew nothing about either of them until my research began in more recent times. On Lucy's death her house was left to her nephew Dave Marven, who moved in with his wife Flo. He died in about 1994, and in 1997 I discovered Flo and she showed me photos of James, Lucy and Dave. I immediately went to the small case that had been my Uncle Albert's, containing family photos, and found a similar one with people I had not been able to identify. I showed them to my mother, who immediately said, 'That's Uncle Jim!'. I should have shown them to her earlier!

I have already mentioned my Great-grandfather pictured outside St. Paul's Mission Hall in Highfield Row, as the Road was then called. He had played a large part in the building of the Hall and the photo at Plate 12 was taken on the day after its completion, which I believe was in 1887. The St. Paul's Newsletter for 1888 states that the Hall was in full use from January of that year. He died on 3rd December 1889. I loaned the snap to the late Alan Dumayne and he published it in his book on Southgate, also using it as a slide for display in his brilliant talks on Winchmore Hill. He is sadly missed, and I was pleased that you are thinking of posthumously publishing an account he gave you in this volume.

I am also quite happy for you to borrow, and publish, a few other old snaps I have. One of these is from about 1908 and features my Aunts Eva and Lilian. (See Plate 13.) Aunt Lilian was born at Hescott Terrace in Vicars Moor Lane in November 1901. Grandpa's elder brother Great Uncle Jim also lived in the terrace at one time. As you can see, the teachers, Mrs Fielder and Miss Mellership, are in the same dress and positions as in the two school shots published in your *A History of Winchmore Hill* and the original 1991 *Winchmore Hill Lives.* I therefore agree with Mrs. Webb's suggestion that they were taken on the same day.

At Plate 14 is a photo' is of my mother's brothers, Uncles Ernest (born December 1917) and Albert Gladwin (born March 1916) outside No. 1 (later No.31) Highfield Road, taken in c. 1923. Ernest joined the Royal Marines and became a member of 45 Royal Marine Commandos. As an instructor he was not required to take part in the Normandy Invasion, but he insisted on joining his mates. On 7th June 1944 they arrived to take Pegasus Bridge, but seem to have been diverted to Merville, where 9th Parachute Regiment had been attacking the gun emplacements. We do not know what actually happened, but he was officially classed as being "Killed in Action" on 7th June 1944. His brother Albert served in the Army during World War II in Ireland, Burma and Italy, and maybe elsewhere. On his return he worked with my father at Enfield Rolling Mills (now Delta Metals) and lived in Gordon Road, Enfield until his death, aged 76, in 1992.

I also have a rather faded shot of what I presume to be nurses at Highlands in the dim distant past. In addition I have just been gifted a lovely large aerial photograph of the area taken in about 1960, which I am quite happy for you to use as you see fit. I have no idea who took it, but you can see that the Capitol Cinema, which closed in December 1959, had already been replaced by the current tax offices. Another feature you can pick out, in Firs Lane, are the old barracks, later a Prisoner of War (POW) Camp. The German POWs ran a football team and attended the local Baptist Church in Compton Road. After the Germans had been repatriated the premises were used for Polish refugees for a while.

Thank you for your own good work in keeping memories of Winchmore Hill in the public arena. I have lived and/or worked here for 64 years and though there have been many changes, not all for the better, I love this area, which has been the 'family home' for about 200 years.

Author's Notes

1. *Another Gladwin household appears in the 1841 Census based in what was called 'Bourne Hill', which is most likely to be what we now call The Bourne (Bourne Hill of today then being called Dog and Duck Lane). The Gladwins listed were Shoe maker William (20), Eliza (13), Samuel (10), Frances (5) and Anna (9 months). All are indicated as having been born within the County. One can only speculate as to how they might be related to George Gladwin's household.*

Also listed as living in Bourne Hill in that Census are Agricultural Labourer Richard Daniels (35) and his family of Anna (35), Mary (10), Dinah (8), Sarah (6), Ann (4) and Daniel (6 months). All were bom within Middlesex. Living in the same household as the Daniels is Mary Furrell (65), a Female Servant bom outside the County. One wonders if Richard Daniels is Ann Gladwin's brother. If so, it would be quite an interesting thought that their next door neighbours, the Abery family, are featured in Mrs. Collins' account in More Winchmore Hill Lives. The two families would then still be living within a mile or so of each other 165 years later, in an area of the country where there is a comparatively high turn round in the population.

There are pre Victorian Gladwins known to be in the area who Mr. Cook is also unable to shed any light on. In his 1949 book entitled 'Old' Southgate Herbert W. Newby tells us that under the Edmonton Enclosure Act of 1800 land in Southgate was allocated to, and also purchased by, R. Gladwin, who was 'the great-great grandfather of Mrs. Miller (nee Gladwin) of Park Road.' Newby stated that this R. Gladwin and his own great-great grandfather, 'are the only two freeholders of 1777 who have as far as I know, descendants now living in Southgate'. Another mystery Gladwin appears in the 1826 Pigot & Co. Directory for Southgate and Winchmore Hill. It lists 'Tradesmen, Shopkeepers, & c.' and one of these is a 'Wm. Gladwin, smith and bell hanger'.

2. *There isn't the space to publish all the items Brian was good enough to give me. After taking his account in 2005 I contacted Nesta Gibbs (nee Rowe) for an account and, as explained in the introduction to this book, I made something of a mess of that, but I do remember that Nesta said that the reason Iris Chamberlain was found in someone else's house was because the blast of the V1, which removed her legs, was so great that it blew her about 60 feet through the air! Only months before going to the printers with this book I managed to obtain a further account of the V1 attack from the Pettengell family of Carpenter Gardens, reproduced later in this section.*

3. *In about 1960 Southgate County moved to Oakwood, and around ten years later converted to being a Comprehensive. With the demise of the Grammar Schools in this country I asked Brian if he could try and contact some of the older pupils to assemble a set of recollections on what life was like at the old Grammar in Fox Lane. He agreed to try.*

Robert Cook - 'Old Bob'

I managed to get in touch with Bob Hill after having seen him mentioned in the Edmonton Hundred Historical Society Newsletter of February 2010. He had written in to try and get the woodman on this section's facing sheet identified, and the editor Jim Deamer duly obliged by quoting the following article entitled, "A Winchmore Hill Celebrity" in the *Enfield Weekly Herald* of 25th April 1924.

'One of Winchmore Hill's oldest inhabitants was buried at Southgate cemetery on Thursday of last week. His name was Robert Cook, better known in the neighbourhood as "Old Bob", who died peacefully, after a brief illness, at his cottage, No.4, Salisbury Cottages, Hoppers Road, in which he had lived for over 50 years. Among the many floral tributes were wreaths from the Southgate Council and staff (he was for many years an employee of the Council), his Winchmore Hill neighbours, and the "old Boys" of a Bible class which was held some years ago in St. Paul's Institute.

"Old Bob" came to Winchmore Hill from Suffolk, where he had been in the employ of Mr Sexton, who was responsible for the first stud book of the famous shire horses from that part of the country. From his earliest days "Bob" had been associated with horses, and he came to this district as stud groom to Lord Dereham, who had his stud farm at Palmers Green, on what is now known as Huxley Farm (the shooting grounds of the present North London Gun Club). For some years he was in charge of some valuable bloodstock, and when Lord Dereham gave up the farm, "Bob" went to another bloodstock owner, Thomas Denton, who had a big farm in the part of Palmers Green known as Fox Lane, where the Southgate County School and Palmers Green Congregational Church now stand. In his employment of stud groom, Cook travelled extensively, and his name was very familiar in all the Hertfordshire and neighbouring market towns, especially in those where annual fairs are held, such as Barnet and Waltham. On one occasion he took pedigree horses to Denmark, and in his later years was able to give some interesting reminiscences of his journeys and experiences. He was a wonderful judge of horseflesh, and was justly proud of his knowledge of equine vagaries and value.

Twenty-nine years ago he became an employee of the Southgate Council and continued in that capacity until the age of 81. After 25 years service, he retired on a pension, and since then has enjoyed a well-earned rest. On fine days he was to be seen basking in the sun on the old village green, his ruddy complexion and white beard and locks, surmounted by his old-style wide awake hat, giving him a benevolent and cheery appearance, in keeping with the days when Winchmore Hill was a real old-fashioned village. He enjoyed excellent health and was a great believer in the open air and plain food. He was not averse to a glass of ale, and used to tell some of his experiences in the "old days" when, with horses at fairs, some of the "horsey" fraternity used to get rather "frisky" under the influence of strong ale. His wife died some years ago, and his only daughter is the wife of Mr Wright, a bootmaker and repairer, who lives at 2 Church Hill, Winchmore Hill. "Old Bob" had lived by himself in his snug little cottage since the death of his wife, his daughter being a frequent visitor and seeing that he was "all right and comfortable".

He will be missed by all the residents near The Green, and the news of his death will be received with regret by the many residents who recollect with pleasure "Old Bob's" cheery "Good - day" and happy face in all weathers. He carried on his duties of street cleaner in various parts of the district.'

At Page 108 of his *'Old' Southgate* Herbert Newby identified the site of the photograph as being the former style to the Bourne Hill entrance to Winchmore Hill Wood, marked today, approximately, by the southern start of Broad Walk.

Salisbury Cottages are pictured at Page 48 of my *A Look at Old Winchmore Hill*. They were situated just south of the old *Salisbury Arms*, which was replaced by the current building in the mid 1930s. There is much more information on that stretch of Hoppers Road with Norman Last's original account in my 2004 *More Winchmore Hill*

Lives. Mrs. Webb's Hemington family were also featured in that book, and at Page 29 of it there is a photograph of William 'Rat' Hemington (1857 – 1945), for many years a neighbour of 'Old Bob' at Salisbury Cottages.

The Downes Family

The Downes clan lived in the old village over two hundred years ago, as a result of which there are many names associated with the family. In the 2004 *More Winchmore Hill Lives,* when presenting Val Darvell's account, I found the easiest way to make sense of things was to think in terms of three strands of the family. Miss Darvell's grandfather was James Downes (1864 - 1952), whose line included the men pictured at Plates 16 & 17 (the three brothers). One of his brothers was John Thomas Downes (1857 - 1940), who ran a well known business on The Green, as recounted by his decendant Bob Hill. Another brother was Charles Downes (1866 - 1940), pictured at Plate 25, who ran a shop next to *The Dog and Duck,* and who is featured in Janet Palmer's account. I hope this brief introduction helps bring these three Downes accounts into context.

The Downes Brothers - Interview 28th August 2005

Some readers will recall that Val Darvell, granddaughter of James Downes, featured in the 2004 publication *More Winchmore Hill Lives* because of her family's links with the area that go back over two hundred years. At P20 of that book is a 1936 picture of James and his wife Mary along with their then surviving children, including Miss Darvell's mother Elsie. The text next to the picture reads, 'After the Great War, when women were called upon to keep industry running, my mother and her sister Jessie worked as conductresses on the 521 and 621 trams that ran from North Finchley to Central London. Their brothers Will and Jim served in the Great War and Jim later drove a 29 bus from Southgate to Victoria. Uncle Will and his younger brother, Uncle Harry, then worked in the stores at the Northern Hospital (Highlands) and are featured in a postcard I have supplied for publication at some stage, should you wish.....' That picture is now to be found at Plate 16.

Since giving her original account Miss Darvell has informed me that Jim suffered a stroke whilst at the wheel of the 29 bus. Fortunately Jim managed to steer the bus to safety before passing out, although regretfully he never made a good recovery. Jim's younger brother Will had three sons - twins Don and Les, plus the younger Eric. I was flattered when Miss Darvell invited me to a large Downes family get-together at Bounds Green on 28th August 2005. The sun was kind enough to shine on an afternoon in which everyone was listening for news of the latest developments in the Fourth Test against Australia at Trent Bridge (won by England in tense scenes that evening), and I took the photo at Plate 17. I was able to ask the brothers about their association with the area. The following is a summary.

All three brothers were born at Church Street, Edmonton, on the borders with Winchmore Hill. Twins Don and Les were born in 1924, Eric in 1926. They walked to Highfield Road every Sunday morning to visit their grandparents and all three passed the exam needed for attendance at Latymer Grammar School which, of course, still enjoys a high reputation. The house of James and Mary Downes was just next door to the gravel pits, whose Caretaker went by the name of Kersey. Being next door to the sand and gravel didn't cause the nuisance that you might expect. Behind the pits were Jifkins' orchards, stretching all the way to Barrowell Green. Don knew the Gladwin family featured elsewhere in this book.

The brothers reminded me of the family's links with the now disappeared Highlands Hospital, with their granddad being a stoker there in its early days, followed by their father and Uncle Harry, both of whom, as mentioned earlier, worked in the Stores. The brothers told me that when their Grandfather was working at the Hospital at weekends in the summer, he would sometimes be late home because he would get off his bicycle and stop to watch the cricket at Paulin's Ground. I noticed that a few times they actually referred to it as the Paulin and Manns' Ground. They also enjoyed watching the cricket there and 'spent their summer holidays' at the Swimming Baths in Barrowell Green.

There was an amateur Winchmore Hill Football Club in the boys' younger days and, as with the cricket club, you had to pay a high fee to join. This fee was invariably above the level that they and other less affluent families could afford. Don and Eric played for Edmonton, and then Southgate Olympics, in leagues run by the Amateur Football Alliance. The larger amateur clubs, such as nearby Enfield, played in leagues run by the Football Association and they paid 'expenses' to their players each game. That was a means of effectively paying a fee or wage to players within the rules.

All three brothers left the area when they got married. Don married Dorothy and was currently living in St. Albans. He had two sons. Graham was at the gathering with his wife, the other son Michael was on holiday. Les now lived in Cuffley. One of his daughters, Laura, lived in Tonbridge, Kent (though has now sadly since passed away), the other, Anne, lived in Palmers Green. Eric, like Don, lived in St. Albans. Their grandchildren were also present. Phillip, the adopted son of Ethel and Charlie Green, still lives in the original family home in Highfield Road. Roy Parrott, grandson of Jim and Lucy Downes, still lives in Hyde Park Avenue.

Author's Notes

1. *At P19 of More Winchmore Hill Lives there is a picture of a representation of the Downes family home in Bourne Hill c 1800. Family member Geoff Young told me, at the gathering, that the model had been in the old Museum in Broomfield House. He believed that the Council had been able to retrieve the model after the fire that ruined the mansion, and that it is now stored at Forty Hall, in the basement. (See, also, Bob Hill's comments.)*

2. *I have incorporated the accounts of Bob Hill and Janet Palmer next, out of alphabetical sequence, because of the Downes connection.*

Bob Hill of the Downes Family - Letters 2010-11 Memories of a Winchmore Hill exile 1944-1956

Like many stories, mine is perhaps best started at the beginning, when on Friday 22nd September 1944 I was born at the Semon wartime emergency maternity hospital at Ilkley, W. Yorkshire.

My mother, Ivy Hill (nee Downes), was born in 1914, at 6, Wilson Street, Winchmore Hill. With my 2 years elder brother Malcolm, she had been evacuated away to Bradford, Yorkshire, because of the German bombings of London. My father, Ronald Hill, was at the time of my birth away in Europe with the army, having arrived with the leading contingents of the D-Day offensive at Normandy on June 6th, 1944. (Young Malcolm and Bob are at Plate 18.)

My mother's grandfather John Thomas Downes (JTD, b1857) ran a coal and corn chandlery business from a shop at 16, The Green, which he had taken over from a Mr Gabriel in about 1910. (Note 1.) Prior to that, according to the 1901 census, he lived at Woodside Cottage, adjacent to The Green, near to where today's Broad Walk begins. My grandfather Robert Downes (b1882), together with his other nine siblings, attended St. Paul's School on Church Hill.

The coal side of the corn chandlery business was developed to service rapidly increasing local needs as with the spread of urbanization, all the fields became built over with housing. With this the equine and farm animal population in the area became ousted, diminishing the corn chandlery and animal feed demand. The business was staffed almost entirely by great-grandfather JT Downes's family. (See Plates 19 & 20.) The coal was conveyed by railway to the wharf (sidings) at Vicars Moor Lane in J.T. Downes (JTD)'s 'private-owner' railway wagons. There were also horse-drawn vehicles for deliveries in the locality. These, I believe, were kept variously at the rear of 16, The Green and elsewhere, and the horses at 'Downes's Fields', in the vicinity of the road named after him, Downes Court.

By the mid-1930s he (JTD) was in his latter years and in rapidly declining health, and because of the absence of younger males in the family to carry the business on (there had been far more females, and all were by then ageing) it was decided to dispose of the business. It was sold shortly before the war, I think in 1939, to a Northern conglomerate known, I believe, as Reckett Cockerell. Apparently the contractual arrangement in selling the business provided that JTD and his three remaining spinster daughters who resided at 16, The Green, should retain occupancy of the premises until their demise. JTD died in 1940, and the three daughters in the late 1960s. "The Shop" as it was known for so long within the family, then changed hands to become a florist's.

I noted the picture of No. 16, taken in 2000, in Stuart's '*Winchmore Hill Village 1780 – 1830*' and can verify that inside the premises there was a clear variation of appearance based on the differing ages of parts of the structure. What that picture doesn't show is that the bottom of the upstairs front room window is at the floor level of that room. I am sure I can remember seeing, when young, a photograph of the front of the building, showing a winch fixed to the upper part of the building, for raising and lowering sacks of corn, which were taken in through where the window now is.

My father, born in 1915 at then-fashionable Brixton, South London, came from a wealthy family in the legal profession. A constable in the Metropolitan Police, his marriage to my mother brought him a posting to Winchmore Hill police station at Green Lanes (near the bottom of Compton Road - see Plate 43). He lodged briefly with my mother and her parents at number 72, Compton Road, until obtaining a flat (I believe upstairs) at 64, Derwent Road, Palmers Green, where in October 1942, my late brother Malcolm was born. By 1943 my father was called up into the army. Apparently because of his linguistic and other intellect skills he was drafted into the Royal Signals for communications duties in the 'D-Day' offensive on 6th June 1944.

On 15th November 1944, a V2 rocket landed in Ringwood Way, at a time when my mother was out pushing me in a pram somewhere in the vicinity of the strike. Being a baby of just two months of age my hearing received irreparable damage from the blast, and this hearing defect has caused me considerable trouble all through my life, one way or the other. The irony of it is that I was born in Yorkshire, where my mother was evacuated, and she (we) came back to London because it was then considered 'safe' to do so.

As one of the conditions of my parents' divorce, engineered by my paternal grandfather and my maternal grandmother, provision was to be made for my brother and myself to be educated at the Royal Alexandra & Albert School at Reigate, Surrey, which despite it's imposing name, was in essence a charitable orphanage and boarding school for displaced children from broken families, most usually those with armed forces connections. At that time (1947), as may be imagined, there was little shortage of applicants, and it seems my wealthy paternal grandfather was influential in securing our acceptance. At about this point all ties between our two families were acrimoniously severed.

As well as having to juggle, as a now single, income-less mother in the austere post-war years, the upbringing of two boisterous infants, my mother also had the burden of her elderly and ailing parents, with whom we lived at Compton Road. In the case of my grandfather Robert Downes, he had forfeited much of his health with the army throughout the First World War - he'd been, in his five years in the war, gassed and shelled in the trenches in France and Belgium - as well as being in actions in Palestine & Egypt. He'd been wounded three times, and went back three times - such was the nowadays questionable loyalty and patriotism then. He not only forfeited his health, but he also forfeited experiencing the first five precious years of my mother's childhood. In return, the grateful King and country they fought so hard to protect, promised them much, but sadly gave them little - if indeed, anything at all, in return. Thus my grandpa in the grim interwar years of 1920s and 30s depression and unemployment, had by necessity to mortgage his health even more by working for his father (JTD) delivering coal. In those days the sacks were not the smaller much more humane and convenient 56 lb/ EU metric equivalent of today - they were a backbreaking 112lb (1 cwt), forbidden in today's 'Health and Safety' obsessed society. Counting themselves lucky in those desperately straitened times merely to have employment, even heroes put their medals away and rolled up their sleeves.

My grandmother Minnie Downes (nee Butcher, b1877) came from Hoxton. She was very upright - religious, and rather strict, and having been 'in service' (to Lady Paulin), was unsurpassable as a cook. She was nonetheless, a veritable fount of Victorian wisdom. She and grandpa were married in 1907 and were Quakers, but grandpa stopped going to the Meeting House (at Church Hill) quite a long time before I was born, I think, probably because of his deteriorating health, and mobility problems. He was however, a cheerily optimistic old soul, and enjoyed listening to the wireless following his beloved Arsenal football team, smoking his pipe (Lloyd's 'Bondman' tobacco in a round tin) and Will's 'Woodbine' cigarettes in green packets of 10, that my brother and I used get for him from either Guy's newsagents next door to 'the shop' at 16, The Green, or Hunter's tobacconist on the corner of The Green and Wilson Street (the street where many of the Downes family had lived, including my grandpa, and where my mother was born, at number 6).

The smells within Hunter's were glorious, with the aromas of the many different tobaccos stocked - mostly in glass jars; there were special brass scales mounted on a polished mahogany plinth on the counter, for weighing out the tobaccos. Most of the brand names have now, I suspect, long gone; Will's 'Passing Cloud' always took my fancy, but there were many others. The one Grandpa smoked, Lloyd's 'Bondman', came in a circular tin. (Note 2) I have little doubt that had my Grandpa been more wealthy, or the Old Age Pension more realistically generous, he might have been able to indulge himself with some of the seemingly more exotic grades and brands on display. The 'olde-worlde' ambience of Hunter's shop was even more fully set off by the austerity of the bare wooden floorboards, and the varnished wooden shelves behind the counter, upon which the glass jars were displayed. Latterly, after my brother tragically died (aged 10, when we were away at school in late November 1952), it fell upon me to take over the running of such little errands during school holidays as my grandparents' health worsened.

Grandpa, bandy-legged from childhood rickets, was, with his walking stick and somewhat Chaplinesque gait, instantly recognizable around the village. Characteristically, he wore a suit (albeit perhaps baggy and threadbare) with waistcoat, starched collar and tie, highly-polished brown brogue shoes, and trilby hat. With the suit he always wore his treasured silver 'Albert' pocket-watch and chain, which I believe was given to him by his father (JTD), which he frequently consulted. I still have this, and of course I cherish it dearly. People in those days didn't slouch and slop around tieless, unshaven and slovenly like today. Grandpa's military experiences and pride stuck with him. That was another one of my errands, that I took over from my late brother. We (my brother and I) when home on school holidays had enjoyed running errands for our grandparents, using our "Mobo" scooters (a larger and more substantial precursor of today's puny examples), one such errand was to exchange grandpa's collars at Wragg's gentlemen's shop at The Broadway, adjacent to Station Road.

We usually combined this with other errands - for instance, starting with the Co-Op at the bottom of Compton Road, opposite the Baptist Church, we'd queue as patiently as possible for attention, reminding each other to give Grandma's number (indelibly etched even now upon my brain) for the 'divvy'. Modern self-service supermarkets were light years away then! From there we might proceed to the nearby chemist to collect a prescription, or to Sainsbury's some few doors along, next or near to which was a toy shop, to which we were of course attracted, debating for instance, how many of those little pink circular boxes of caps we might be able to afford, for our 'Lone Star' six-guns! There was also a tobacconist/sweet shop near Wragg's, adjacent to Station Road, where we'd get some 'Woodbines' for Grandpa, and of course we'd have sixpence (6d) to spend between us, for going. Back in pre-1952 it was surprising what you could get for 6d - if it wasn't still on ration! A packet of Spangles sweets was 3d, whilst a Mars bar was 4d, as was a packet of Smith's crisps.

My early memories from our walks with Grandpa around the village - for it was indeed still that then - even up to early (Jan)1956 when at eleven I left, remain forever fondly etched in my mind. I recall people greeting and addressing him with much respect - I felt really proud of my beloved Grandpa, and being of the 'Downes' family. I was alas never to see my grandparents again after what proved to be the final parting in January 1956, when I left once again for my boarding school, for in the following month I learned they both died within two weeks of each other after moving away to Ilford, Essex, to a house which had been purchased by my then stepfather-to-be, also formerly of Winchmore Hill residency. He was very kind and absolutely respectable, but somehow he was one of those people who you feel you never get to know completely.

Having just said that, I would like to say a few words about my step father, Samuel Jeffs – Hall (b. June 1901), who was a brave man to take on a new wife and somebody else's children in straightened circumstances. (See Plate 21.) He was around 14 years older than my mother, and during the war he worked locally at Thomas Salter's, the toy manufacturer, as an engineer making munitions, and at the same time he was a Leading Fireman in the Auxiliary Fire Service (AFS), on call 24/7. He told me of the night when a heavy German air-raid was on, how he was driving an open top pre War Merryweather fire engine along Bourne Hill, near its junction with Green Lanes, heading from Southgate to the East End Docks. It seems that a German bomb ricocheted off some masonry - possibly St. John's Church – and flew almost horizontally towards the vehicle, clipping the top rail of the windscreen, before continuing its journey, and exploding elsewhere. No doubt he faced many other harrowing incidents in his night time fire duties in the East End.

I never knew much about my stepfather's past, nor his background in the locality, but at the time that his relationship with my mother started, probably in the early 1950s, he was living at 13, Compton Terrace, known as *Hillsboro*, which at the time was being used as a ladies hairdresser. That business was carried on in the front room parlour, but other rooms were let out to various (mainly) middle aged men, who like my stepfather were presumably displaced because of the war, and had like many of that era, to suffer sharing.

A frequent walk with my Grandpa was to The Green, most often to 'the shop', to see 'the girls' (three equally elderly sisters, Lucy the eldest, after her mother, then Daisy, and Nancy) where we'd stop for a cup of tea and a (lengthy) chat, before perhaps proceeding further, to Wades Grove (No 13 - which backed onto the Quaker's cemetery) to call on Jane Cormell, his closest (oldest) sister, long since widowed, who had in previous years worked at 'the shop'. In doing so I would, of course, pass the Victorian horse trough opposite *The King's Head*, which is similar to the one at the base of Compton Road. Someone told me – Grandpa Downes I think – that these and many others like them around the London area, were made by prisoners at HMP Dartmoor from the local granite there. This was by hand, as at the time they were made there wasn't the machine technology to manufacture in large numbers. (Note 3.)

Aunt Jane's, at 13, Wades Grove, was literally a 'time warp' from Victorian/ Edwardian days; the table in the front-room parlour had a heavy tasselled brown velvet cover that reached to the floor - exactly identical to the one my Grandparents had; there was no electricity in the house, only gas, by which it was lit - how I recall the strangely soft glow of the gaslight, which used to emit odd popping and hissing sounds. Also in the front parlour was a lovely wooden (I think teak) pendulum clock on the wall, almost identical to that in the waiting-room at the (Winchmore Hill) station. Its timelessly rhythmic "tick- tock" sound is one of my most enduring memories of that small house, where, as at 'the shop' we always had cups of tea, and buttered "Osborne" biscuits.

She (my great-aunt Jane) had a little wire-haired fox terrier called Peter, which I often took for walks to Grovelands Park, and around the locality, initially with my late brother, but latterly alone. When we got back from our walks in the early evenings of the late summer (August) school holiday I was usually provided with a cup of Ovaltine, and we'd listen to "The Huggets" (featuring Jack Warner and Kathleen Harrison) on Aunty Jane's battery-powered (Vidor) radio, to wait for my mother to escort me back to Compton Road in the gathering dusk.

At such times we might encounter the lamp-lighter, a man who rode a bike, and carried a short ladder with which he accessed the gas street lamps around the Station, Broad Walk - and I think, nearby Seaforth, Branscombe, and Denleigh Gardens - for my mother and I might on a nice evening, take a roundabout route, via Downes Court, back home to Compton Road. I recall such perambulations at that time being quite tranquil, with an almost total lack of road traffic and proliferation of parked cars such as there are today.

On the way back to Compton Road across The Green from Wades Grove, at the corner of Hoppers Road, was Chalkley's the bakers, where Grandpa and I would often call in (the lovely smell was really unforgettable) for a wholemeal loaf which cost 4

¼ d (four pence-farthing), or (for my brother and I) maybe something tastier, added to which old Mrs Chalkley would invariably pop a couple of 'little extras' into the bag, *gratis,* for us. Such were the times - and the people. We'd then proceed at Grandpa's so-slow rate towards Compton Road via Compton Terrace (part of Hoppers Road). I expect it's gone now, but if I recall correctly, the 'pavement' along Compton Terrace consisted of a sort of cream-coloured profiled surface not at all unlike squares of 'white' chocolate.

Turning into Compton Road by the triangle with the lovely old horse-chestnut tree at its centre adjacent to the *Salisbury Arms* public house, and slightly nearer Holly Lodge (the original, not the later flats), there were diamond-shaped cast-iron signs of the former Great Northern Railway (GNR) origin adjacent to the railway bridge, forbidding the operation of 'locomotives' in excess of a certain weight across the bridge. This always perplexed me, as in my juvenile mind a 'locomotive' was steam-driven (as were all of the trains on that line in that era), and trains ran on rails, NOT roads. Obviously I can see now that those signs referred to a long bygone age when traction on the roads before diesel lorries, was by steam. There were also the later blue enamelled metal "British Railways" signs forbidding trespass on the railways, for fear of a fine of 'no less than forty shillings' (40/-). I daresay those signs, long since disappeared, now adorn the walls of some latter-day 'railwayana' enthusiasts?

It was on this bridge that my brother would often hoist me up so I could peep over the parapet to see the trains passing. In the summer months, particularly in late evenings, a genial man, known to us as Mr Last (presumably from the family featured elsewhere in this book), might have bonfires on the allotment on the railway bank adjacent to Compton Road railway bridge; we used to 'help' him sometimes, my brother and I returning home to supper and bed reeking of bonfire smoke, and having to have a bath before anything else!

As we grew, Malcolm and I ventured further. We'd often go up in the park - Grovelands, where we'd spend practically all day playing together; 'hide-and - seek' in the wooded part (the remainder of the one-time Winchmore Hill Wood, so old Grandpa told us) that we entered from Seaforth Gardens, having crossed Broad Walk from Downes Court, which we knew was named after our great-grandfather (although we didn't know quite why). We were always delighted to watch the antics of the grey squirrels in the wood, which were then classified officially as vermin - ruinous invaders from America, we were told at school, and if you killed one and cut it's tail off, you could get *5/-* (25p) for it. Although quite where one went to exchange one's squirrel tail for the 5 shillings offered, was never clear to me.

Of course one of our favourite attractions at Grovelands (and it seemed many other peoples' too) was feeding the ducks. Quite how we should have ever had *any* spare bread in those difficult times, I cannot now imagine, but feed the ducks we did - and from the very earliest age that I can remember. That in turn reminds me of the cold winter of 1947, when I was 3. Our mother took us up to the park with wooden sledges that I think Grandpa had made in his shed - there was a bit of a hill (or undulation) as one walked into the park from the main Broad Walk entrance, towards the cafeteria, adjacent to the bandstand, if I remember correctly, and there, together with hundreds of others, we were launched at seemingly great velocity across the expanse of quite deep snow. The lake then was of course frozen over, and the ducks took much advantage of the sudden influx of visitors with their generosity in feeding them!

Grandpa would sometimes take two of grandma's jars that she used for making jam, or pickling things in, and fix string handles to them for us to take, when we'd play by (or most often, in) the brook that tinkled it's way through the park from the lake towards Church Hill, and the park-keeper's house nearby. Sometimes (usually on a Saturday) there'd be a fishing match on at the lake, and we'd go and talk to the anglers to see what was being caught - not much more than the minnows we abstracted from the brook, it often seemed!

One of the big attractions that our mother accompanied us to Grovelands for, were the Saturday afternoon performances of the brass band concerts from the bandstand. They were extremely popular, and one had to ensure arriving in good time to get a good seat (deck chair) or space nearby on the grass. They are among my fondest memories of that time. Our Mum used to be well prepared, bringing a picnic lunch for us, which among other things, nearly always consisted of egg sandwiches. We might if we were lucky, supplement that with a bottle of Tizer and a packet each of "Smith's" crisps obtained in the park cafe; the chief attraction of the crisps I think, was locating the little blue twist of paper containing the salt - the vital ingredient without which crisps are quite bland and tasteless!

Throughout the summer months a popular pleasure in Grovelands Park was boating on the lake; rowing boats were hired out, and plainly it was a much enjoyed activity. Visiting recently (2009) I came to understand that this facility has long been withdrawn, due to vandalism and anti-social behaviour that has sadly become endemic throughout our latter day society. (Note: See footnote 4 to John Lucas's account.) In the vicinity of the lake was the aviary, appearing, I think, around 1953-54, containing hundreds of tiny brightly coloured little birds, mostly canaries, budgerigars, and finches, as I recall, which as a 9 -10 year-old I found a source of much fascination. Of course we made good use of the roundabout, swings, see-saw, and other such standard children's amusements.

As well as Grovelands Park, in the summer my brother and I used to go to Barrowell Green open air swimming baths, or lido, as it was sometimes referred to. I can't remember how much it cost, as my brother was always in charge of the money (6d maybe?). Of course I know it's not there any more, but in those days (1951-2) it was jam-packed with shrieking kids all day long! I would think one could have located it blindfold, just relying on the sounds of the children! Sometimes we met up there with some slightly older girl cousins from Hackney. Although I couldn't yet swim then, it was wonderful fun, and we'd both plod back home for dinner starving hungry and thoroughly worn out! Incidentally, in the early post-war days our Mum made our swimming-trunks - knitted - from wool. Okay when they were dry, but once they were wet – well ..... hence the term 'droopy drawers', perhaps?

Talking just now of Green Lanes reminds me of trips by 629 trolleybus to Palmers Green, to Woolworths, just past Aldermans Hill/The Triangle. This really ripped along at a rate of knots. Mind you, there was nothing like the amount of cars on the roads then, to hold them up, as there are now! We used to sit on the inside-facing seats over the twin back wheels. You had to be seated fairly promptly before the bus pulled off, as the acceleration was phenomenal - we'd all lean back (sideways) at this point, towards the open rear platform of the bus, which I recall having the familiar large London Transport logo featuring the red circle with broad horizontal blue stripe, on the back window.

And talking of Woolworths at Palmers Green, I still have a small suitcase bought by my mother in August 1949, for me for starting at boarding school in September of that year. Actually, she bought two - the other being of course, for my brother, for the same purposes of travelling to and from boarding school. The day my mother bought those suitcases, strangely enough, I remember as clearly as though it were last year, not 61 years ago; I was almost five years old, and my brother was approaching seven. It was a lovely sunny day, and we got off the 629 at The Triangle, and going into Woolworths we were both weighed on the enormous machines that they had inside the store in those days. Having bought the suitcases, my brother and I carried one each, and we made our way to Lyons' for refreshment, which I distinctly recall was when I had my first-ever cup of coffee. We then proceeded towards the cinema, to cross over on the Zebra for the bus back home, when there was some commotion there; it transpired that someone had been run over by a bus. I recall seeing the unfortunate person lying in the road (which I thought rather odd) looking not at all well, the subject of much attention from passers-by!

No mention of Palmers Green would be complete without recalling my <u>very earliest</u> memories - of travelling by *<u>train</u>* with my mother, as a toddler from Winchmore Hill in the mornings, to Palmers Green, for the Day Nursery some way up Aldermans Hill. I think the name of the house, if not the establishment, was (possibly) "Holly Lodge" - in this respect I hope I'm not confusing with the building of the same name on the corner of Hoppers Road and Compton Road. Somehow I associate this name with it, and it is where I was deposited for the day in order that my mother could go to work in London to earn some money to keep us. There were not the number of State Benefits around in those days as there are now, and as I mentioned earlier, my father reneged on the alimony payments - he never ever contributed a single penny towards my brother and me whatsoever. This (day nursery) arrangement commenced after my brother had started at the boarding school, in September 1947 (there was exactly two years between us), and obviously my trips to and from the Day Nursery had to be made twice daily, coinciding with my mother's train journey to and from her job as a shorthand typist in the City.

For a number of reasons, railways - and in particular steam trains - had long become an integral part of mine, and my family's life; living right next to the railway line (the Hertford Loop) on which Palmers Green and Winchmore Hill are situated, it would have been difficult for that not to be so. In the very early post-war days of my childhood, the railway was busy by day with alternating passenger and miscellaneous goods trains, and even busier through the night with extensive freight workings, which varied between very lengthy coal trains, and equally lengthy trains conveying military (wartime) materials - tanks, guns, lorries, and much other associated equipment, that the war-damaged roads at that time would have been unable to take.

Most of these goods trains were "unfitted" - that is to say, not fitted with the continuous vacuum braking such as passenger trains had, relying on the braking provided by the loco at the front, and the brake-van at the rear. Slightly to the north of Winchmore Hill station, adjacent to my great-grandfather's coal sidings at Vicars Moor Lane, stood a signal box (now gone) which controlled the section, and since these huge goods trains were unbraked and therefore speed restricted, they were not infrequently held at the signals (all semaphore then), to give the faster passenger trains priority. That was fine, except re-starting these weighty trains from a stand more often than not proved difficult, as the locos slipped on the damp rails, struggling to get grip, as the driver juggled with the controls. As well as the noises of the engine, the pyrotechnic effects in the night sky, as huge lumps of white-hot coal from the fire were blasted upwards from the chimney, were something to be seen - not to mention the ensuing racket of the loose-coupled wagons crashing and buffering up against each other as the engine alternatively gained momentum and then lost it. My brother and I would frequently get out of bed to watch these spectacular displays; sometimes the engine would still be struggling as it passed falteringly through Winchmore Hill Station and the cutting towards Compton Road bridge. Indeed, I can recall instances of trains coming to a complete stand there, and us watching as the footplate crew repaired the fire (most of it having gone up through the chimney) and 'brewing - up' to restore the exhausted steam pressure in the boiler.

Other little excitements were the winter fogs that we used to get, when visibility was very often hardly an arm's length! On the railways at such times signalmen and station staff used to place detonators on the rails to warn enginemen of the proximity of signals and stations. These explosive devices were of course by their very nature pretty loud, and many were the times when foggy evenings were punctuated by sounds of detonators going off as the trains ran over them. Curiously, these thick fogs (or smogs - known as 'pea-soupers' because the atmosphere resembled that brownish-green colour) tended to muffle the otherwise more plainly heard sounds of the trains, so the detonators also alerted waiting passengers and railway staff of approaching trains too.

At that time most if not all of the locomotive stock and infrastructure in the country had been hideously neglected and starved of maintenance during the war years, so faults and failures at the approach of nationalization in 1948 were par for the course. How I can still recall one regular loco on the coal traffic - what I've since come to know was an LMS Stanier class 8 - a 'foreigner' on LNER metals - but a one-time proud thoroughbred cart horse if ever there were such things, that I could recognize way before it even came into sight, because of its characteristic woeful collection of wheezes, gasps, and clanks as it slogged and struggled gamely with its enormous load. How faithfully those old steam locomotives served the country in those grim days - one wonders how modem 'hi-tech' traction could perform in comparable circumstances, bereft of maintenance?

I made mention previously, of the Downes family's shop at The Green, and the coal business; as my brother and I grew up (i.e., when we were around 7 or 8) our Grandpa sometimes took us down to the coal sidings at Vicars Moor Lane, where we'd sit by the railway and watch the trains go by; Grandpa 'happened' to know the signalmen, and it was often just a matter of time before we crossed over the tracks and climbed up into the elevated cabin of the signal box, which from its lofty height gave us a superior view of the railway. The cabin itself, with its numerous levers all labelled and painted different colours, was fascinating; even more so when various bell codes via the telegraph system activated different instruments in polished wooden cases mounted on a long shelf running most of the length of the cabin, behind the levers. At such times the signalman would acknowledge the bell code, and send another off. On receipt of this, he'd pull certain levers and re-set others, then another bell code would sound, which would be acknowledged.

As trains passed, entries were made in the log book to record them, and sometimes telephone calls were exchanged between the signal box and that at Winchmore Hill station. In between times much use was made of the anthracite stove and the constantly-boiling kettle, in providing cups of tea, and we were regaled with a running commentary on the ever-changing train movements of the day, as they progressed. It was a lovely place for a small boy to be in the 'steamy' days of the early 1950s, particularly as just then they were quadrupling the East Coast Main Line (ECML) at Potters Bar and putting another tunnel through at Hadley Wood, so for a while all the big front line 'Pacifics' and 'namers' (prestigious named locos such as the "Flying Scotsman") came by on our line, to rejoin the ECML further up past Hertford North. Many of the loco crews appeared to know the signalmen, and had their own personalised forms of greeting as they passed - for some it would be a couple of 'pops' on the whistle, and for others, somewhat lengthier 'crows' - it was here in the signal box that I became aware of the differences between LNER and LMS loco whistles; they were quite marked, and with practice one could identify pretty well the type and class, just from the sound of the whistle!

It might not be surprising for me to mention that having been brought up to the sights and sounds (AND SMELLS!) of steam trains passing close by, as an infant the sounds and vibrations - sash windows rattling! - of the trains lulled me to sleep at night. When I later (at the age of 5, in 1949) went to a remotely-located boarding school in the heart of the Surrey countryside, I was most distressed at the absence of a railway nearby, and had tremendous problems with trying to sleep without the comforting cacophony of train sounds that I'd been so used to. It may be of some interest to note that some of my Downes forebears worked on the emergent Great Northern Railway branch at Winchmore Hill when it was first opened, in 1871. There was in fact a somewhat romantic story within the family, of how my great-grandfather J.T. Downes, then a mere teenager employed as a porter, encountered a certain young lady alighting from the train, *en route* for a 'situation' with Lady Paulin's household. This young lady having caught my great-grandfather's eye was then amorously pursued; in time they married and she, Lucy Bamaby from the tiny Lincolnshire village of North Owersby, became my great-grandmother-to-be.

With the Downes family being so long established in the area, and so widely dispersed, it is not an easy matter to discuss briefly in context with this narrative, without confusing the subject (and the reader!), as for example, it seems for several generations at differing times, sons were named after fathers, with no middle name to identify who was who. Hence may be realised some of the difficulties I have had of sorting out my family line. Whilst all Downes variants in the district can be considered related as far back as at least the 18th century, it is only with yet more research that I might better establish my own ancestry!

At its inception I believe the local railway line's intended limit was Enfield. In anticipation of all this destruction and upheaval, one far-sighted ancestor (apparently my 3 x Gt-grandfather's uncle) made a model of our 1800 cottage, which placed within a specially-made glass case, was apparently on display at later generations' places of abode - and perhaps mostly so - at my great-grandfather J.T. Downes' homes in Hoppers Road, Woodside Cottages, and subsequently at the shop at 16, The Green. Bringing the story round to full circle perhaps, prior to my gt-grandfather JTD's demise in 1940, it was apparently decreed that the model, together with other Downes family artefacts, should go to the Broomfield Museum in Broomfield Park, where they did in fact remain until the arsonist's fire in the 1980s, wherein many local history artefacts were destroyed.

By sheer chance and good luck (and not to mention the efforts of the salvage team) not all was so completely lost - in my recent (May/June 2009) visits to Forty Hall Museum. I (together with the splendid efforts of Val Mundy) located the historic model of my Downes ancestor's cottage, in unbelievable condition - looking far better than in the 1936 "Palmers Green & Southgate Gazette" photo - totally undamaged, and still in it's original (also undamaged) glass case. Even though it wouldn't make the national news on TV, for me that's something really nice to know, as in the last couple of years since retiring I have been involving myself with researching my Downes family background that I wasn't able to do during my younger days. (Note: *More Winchmore Hill Lives* contains further information on Miss Valerie Darvell and the Downes family, including a reproduction of the 1936 newspaper illustration just mentioned.)

Reflecting further on my Winchmore Hill childhood, it may be of some interest to recall how later, my brother and I when home on school holidays around 1951-2, used to wait at Winchmore Hill station to greet our mother from her train home from work in the evenings; the station, as indeed had the railway, from earliest days figured quite centrally in our lives, and my memories of it as it was then, still remain clear.

It was built in identical style to that at Palmers Green, straddling the tracks, and was entered at street level. It had a booking (ticket) office booth located centrally within the entrance above the tracks. This was constructed sturdily from timber, which was varnished; it was of an oval shape, and was glazed with substantially-thick, bevelled glass, which I think on certain panes was etched the old "G.N.R." logo. There were two cashier's windows to the booking kiosk - one each side -for 'up' and 'down' journeys respectively; passengers were channelled past stout varnished timber handrails and barriers. There were two large, since bricked in, windows, looking out over each running track, that both faced north. The wooden floor boards were uncovered, and the flights of stairs descending to each platform were also of timber, with a roof covering of curved corrugated iron for protection against the elements. Suspended horizontally beneath the bridge/station structure directly above the running tracks, were smoke-shields which deflected the sparks and sooty emissions from locomotives.

The 'down' (northbound) platform had a somewhat shorter waiting room than that on the opposite 'up' (London) side, where there was also on the 'up' platform, a small signal box under the stairs. There was at the foot of the stairs on the platforms, a small 'sentry-box' for the ticket collector to sit in. I don't suppose it's there now, but I recall very strongly there being a metal (iron) mud scraper being at the station entrance - possibly built into the wall, adjacent to the Royal Mail postbox that I also think was built flush into the wall. The mud scraper, I think incidentally, alluded not so much to Winchmore Hill's rural past, but to the horse-drawn traffic which prevailed when the station was built, and the inevitable unsavoury deposits that resulted on the roads! Another anachronism at that time, was the illumination of the station and platforms, by gas light. Signalling in that era of steam was of course, semaphore, and there was a signal gantry located on the 'up' line just immediately south of the station, combining, I believe, a 'home' and 'distant' pair of signals. This was visible to us from our bedroom window at Compton Road.

With our regular evenings' frequenting of Winchmore Hill station to wait for our mother's train, my brother and I evidently became well known, as several of the exiting passengers arriving from their travails in the City would quite often give us bags of confectionery, or fruit such as oranges and bananas. Bearing in mind that rationing was then still very much on, these sort of treats were very gratefully received indeed - especially considering our mother's parlous financial situation.

In that latter respect, I have never forgotten one very kind gentleman who stood out; somewhat elderly in appearance (to us then), he was always immaculately dressed in a quaint way, that was old-fashioned even in 1951-52 - a dark pinstripe suit with waistcoat & silver 'Albert', 'butterfly' collared shirt and tie with (probably rather valuable) jewelled tie pin, grey spats, and the most highly polished black brogues you ever saw. As if all this were not enough to distinguish him, he wore a black bowler hat, a monocle, and displayed a silver, waxed moustache - and, I'm sure in thinking, with a red carnation in his buttonhole every day. His name, we learned, was Mr Steiner, of plainly Jewish origins, and from out of his leather briefcase he would produce, like a magician with white rabbits, bars of chocolate and/or bananas, which he, arriving as always on the same train as our mother, would give to her to give to us. I believe he lived in nearby

Ringwood Way, off Station Road. Again in a quaintly old-fashioned way, he was most polite and genteel, and although I don't recall seeing him for around a year before I left Winchmore Hill in 1956, I never forgot Mr Steiner; I'll never know his circumstances, but I'm quite sure he quite accurately guessed ours.

As I may previously have mentioned, we lived at number 72, Compton Road; this was the second house away from the railway, and directly opposite the Congregational Church. Our neighbours next to the railway (74) were the Smale family, which consisted of two or three children slightly younger than us - and three golden Labrador/Retriever dogs, which were often very noisy (both the kids and the dogs!). I'm not too good on names, but I think our other next-door neighbour was old Mrs Poumier (don't hold me too much on the spelling), then (I think) it was Mrs Rossiter - then Mr & Mrs Waymark, and then at the end (corner of Roseneath Avenue) old Mrs "Nanny" Court. She had a scruffy looking little dog that was quite vociferous, snapping and barking whenever anyone passed by; we two boys (my brother and I) often teased it when its snout protruded under the gate. With the Congregational Church opposite, clearly we had no neighbours from that direction, and apart from the Smales next door, I knew of no other children in that immediate locality.

It wasn't until some two years after my brother's death in 1952, that I became aware of the Parry family diagonally opposite at number 73, next to the alleyway that led (directly opposite Roseneath Ave) through to Orpington Road. By that time I was almost 10, and it turned out that Mr & Mrs Parry, a very pleasant and friendly youngish couple, as well as having a Jowett Javelin car (I was beginning by then to pick up on such things), had two boys, James and David; the eldest being James, the same age as myself, whilst David was perhaps 18 months younger. Quite how we palled up I cannot recall, but the three of us became close friends. Whereas I'd never associated with the next-door Smale family, the Parrys sort of 'clicked' with me, and we got on really well together. At a time when I was still a bit 'shaky' after losing my brother, I think I derived a great deal of benefit from their friendship & company. However, this was to be short-lived, for as previously mentioned, my mother and my grandparents had to move away very early in 1956. (Note 4.)

That move, it is fairly apparent, was strongly instrumental in hastening, if not directly causing, my grandparents' demise at that time. That in turn meant that due to the unready state of the house in Ilford, I couldn't return there for school holidays, and so for that year I was fostered with a family in Worthing, Sussex, which comprised a boy and girl almost exactly the same age as myself, and a small dog, and turned out to be one of the brightest spots in my childhood - certainly after the loss of my brother just over three years earlier. Alas Worthing was, as with my friendship with the Parrys, a woefully short period in my life - but that is another story, and I suddenly realise, I am talking of the start of my time in exile. I've certainly enjoyed recalling my cherished early years in Winchmore Hill, and hope that there is something in these reminiscences that might appeal to others.

<u>*Author's Notes*</u>

1. *The 1911-12 Kelly's Directory shows 'Gabriel William, corn and seed merchant' as occupying 16, The Green, whereas in the 1912-3 Directory he had been replaced by, 'Downes Jn. Thos. Corn mer.'.*

2. *When talking of his visit to Hunter's Bob didn't want to 'clutter up' his account with a list of brand names, but in his notes in the margins he reeled some of these*

off. When it came to cigarettes Bachelors, which had embossed male and female faces, Park Drive, Craven A, Black Cat, Capstan, Weights, Balkan Sobraine (Black Russian), Camel, Senior Service and Player's Medium Navy Cut were amongst the very many popular brands. Pipe tobaccos that Bob remembered were Erinmore, St. Julian, and St. Ogden. He says that those who didn't smoke, in those days, were very heavily outnumbered.

3. *The inscription on both drinking troughs reads, 'Metropolitan Drinking Fountain & Cattle Trough Association.' On the eastwards face of the one on The Green are the additional words, 'In Memoriam Doctor C. Highett 1896. Erected by C.F. (then faded out)'*

4. *The 1953-4 Street Directory for the part of Compton Road where Bob lived contains the following entries – South Side: '65. Lyons, Bartram, 65. Smith, Leonard 67. Vacant 69. Parsons, Edward W. 71. Wimpenny, Lionel H. 73. Parry, Norman F. (no 75) 77. Canning, Leo. C., Compton Road, Congregational Church, 'Holly Lodge' Grant, Wm. (Hoppers Road).' North Side: '.... (Roseneath Avenue) 64. Hopkins, Thomas E. 66. Robinson, William W. 68. Parr, Geoffrey 70. Waymark, William G. 72. Downes, Robert 74. Mc Kever, May T. 74. Smale, William 74. Sturge, Wm. V.'*

5. *On seeing this listing Bob commented that he remembered Mrs. Parr at No. 68, whilst he thought William Robinson at No. 66 might be a misprint for Rossiter, the lady of the house possibly being one of his Grandmother's friends from the Quaker Meeting House.*

Janet Palmer, nee Humphrey - Letter 7th July 2005

Dear Mr. Delvin,

Many thanks for your letter. My apologies for not getting in touch sooner. I have put together what I know about the Downes family and my connection with them through my aunt Evelyn Downes. Although all the Downes members mentioned in my notes are no longer with us I am pleased to say their grand and great-grand children are keeping the line going. Firstly I can add a little more to Miss Valerie Darvell's account of the Downes family, mentioned in *More Winchmore Hill Lives.* I am related to the Downes family through my mother's sister, whose father-in-law was Charles, the brother of James and John Downes.

Charles and his wife Charlotte (nee Jupe) had three children, Charlotte (k/a Lottie), Cassandra (k/a Cassie) and a son Charles Henry. They lived and ran the General Store at 72, Hoppers Road, Winchmore Hill, close to the *Dog and Duck* Pub. (See Plates 23 & 24.) Their daughter Charlotte married a Mr. Geyelin and had two daughters, Jean and Josie. Their second daughter Cassandra did not marry, and their son Charles married Evelyn Sudul and had one son, Alan.

My godmother Evelyn Sudul was my mother Marjorie's sister. She married Charles Henry Downes on Saturday 6th July 1935. My mother Miss Marjorie Sudul was chief bridesmaid, the other bridesmaids were Miss Jean Geyelin (the bridegroom's niece), Miss Dorothy Page (the bride's cousin) and Miss Ivy Downes (the bridegroom's cousin). Mr. Clifford Humphrey (at the time Miss Marjorie Sudul's fiance) was best man. Charles and Evelyn were married at the Holy Trinity Church and their reception was held at Firs Hall, Winchmore Hill. (See Plate 25.)

Following Mr. Charles Downes Senior's death on 8th March 1940, his widow and Miss Cassie Downes, continued to run the business at 72, Hoppers Road, which they later turned into a sweet shop. I now turn to the maternal side of my family, the Suduls.

My grandfather, Arthur Sudul, purchased 29, Elm Park Road, Winchmore Hill in 1926 and moved there from Hertford Road, Waltham Cross, with his wife Annie Sudul and his two daughters Evelyn Sudul and Marjorie Sudul (my mother). Evelyn was about 19 years old at this time and Marjorie about 15. They continued to live at No. 29 until they got married. During the 2nd World War my grandfather Arthur had an air raid shelter built in the back garden of No. 29, which was still there when we moved in 1960. In his younger days Arthur was always known as 'Johnny' and even in later years he was always known as 'John'. He was a good sprinter for the Highgate Harriers and later became the first president of the Southgate Harriers.

My mother Marjorie married Clifford Humphrey on 25th March 1939 at the Holy Trinity Church, Winchmore Hill. They spent the first few years of their married life at 11, Green Lanes, Winchmore Hill. I was born in 1945, and following the death of my grandmother Annie Sudul in December 1946, we moved to 29, Elm Park Road so my mother could look after her father, Arthur Sudul. My grandparents Arthur and Annie were both buried in Southgate Cemetery, Waterfall Road.

Although I now live in the Midlands I was in Winchmore Hill earlier this year and went down Elm Park Road. I was sorry to see Firs Hall had gone but No. 29 looked much the same as I remember it. I also visited Grovelands Park, where I spent a great deal of my childhood. I was pleased to see it hadn't changed at all. My early memories of Winchmore Hill are in the 1950s.

My mother did her daily and weekend shopping at a general store run by Mr. and Mrs. Eames. It was on the same side of Green Lanes as Elm Park Road, just up from the Post Office. My mother used to give her shopping list for the weekend to Mr. Eames on a Saturday morning and he used to deliver it late that evening after he had closed his shop. Opposite his shop on the other side of the road was the Milk Yard, where the carts were loaded up ready for the horses to take the milk round the streets. (I think there is a dancing school now on the site of the milk yard).

Further down on the same side of Green Lanes lived my best friend Jacky Hands at No. 817. Her father, Bernard Hands, ran a building and decorating business called Ricketts Builders, and their yard was in Berry Close. My friend Jacky used to go to Iris Caldicott's Dancing School, which was above the butchers near *The Green Dragon.*

Both Jacky and I attended a Nursery School in the early 50s run by Miss Geddy. It was held in the Church Hall in Compton Road and I remember there was always a big coal fire burning in the grate during the winter months.

There were two greengrocery shops, one on Green Lanes, near *The Green Dragon,* and the other on The Broadway. They were run by two brothers, Alan and Ivor Burke. Further round on Green Lanes, opposite *The Green Dragon,* was the sweetshop where my friends and I used to go to spend our pocket money. It was run by Mrs. Penn, who was always very patient while we made up our minds which sweets to buy. She always made sure we got as many sweets as possible for our 3d or 6d.

I can also remember the hardware and do-it-yourself shop which was run by Mr. Hanley. It was like an Aladdin's cave, with everything from nuts and bolts to brooms and washing soap. There was a Sainsbury's on the Broadway, which was a long shop with black and white tiles on the floor covered in sawdust, which I used to kick up while I was waiting for my mother. The counters ran both sides of the shop, one for bacon and meats, and the other for cheese and dairy products.

On the corner of Green Lanes and Fords Grove was the Capitol Cinema. (See Plate 64.) I used to go there with my friends on a Saturday morning to watch the children's cartoons programme. Years later it was knocked down and an office block built called Capitol House and I worked there from 1966 to 1973, when I moved to Leicester.

Yours sincerely,
Janet Palmer

Alan Dumayne - Letter 27th September 1984

Many readers will remember the late Mr. Dumayne for his numerous talks on the area, and his valuable, impeccably produced, books. The books, of course, remain on the shelves for us to read even now, but many younger people will be unaware of just what a full schedule of talks Alan gave around the Borough. For example, in his letter to me of 27th September 1984 he wrote,

'I am giving my slide lecture, - Southgate & Winchmore Hill, A Glimpse From The Past: - U.R.C. Women's Fellowship 2 p.m. 3rd Oct. '84; Minchenden School 9 a.m. 4th Oct. '84; St. John's Social Club 8 p.m. 16th Nov. '84; Camera Club, Bramley Road 8 p.m. 30th Jan. '85; W.R.V.S. Walker Hall 2.15 p.m. 4th June 1985; St. Mary's Enfield 19th June '85. Also I am giving a talk on Tommy Lipton called 'The Lipton Story' to the Walker Social Club on 10th Oct. '84 at 8 p.m. I am normally allowed to invite any guests I so wish to any of these (except Minch. School) but should like due notice if you do decide to attend.'

It is a long time ago now, but as far as I recall I attended Alan's Lipton talk in 1984, and in later years various other heavily illustrated lectures on Winchmore Hill, including one, I seem to remember, in late 1992 with both my wife and mother, at the premises of Alan's old school in Fox Lane. It is amazing how Alan kept up such a punishing schedule at that time because although we were never what you would call friends, I had visited him in about 1990 when he was seriously ill in St. Bart's. in the City. At the time I was working literally next door to the hospital, and so it was easy for me to pop in one evening on the way home. Even though he was obviously up to his eye balls on medical drugs he was still sufficiently 'with it' to say to me (a friendly rival), 'Keep on researching Stuart, keep on digging away.'

I have kept digging away, as Alan urged, and have continued to write on Winchmore Hill, as opposed to Alan's wider grasp of the area. I think we should remember Alan not just for his writing, but also for his great impact as a lecturer, feeding into older folks' own youthful memories, and explaining something of the background to these with his wonderful array of slides. Alan was, in effect, a one man local history association in his own right, and I think his passing left a huge gap in the fabric of our local society which has never been adequately filled.

I am grateful to Alan's widow, Sheila (who appears in the 2004 *More Winchmore Hill Lives),* for permission to publish this account posthumously, and also for allowing me to copy Alan's files of research material on Winchmore Hill. More detail on much of this summary account can be found in his 'Fond Memories of Winchmore Hill'.

'I was born in Harringay in 1929 and then in 1933 my parents moved to Winchmore Hill (83, Farm Road), which was then still developing as a suburb. I think the new 3 bedroomed semi – detached houses were generally being sold at prices between £750 and £850, but ours was a corner plot with a large garden and cost £900. I attended Winchmore Hill Junior School in Highfield Road between the ages of 5 and 11 (1934 – 1940). In 1940 having passed my eleven plus exam, I went to Southgate County School in Fox Lane and was there from 1940 – 1946, where I gained matriculation and my Higher Schools Certificates. These, of course, were the war time years. Immediately after the war I served an apprenticeship in my late father's building firm as a joiner, after which I was called up for my two years National Service (1950 – 52). I have remained a 'local boy'; I married a girl from the area in 1952 and we lived initially in Winchmore Hill. Since 1958 we have lived in Southgate.

Pre - War Memories.

I remember the trams running in Green Lanes and that lovely sound they made going along. I also recall my schooldays at Winchmore and all my teachers there quite vividly. Miss Peryer was the headmistress and there was Mrs. Hemmings, Miss Prince, Miss Maynard, and Mr. Allders. I recall the sweet shop near the school, then called Davidsons, and the halfpenny bars of blackjack we used to buy. There was a little shop on the hill near the humpback bridge and I can see the owners Mr. and Mrs. Gandy now as clearly as though it was yesterday. They sold everything from groceries to haberdashery. Many commodities were sold loose from sacks on the floor and the Gandys would use scoops to weigh out ½ lb. of rice or whatever you wished. You could buy an ounce of pins or a yard of elastic and the whole shop retained an air of organised chaos. Mr. and Mrs. Gandy were lovely people. I wish they were still alive. (Note 1)

I looked forward to the ice cream tricycles coming round in the summer ringing their bells. 'Walls' used to sell 1d snowfrutes (a triangular bar of fruit flavoured water ice). If we were really flush, we would have a 2d ice cream bar which came in a wrapper, with two wafers thrown in. I remember the rival ice cream sellers, 'Eldorado' and 'Dairy Ice Creams'. The 'Walls' trike was always dark blue with a notice 'Stop Me and Buy One' on the front. The baker and his push-cart come to mind. If he was in a good mood, the baker would give me a scoop of the fine bread crusts from the bottom of his cart for nothing. I played football and cricket in the streets with my chums. There was so little traffic then that many of the streets were simply our playgrounds. Our side garage gates served as a goal for football and, with appropriate chalk marks, as a wicket for cricket. We would play for hours.

I remember the family going to the cinema each Monday and Friday regardless of the programmes. (See Plate 64.) We would go to the 'Capitol' cinema in Green Lanes every Monday evening and to the 'Odeon' Southgate on a Friday evening. Both of these lovely cinemas were once very well patronised, both now having been demolished. The 'Capitol' always had a lovely smell and I loved the upstairs restaurant where Mum occasionally took me during school holidays for afternoon tea. I remember the larger than life portraits of the idolized film stars that adorned the walls. (See, also, the account of Brian Bennett of The Shadows.)

Wartime

During the air raids we slept in the shelter and suffered the noise of the anti – aircraft guns firing from the Firs Farm site in Firs Lane. We could hear the command 'FIRE' from our house. Somehow as kids, though, we knew no fear. I recall the night the V1 – or was it the V2? – dropped in Carpenter Gardens. I can see that ball of fire now. I felt sure it was going to hit us. (Note 2). I also remember the night a landmine dropped and wrecked Prince's Dance Hall, Palmers Green. There was a high loss of life as a dance was in progress at the time. I remember my days at Southgate County School with affection. There were frequent interruptions when the air raid sirens sounded and we were marched off to the air raid shelters on the school playing fields. Although we missed out in so many ways, there was a great espirit de corps.

The cinema was still the main source of entertainment and we went regularly. If the air raid warning sounded a notice would be projected saying something along the lines of, 'We have to advise our patrons that the air raid alert has been sounded and that those who wish to leave the cinema should do so now'. Nobody ever moved!

As I grew into my later teens the Saturday night dance became an almost regular feature. The well known local bands would perform and play a mixture of quick steps, waltzes and foxtrots. So many friendships formed on the dance floor, blossomed into courtship and then into marriage. In those days it was almost unheard of for people of our age group to frequent the pubs. Pubs were for the much older folk – particularly the men with their pints. How times have changed.

My Dad and I were great Arsenal supporters and I had a season ticket from the age of 7. During the war Arsenal's home matches were played at Tottenham's ground, since Highbury was used as an Air Raid Warden's H.Q.. The League was zoned to avoid long journeys so Dad and I were able to cycle to all matches, both home and away. I say cycle because petrol was rationed and cars could only be used for essential purposes. Dad worked every Saturday morning and I would often help dig out back gardens to accommodate Anderson Shelters. Father would usually tie our bikes on to the back of his car, which he could use for business, and then we could cycle on to see the Arsenal if they were playing at Millwall or Charlton or somewhere accessible from Walworth. We would buy tea and buns from the stalls outside the ground. For Saturday tea at home we always had fish – kippers or herrings or bloaters or smoked haddock – whatever Mum could get. Dad and I would relive the games we had seen and Mum would join in the excitement.

Brother Ron was in the Army serving in India and we had his picture on the wireless set in the corner of the room. Of course there was food rationing, and clothing coupons were in force all during the war as well as for many years afterwards.

I often used to get the shopping for Mum on the Broadway. There was a lovely 'Sainsburys' there with a very jolly lady who served on the meat counters to sell us our meagre rations. There was 'Burkes' the greengrocers. I remember Mr. & Mrs. Burke so clearly. Later on well after the war their sons Ivor and Alan continued the business. Everything was in short supply but when stocks were expected the word would go round and long queues would form. There was a particular shortage of meat and a new delicacy was introduced - whale meat. I recall the first supplies coming into Mac Fisheries.

I remember all the favourite radio programmes, too numerous to mention here, as well as the tram tracks coming up and the trolleybuses coming in. I think the biggest change in the last two decades has been the tremendous increase in traffic. Lorries and cars now ceaselessly trundle through what were once quiet roads and thoroughfares. Cycling, a great and enjoyable pursuit in my youth, has become impossibly dangerous. (Note 3) Noise and pollution have taken their toll. Great progress has been made in so many ways since the 1930's, but very often at some cost to the quality of life.'

<u>*Author's Notes*</u>

1. *The 1935 Kelly's Directory contains the following entries for the western end of Highfield Road -*

South Side: Cedar's Hall; 2. Sandles, Jsph.; 4. Martin, James; 6. Ganderson, James. grocer – here is Cedars Rd. – 8. Sparrow, Fras., dining rooms; 10 Brickett, Wltr.

North Side: 1 Andres, Geo.........25. Davies, David Alex. Shopkpr. 27. Clarke, Mrs. .... 51. Woodcock, William David; Holy Trinity Parish RM; Solomon & Brown, florists (Fords Grove nursery); Winchmore Council Schl.; Solomon Isaac (White ho.).

It would seem that Mr. Dumayne knew Ganderson as Gandy and, presumably, Davies as Davidson. The 1939 Kelly's still shows Ganderson the Grocer at No. 6 but for No. 25 the occupant is given as 'Leigh O.A., shopkpr.'. The Solomon family is, of course, covered in the Everett sisters' account in More Winchmore Hill Lives.

2. *The 'doodlebug' attack mentioned by Mr. Dumayne is covered in more detail in the accounts of Mrs. Doncaster and Iris Chamberlain in More Winchmore Hill Lives (2004), as well as elsewhere in this volume.*

3. *I think the situation has changed since this was written. There are now many dedicated cycle paths, whilst cyclists often try to navigate around pavement pedestrians rather than endanger themselves on the roadway.*

4. *In the summer of 2010 Sheila loaned me an early draft of a book Alan had intended, entitled My Sporting Heroes, which he briefly alludes to in his Fond Memories of Winchmore Hill. It was written in Alan's early middle age, and I thought that it would be interesting to quote, with Sheila's permission, a fragment from it here.*

'I was sports mad at school. I was a sprinter and athlete of fair ability, became vice captain of the cricket, and captain of the football first elevens. Above all I was an enthusiast, and a very proud captain of the Green House. My progress on the football field was unusual.

By the time I was fifteen I had settled into the outside right position after a spell at centre forward, when an injury forced me to stand down. It just so happened that week the school were without a goalkeeper, and I readily agreed to fill the gap between the posts to help out. I reckoned I was fit enough to play in goal even if I couldn't run around the field. There was no looking back. I became the regular goalkeeper and skipper of the first eleven. I was asked to join Durnsford Rangers, a leading local side in the Southgate Minor League, and gained representative honours when I represented the League shortly after the war on a short tour of Holland.

That was in April 1946. On my return I was told I had been selected to play in some final trial matches for a London Grammar Schools side that was being chosen for a three weeks tour of Norway. In a tour involving much travelling, five matches were to be played in various centres, where the people, as in Holland, free at last, longed to show their relief and gratitude to the mother country who alone had kept the light of hope burning in their darkest days. As you may imagine I was thrilled to hear I had been selected, with the added bonus that Ted Drake was to be in charge of the party. .... As we congregated on the platform at Kings Cross Station that day in 1946, we were individually introduced to our leader ....'

Alan must have had great satisfaction in working under his hero Ted Drake, who some readers will recognise as Arsenal's iconic centre forward from the 1930s. For some reason Alan omitted to mention just how good he was. At the front of his The Old Borough of Southgate was an obituary, following his premature death on 30th April 1998. This told us that, 'At school Alan excelled at cricket and football. He went on to play football for Enfield and an Arsenal youth team, being selected to play for his county and his country in representative matches. An injury put paid to a promising career.'

Eleanor Holder - Letters Autumn 2000

I was born in Barbados and started my nursing career upon arrival in the UK in 1964, moving to the Acute Ward for the Elderly at Highlands in 1974.

The old buildings were set in lovely grounds, whilst the staff and patients were a pleasure to work with. The wards had a Nightingale Setting, which entailed there being up to 30 beds set out in long rows on either side. Food was prepared in the hospital kitchen on a daily basis and the patients enjoyed these meals. Getting to work was easy as I lived in a nurses' home in the grounds until about eleven years ago, when I moved to Palmers Green.

I moved to Chase Farm in 1995 when Highlands closed. Here the meals are cooked in advance, stored and then served to the patients – but they do not eat all the food as they don't find it so tasty. Perhaps this is an area that could be investigated. (1)

I enjoyed my time at Highlands. It had a pleasant friendly atmosphere that I believe is sometimes lacking in modern hospitals.

Author's Notes.

1. *Nurse Holder's comments were brought to mind when I read an article by Lorraine Fraser in The Sunday Telegraph dated 23 September 2001. The article highlighted a report by The Audit Commission, the Government's public spending watchdog, on NHS catering. It said that nearly a quarter of Trusts made no attempt to establish patients' dietary needs, even though these could be essential to their health and recovery. Patients, particularly the elderly, were frequently not given the assistance they needed to eat their meals. Additionally, the food delivered was too often cold or not what had been asked for. Nationally there was a huge variation in the amount spent on each patient – from £3 to £20 per day.*

The Holstius Sisters - Various Interviews (and letters)

The following is based on an interview with Joan Stripp, nee Holstius, together with her elder sister Pauline, at the latter's home on 15th March 2008, with

Pauline only on 7th April '08, and Joan only on 7th June 2008.

Both were born at the southern end of Hoppers Road, in the family home almost opposite Palmers Green High School for Girls. Pauline was born on 23rd January 1916, whilst Joan came into the world in 1921. At Plate 26 is a photograph of a very young Pauline outside the family home of No. 27. Their mother's father, and his brother, (the Flaxmans), built much of Park Avenue, part of Windsor Road, and other local properties, at the turn of the 20th century.

Two doors south of the school was a cottage, built at right angles to the street, occupied by a Miss Dixey. It had a chicken run at the back, which occasionally supplied eggs to the Holstius household. Pauline also told of a man occasionally coming up from the Workhouse in Edmonton to beg in the side passage to their house, and Joan said that their mother would then give him some refreshment.

Joan told me that their father was a great walker, and decided not to buy a car even when he could afford to do so. Most weekends the family would stroll up to Winchmore Hill Station and catch the train to various scenic destinations on the Hertford North line, from where they started their walks. She said that they frequently saw Stevie Smith waiting on the platform to do the same. She stood out, even though not yet famed for her poetry, because of her slightly eccentric appearance. (See the account of Stevie Smith's life later in the book.)

The Fentum/Abery and Downes families, which had been in the vicinity since at least the mid 19th century, were featured in my 2004 *More Winchmore Hill Lives.* Both sisters remembered Fentum's store just north of *The Dog and Duck*, and, just south of the pub, the sweetshop run by Miss Downes, where you could obtain a good number of sweets, such as gobstoppers, for ½ d or 1d. (See Plate 23.) Pauline's recollection was that a penny would buy you 2 ounces of some of the cheaper sweets, whilst a ha'penny would purchase a liquorice dab or fountain. There was a cottage next to the sweetshop, then villas, then a small row of shops. (Note 1) A recent picture of this stretch of Hoppers Road is at Plate 24.

The first shop coming south was a Butchers called Hibberds. Next door was Begley the shoe repairer, at least when Pauline was younger, though later on, she says, the premises fell into disuse, and goods were left in the shop. Next was 'North's Library', which was a second hand bookshop where Joan used to buy her Angela Brazil stories. The corner shop on the north side of Stonard Road, where the Indian Restaurant now stands, was Williamson's Grocers, where their mother sent them regularly for an order of '1/2 lb. wide streaky bacon, no 7, no bone'. On the opposite corner of Hoppers Road and Stonard Road was Peters Off Licence. There was a sweetshop next door, which had a phone booth at the rear (in an era when 'phones were not commonplace), and next to this was the Grocery run by Sillick.

The girls attended the Convent School in Oakthorpe Road, Palmers Green, and usually walked there in the morning, there being very few cars in those far off days. They came home for lunch on the trams that ran along Green Lanes, the tops being open to the elements. The seats were turned around at the end of each journey so that they then faced the new direction of travel. Joan remembered that in those days the nearest south bound stop was on the island at the junction of Hedge Lane and Green Lanes. There was a large tree on it, with an uncovered seat around it.

At that time there was hoarding fronting waste land where there are currently flats at the northern corner to Green Lanes and Bourne Hill. The flats were built after the war. On the eastern side of Green Lanes opposite St. Monica's Church there was also hoarding, concealing waste between Oaktree Avenue and Hedge Lane, the flats there also being built after the war. The flats between Oaktree Avenue and Crestbrook Avenue were built before the war.

Joan remembered two houses, which were set back from the pavement, just south of the Post Office in Green Lanes, Palmers Green, where she once broke her ruler rattling it on the railings in front of them. Pauline remembered hoardings where there are now shops just south of Hazelwood Lane. Further south still both sisters recalled the old thatched cottage by The Triangle, pictured at Plate 28. In their childhood it was Whellock's, the florist, who owned land at the back where, Joan presumed, they grew plants. That plot bordered onto the then extensive grounds of the Oakthorpe Convent School, where today we find the open car park. (Note 2)

Pauline thought that in those days there was more snow, and it was thicker. She remembered well the frequent pea soupers of her childhood, which continued to blanket the capital until the early 1950s. She remembered, less clearly, the Muffin Man walking the pavements with a tray of his wares on his head. She recalled sheep coming up Green Lanes, from what she believes was Palmers Green Station, and then up the western side of Hoppers Road to a 'holding field' just south of the skew bridge. The sheep waited there until Stockton, the butcher next door to the old *Salisbury Arms,* collected them for local slaughter.

Pauline and Joan remembered the Walls Ice Cream 'Stop Me and Buy One' tricycle. If you wanted him to call on you, you put a 'W' in your window. Nix's Dairy on The Green sent a milkman around twice a day, and you went out to fill your own jug from a churn on his cart. There was also a travelling grocers, based in a cottage past *The Orange Tree* in Highfield Road. The Postman would sometimes make one of his deliveries as late as 10p.m.!

Pauline said that in this pre War era Tancock, the florist, featured in *More Winchmore Hill Lives,* had retail premises beyond the end shop at the top of Wades Hill, now converted to a garage for the neighbouring old house. Mrs. Wackett, whose account features elsewhere in this book, used to help the sisters' Mum with her housework. Pauline felt sure she could remember the old coach house, set back from the pavement in Radcliffe Road, near its junction with Station Road, as being a radio repair shop. In 1940 the Holstius family moved to 24, Broadfields Avenue, which then cost £1,200, but would now fetch over £ ½ million!

Joan, like many older people I have interviewed, spoke of Tidey's corner shop on the junction of Hoppers Road and The Upper Green, and Chalkley's baker's on the opposite corner, offering sticky buns. She also remembered Mably's draper's store, now occupied by Blendis the Dentist.

Both sisters were keen to tell me that they 'did their bit' for the war effort. Pauline worked in a bank, which was a reserved occupation, but joined the Women's Voluntary Service (WVS), and for a while did Fire Watching for incendiary bombs at night in central London, though after a while this was stopped as, in those days of inequality, it was deemed to be too dangerous for women. A girl who was killed by a bomb in the Aldwich – Kingsway area was from Winchmore Hill. There was no visible damage to her body, but clearly she had severe internal injuries. Pauline then did Fire Watching at the base of Wades Hill, and occasionally slept in a hut by the stream there. She was an Air

Raids Precaution (ARP) Officer for the 'doodlebug' attacks towards the end of the war, being attached to a large house called The Grange in The Bourne, opposite the cinema, where firemen and others came for breakfast and snacks.

Late in the War, or just after, Pauline helped at Park Side Farm in Hadley Road, cycling there in the bitter cold. She was given eggs and milk, which she welcomed, as rationing went on into the 1950s. In this period she spent many of her holidays and weekends working on the farm without payment, as she loved the work so much! She occasionally milked the cows, mixed their food, cut thistles, helped with the harvest, and all manner of farming jobs. Somewhere she still has a picture of herself on a carthorse. In this era she also spent a few holidays in the Cromer – Sheringham area of Norfolk.

Joan was a Civil Servant who, in 1942, was released to work as a Voluntary Aid Detachment (VAD) Red Cross nurse, attached to the Army at the half mile long Royal Victoria Hospital at Netley, Southampton Water, in Hampshire. At the beginning of 1944 the hospital, along with all other military hospitals on the south coast, was handed over to the Americans, to allow them to build up for the Normandy landings, but after VE Day it was handed back. The bulk of it was demolished in 1966, and all that now remains is the Chapel, which is now a visitors' centre for the Royal Victoria Country Park.

It was at the hospital that Joan met her radiographer husband Bill. They married in 1946, and in 1962 moved to her current address in Beechdale, where she and Pauline had played as girls in the remnants of Winchmore Hill Wood. There were then few houses on the Green Lanes side of Broad Walk. One way to access the woods was in a gap in the housing in Bourne Hill opposite Cranley Gardens, now occupied by a bungalow that looks slightly out of place with the earlier houses surrounding it. There was also another gap in the housing at the foot of Woodcroft, where after the war a small house was built. Joan explained that one reason for mentioning these gaps is that they were 'curiosity items', in that they denoted where new roads had once been planned to run earlier in the century.

Pauline remembered selling national saving stamps to Horace Regnart of the now vanished Stone Hall Estate. Joan told of meeting the comedian Ted Ray (of radio's *Ray's a Laugh* fame) when out for a walk with her Jack Russell terrier, when he told her that Jimmy Edwards, a fellow panellist on radio's *Does the Team Think,* had two like hers. He lived in a house on Broad Walk on the last stretch of it to be built up, between Brackendale and Bourne Hill.

Arthur Pettifer once lived next door to Pauline at No. 54, Wades Hill. Pauline had collected his personal account that I was allowed to use in my original 1991 *Winchmore Hill Lives*, and both ladies were obviously still interested in what went on locally. For example, I learnt that *Jim Thompson's* was soon to revert to being *The Green Dragon* again, and that Mrs. Netherclift, who had contributed to *More Winchmore Hill Lives,* had passed away in her 90s. I was pleased to learn that the publication of Mrs. Collin's recollections in that book had spurred Pauline into re-establishing contact with her childhood friend.

I was very interested to hear that the harness room remaining from Paulin's estate, pictured at P40 of *A Look at Old Winchmore Hill*, had a reputation of being inhabited by a ghost or poltergeist. They explained that the more northerly row of cottages in Harwood's Yard had their entrances facing north, onto what would have been the driveway to Paulin's mansion. He didn't like this, and so made the occupants access their cottages by their rear doors (as they still do).

Pauline also told me that the next cottage up from her own 'Broadfield' was owned in the late 19th century by the locally well known family of Newby, and their stables probably occupied what is now an atrium. (Note 3) She kindly supplied me with her research on the row of houses in the 1891 Census, which I have reproduced with the Paulin family account later in the book.

Joan told me that she considered that the area was at its peak before the War. I took the photograph of the sisters at Plate 27 outside Pauline's front door on 15th March, and thanked them for talking to me, especially as Pauline's health was not good. I was delighted, however, when Pauline asked me to call again after she had found a 'treasure trove' of old photographs, which she encouraged me to copy, with a view to publication.

I should also like to record that as I was about to leave Joan on my visit to her of 7th June, she told me, almost reluctantly, for fear of seeming boastful, that her late husband had been a leading figure in the field of orthopaedic radiography, and had been funded by foreign hospitals to lecture to them in their own countries. Trips to America, New Zealand and South Africa particularly stood out in Joan's mind. She pointed to a photograph on the desk of her and Bill outside Buckingham Palace in 1983, when he received the MBE for his work.

Notes

1. *The following listings appear in both the 1923 and 1930 Kelly's Directories, unless otherwise indicated.*

Emil G.S. Holstius is living at 27 Hoppers Road. On the opposite side a James Dixey is indicated as the occupant of No. 98, below Palmers Green High School. Nos. 76 and 78 are occupied by Fredk. Fentum, whilst Henry R. Lambe is shown as 'beer retailer' at 74. Charles Downes is at 72 with a General Shop, with four private residences, before Charles Hibberd's Butcher at 62. At 60 was Horace A. Begley, Sports Goods Manufacturer. At 58 was Stationer William Marlow (Harry North in 1930), and at 56 (the corner of Stonard Road) was Grocer Herbert Williamson. On the opposite corner, at 54, was Wine Merchant William George Peters. Next door at 52 was confectioner Horace Crocker (Kaza Davis in 1930), whilst at 50 was Grocer Frank Sillick. Then there are residential properties.

2. *In his Once Upon a Time in Palmers Green, Alan Dumayne tells us about Ye Olde Thatched Cottage, pictured at Plate 28. Alan reports that it was built about 1790 by Thomas Lewis, Governor of the Bank of England, as a lodge to a large house called 'The Lodge', which I suspect must be Plot 523 on the 1801/2 Enclosure Map. The estate took up much of the eastern side of the Green Lanes between Hazelwood Lane and the Triangle. The front garden was given up to accommodate the widening of Green Lanes in 1906, and the cottage was used as a dwelling place until 1911. Percy Whellock, FRHS bought the lease and converted it into a florist, and restoration work was carried out in 1916. Whellock developed two acres of nurseries to the rear of the shop. He sold roses, fruit trees, shrubs, bedding plants, seeds, bulbs, and cut flowers. The enterprise achieved fame even beyond these shores. Gradually, though, it seemed to be incongruous amongst the surrounding shops, and in 1938 the cottage was demolished to make way for a new branch of Burton's tailors, since having become Westlakes.*

3. *In his Memories of Winchmore Hill, Horace Regnart devotes one of his early chapters*

to Harry Cox, who was born in the village in 1839, and his family. Regnart says, 'They were driven to Hyde Park to see the 1851 Exhibition by Newby who had a livery stable on Wades Hill on the site of Burleigh Terrace.'

The Gazette of 17th October 1930 features an article headed, 'Water a Penny a Pailful at Winchmore Hill'. It ran, 'Newby, the carrier and fly proprietor, had his cottage, stables and yard where Nos 1 and 2 Broadfield Cottages now stand. Large casks and open tubs of water stood close to what is now the footpath, and when the pump on The Green (which was opposite Chalkley's shop at the corner of Hoppers Road) was dry, the cottagers either paid Newby a penny a pailful for water, or, alternatively, walked down to the Vicarsmoor Well, or to the New River, dipped their pails full, and carried them up the hill.....Newby was a relative of the well known Southgate builders of that name. Broadfields at that date was a farm....'.

Norman Last (Revisited) - Interviews 2005 & 2010

Some readers may recall that Norman Last (b. 15th December 1927) contributed to *More Winchmore Hill Lives,* published in 2004. His account, and the Directory listings for the top of Hoppers Road in his childhood, which accompanied it, were at Page 81 onwards in that book. I subsequently came across a photograph and article in *The Palmers Green and Southgate Gazette* of 31st January 1936 which focused on that stretch of road, and Mr. Last kindly agreed to meet me on 11th April 2005 to help identify more certainly the buildings in the old *Gazette* photograph. At that meeting, and in subsequent telephone chats, Norman also told me a little more of his background. This was added to when I met him at his home on 27th October 2010, his wife having passed away after some illness on 28th September, aged 77. He considered her a wonderful woman, whose fine artwork adorned the walls. The following adds to his earlier account.

Norman reminded me that his paternal grandfather William Last was groundsman at St. Bart's Playing Fields. "Old Bill", as he was known, came to the village in about 1905 and with the original account are two pictures of the old Pavilion. One was taken in 1986, and a better one taken about 80 years previous. It is possible 'Old Bill' was in that latter photograph. Norman now explained that the Pavilion, on St. Bart's Playing Fields, was also his grandfather's home!

'Old Bill' lived at the rear of the building, the accommodation taking up the full length of it. The western end contained the cricket scoreboard and the eastern side stables, the entrance to which are the two dark arches in the older photograph. These are similar in style, Mr. Last points out, to the arches adjoining *The King's Head*, where the village fire engine was once housed. He believes the Pavilion possibly pre dated the opening of the Sports Ground in 1895, though he didn't explain why.

To the west of the Pavilion were three grass tennis courts and during the Second World War the grounds were used for the London Counties cricket league. For many years there was also a Rugby spectator stand on the western (Haslemere Road) side of the fields.

His memory now truly prodded, Mr. Last went on to recall that next to Chalkley's corner shop (now a menswear shop), going down the Lower Green, was Willingham's, specializing in clock and watch sales + repairs. Next-door down again was a butcher's (now a launderette), and then Roseville mansion (now flats).

The Chalkley family appeared to occupy all that area of Hoppers Road from the corner shop up to, and including, the still existing 'Old Bakery' premises. These are now, as then, used as living quarters. Behind them, in the early 1930s, was the actual bakery and behind this, in turn, was a shed for delivery vans. Between the Chalkley premises and 1, Compton Terrace was a drive way, which not only enabled access to the foregoing, but also to a set of four of Chalkley's stables behind the houses at the start of Compton Terrace. The 3rd and 4th stables were behind the Last family home. Chalkley's son apparently married butcher Stockton's daughter. (Note: See the Chalkley family account elsewhere in this book.)

Norman knew some of his neighbours in Compton Terrace in the 1930s when he lived at No. 4. When he was a youngster Mrs. Palmer lived at No. 1 with her two daughters, one of whom was named Ethel. At No. 2 were the Horn sisters – Doris and May. At No. 3 was Mrs. May with her two sons Stanley and Horace, who was better known as Sonny. The latter contracted Polio in his late teens and Mr. Last remembers he used a wheelchair to get to work in Hedge Lane.

Mr. Last and his family occupied No. 4. Apart from Norman there was maternal grandfather Jack Westbrook, who looked after Nix's horses in stables in Wades Mews, mother Alice, father Bert, brother John, Uncle Arthur, and Aunt Doris, the last named remaining unmarried. In addition there was Elsie Westbrook, who became Mrs. Bennett, and Frederick Westbrook.

Mr. Wells, who was a Postman, lived at No. 5 with his wife. Norman knew them as Uncle and Auntie Wells. They had a son named Alec and a daughter, Winnie, who married a Mr. Halliday. At No. 6 were the Walker sisters, who were never best pleased when tennis balls strayed onto their premises. At No. 9 was the Turner family, and No. 14 was a hairdressers for some years. (Note 1.)

On the other side of the road, Mr. Last explained, Walker's fields ran to the south of his yard and, so, behind Esther Cottages, Stockton's, *The Salisbury Arms* and the old Salisbury Cottages (pictured at P48 of my 'A Look at Old Winchmore Hill'). He remembers the Esther Cottages as being clapperboard in nature (i.e. like the ones at the base of Church Hill) and recalls looking out from his bedroom window onto Walker's fields, which were visible where the building (shop) currently adjoining *The Salisbury Arms* is.

Since last talking to Norman about his account in October 2010 I have located the picture at Plate 29. This shows the stretch of Hoppers Road he has just described, as it was prior to its redevelopment in the mid 1930s. In that photo' the clapperboard Esther Cottages are hidden by the brickwork of Stockton, the butchers.

When he was a youngster his mother used to take him to Dr. Goble of Grove Lodge in Station Road. He was a kindly old man with white hair who charged 2/6d, as far as could be recalled, which was less than Dr. Simpson of Roseville's fee. (Note 2.)

Mr. Last then spoke of the war years, and with Mr. Last's permission I cover that period by quoting his *Come to the Front Norman*, written as reminiscences for his family. Talking of his time at Southgate County School in Fox Lane during the academic year 1942-3, Norman writes,

'It was during that school year that the war was brought home to us. Bombs and land mines were dropped during enemy raids. Two landed on the school's sports field; in both cases, on the boys' football pitch. The first landed on the goalposts at the far end, creating, in the future, a football pitch that was minus the final ten yards. (We boys, however, played on.) The second landed slap bang in the centre circle a few months later. (We boys called it a day then, even the great Stanley Matthews couldn't dribble a football whilst navigating a hole twenty feet wide by ten feet deep.) In fact, the second explosion happened whilst school was in session. The shelter we were in was the one nearest to where the bombs actually fell. We were rocked about, us and the shelter both, as the explosion detonated, the hurricane lamps flickered and the next second, they all went out! We were now in utter darkness! A young voice called out, "Who's pinched my gobstoppers?" Immediately all was forgotten and the confectionery hunt began......

.... At home during those war years, Dad (who when young had his left leg amputated beneath the knee) had been a very frustrated man. Like all "True Blue Brits" Dad wanted to be "up and at them" when war was declared in 1939, but because of his disability he could never pass the medical examination. He finally found an outlet for his frustration just as the Blitz began. The company Dad worked for was in the City of London, very near the Tower of London. Incendiary bombs were being dropped every night, everywhere, resulting in fire and destruction on a large scale. Dad volunteered for permanent night duty as a Fire Watchman. So, for the rest of the war, off Dad would go at about 5 p.m. every evening and return home the following morning at about 7.30 a.m. He never once complained, although he must have had, to put it mildly, some very trying times, nor did he ever speak about his time away.

Each morning he would be asking John (Norman's younger brother) or Mum or me what we were going to do that day. I know Mum was worried, but like all good mums, she would smile, straighten her apron and get on with cooking breakfast.

One morning Dad came in with very muddy boots and trousers that were scorched around the turn ups. "What on earth have you been up to Bert?" Mum asked. Dad smiled all over his face, "Playing football of course! On the roof at work." Mum sniffed, "Oh Bert, really!". She slapped Dad's finger away as he toyed with a sausage still in the frying pan. Dad said, "Ow!" as John and I laughed and the football matter was forgotten. It wasn't until many years later that I found out, quite by accident, that Dad had actually been putting his artificial leg to good use that night. He had kicked some burning debris from another building off of his own company's roof using his artificial leg to kick with, thus scorching his trouser turn ups. So the mystery of Dad's night time football match in London was finally laid to rest.....

.... One day, Dad noticed a poster about salvage and then saw an empty shop on The Green. He contacted the local Council, obtained the keys and "Bert's Salvage Shop" appeared. All the old metal, beds, bikes, kettles, cans – basically anything that could be converted into "armaments for the lads" – were brought to the shop. The Council lorry collected weekly, all the goods having been duly sorted by Dad. One morning, a lady brought in a rusty lawnmower and a box of old gardening tools. The goods were sorted out, leaving just the wooden box. Dad thought about it for a moment and yet another scheme was born.

Whenever there was a spare moment in the shop, Dad's hands were busy making doll's houses, forts and motor cars, etc. These were shown in the shop's window and raffled off, the proceeds going to all the different wartime charities. John and I had one of the forts Dad had made specially for us. It wasn't put in the shop window for raffling, it arrived at the bottom of John's bed via Santa Claus.

Dad's day during the war was as follows:- Morning – salvage shop.

Afternoon – sleep and then allotment (this was Dad's night in either a deck chair or bed). Evening/night – fire watching for at least 12 hours. This was typical of so many British "Civvies".

During the height of the Blitz Dad insisted that Mum, John, and I should go away for a month's holiday .... to Silloth, via Carlisle .... When we returned to London, fully refreshed and ready to go again we found several houses in our locality had been damaged by enemy action; our own house was untouched but houses in Station Road, Compton Road and Church Hill had all been badly damaged. The winter of 1943/4 gradually showed a slackening off ......'

When chatting about his school days in October 2010 Norman added that at Southgate County Grammar he was two years above Peter Baker, who was Spurs' right back in their great team of the early 1960s, and four years behind Warren Mitchell (his later stage name), who starred on television for many years as the awful Alf Garnett. The latter was also a good, tough footballer. Mr. Last played for the school team as a right footed left half, and confirmed that his late friend Alan Dumayne had indeed been on Arsenal's books as a goalkeeper when young, but an injury had cut short his early promise.

Norman spoke warmly of all his teachers at both his schools, and was proud that even after all these years he could remember them all. His Southgate Chemistry master Mr. Auger, who always walked with two sticks, was someone who taught Norman to rise above adversity, which Norman had to do before being badly injured in a road accident in 1959.

<u>*Author's Notes*</u>

1. *The listing for the top part of Hoppers Road, east side, in Kelly's 1934 Street Directory is: Chalkley Wilfred F. corn merchant. Chalkley Harold William. Compton Terrace: 1. Palmers Mrs. 2. Horne Edward. 3. Burrows John 4. Westbrook Arthur Henry 5. Wells James Alexander 6. Walker Misses 7. Cressee Miss 8. Mortiboy Edward 9. Turner Hy. Edwin 10. Fuller Miss Hilda 11. Chalkley Archibald F. 12. Teer William Thomas 13. Maison Ivy, hairdrssrs. – Freeman Wm. Hy. (HIllsbro') ... here is Compton rd. .....*

This listing features some familiar names. The Teer and Chalkley families are featured elsewhere in this book, whilst some readers will know that Fords Grove was known as Mortiboy's Lane in Victorian times, after the family's farming efforts in the vicinity. The 1899 – 1900 Kelly's Directory indicates that cow keeper Edward Mortiboy occupied Fords Grove dairy in the country lane, as Fords Grove then was. Perhaps the 1934 Edward Mortiboy was this same man, who would have been made homeless in 1911, when Southgate Council issued a closing order on the aged dairy farmhouse, owing to its poor state. A few readers will also probably recognise the name Cressee from the listing of land associated with the 1800 Edmonton Enclosure Act. David Cressee Senior then owned a plot off of Wades Hill near where the flats on the southern junction with Cresswell Way now stand.

2. *Dr. Goble's name has cropped up a number of time over the years, and he was obviously an important member of the local community. I was therefore pleased to come across an article in The Middlesex Gazette of 10th August 1939 in the David Hicks Archives which told us a bit about him. The Gazette article reported the death of Dr. Edwin Wallace Goble the previous Thursday from a cerebral haemorrhage. He had been educated at Merchant Taylors' School, and qualified at Guy's Hospital,*

where he became a house surgeon and physician. He later held the post of medical officer at the Queen's Hospital for Children in Hackney.

Dr. Goble came to Winchmore Hill in 1904, when it was still very much a village, practising at first in Compton Road, before moving to Grove Lodge, next to the station in Station Road. During the Great War Dr. Goble served with the Royal Army Medical Corps in both Italy and Gallipoli, where he took part in two evacuations. He won the admiration of the villagers with his devotion to duty, and made many friends. He was vice president of Winchmore Hill Cricket Club and a playing member of Crews Hill Golf Club. Dr. Goble was, up to the time of his death, medical officer for Halliwick Cripples' Home at Bush Hill Park, which was demolished in 1993. He was also a member of staff at Wood Green and Southgate Hospital.

Dr. Goble's funeral service was held at Christ Church, Southgate and the large number of attendees included Dr. Robert Simpson of Roseville, virtually opposite Grove Lodge. Other mourners included the well known locals Mr. E.J. Westoby and Mr. Frank Vanderpump. The Middlesex Gazette article included a photograph of the good doctor in his younger days.

John Lucas - Interview 17th May 2005
A Childhood That's Always Green

Winchmore Hill and I are old friends. And whenever I pass that way these days, from my present home in Potters Bar, I pop into *The King's Head* , opposite the 400 (stet) year-old-Green, and drink a silent toast to the village, which is bestrewn with my earliest – and among my happiest – memories.

One of these is prompted by that redundant old horse trough opposite *The King's Head* – filled these days, not with water for horses, but flowers to be admired. The memorable occasion occurred in September 1933. I was six and was taken up to The Green by our maid, Daisy, and sat on the trough and watched local history being made by HRH Prince George of Kent, husband-to-be of Princess Marina. He was driven by on his way from Oakwood Park, where he and the Charter Mayor had each planted a commemorative tree to mark the Prince's presentation of Southgate's Charter of Incorporation as a Borough. (Note 2)

That was not my earliest memory of Winchmore Hill, but it was one of an important occasion for Southgate. A more personal event occurred the day a year earlier when I started at St. Paul's Church of England School. I celebrated my arrival by bursting into tears at the prospect of being with strangers! But Mrs. Johnson, the kindly headmaster's wife, pacified me in the school house, and soon all was well. Miss Perkins, the dear infants teacher, who once came home to tea, helped settle me in, too.

My home was around a mile away in Sherbrook Gardens, (Note 3) near *The Green Dragon* (now *Jim Thompson's)*. My parents bought our three-bedroom house in 1926, soon after they married. It stood on New River Company land, opposite Firs Lane, and cost £800.

To get to school, my brother Ray and I – he started at St. Paul's a couple of years after I did – would first walk up Vicars Moor Lane, past Rose Cottage (where that prolific writer and poet Thomas Hood lived in 1829), then left along the railway passage towards Winchmore Hill station (which, surprisingly, was completed as far back as 1871), to Wilson Street. Turning right, we would pass through the always intriguing bottling plant of George Nix's dairy, then past the ancient Quaker Meeting House. St. Paul's school itself was a Victorian building next to the church, with the date inscribed on a buttress in the playground of 1859.

It took a little time to settle in – in particular to the quaint eccentricity of the head, Mr. John Nathan Johnson, a First World War victim of shell-shock. He seemed obsessed with Time, frequently glancing at the wall clock and searching the faces of the class for any of us who had stopped working.

Johnson's deputy was Henry ("Pop") Hallam, a model teacher – and literally so. He was always making models, whether a plaster-of-Paris relief map for a geography lesson, or a vivarium, complete with newts, small rocks, sand and weed for nature study. I recall him getting us all to make a nature box for specimens, and if possible a toy microscope. My father bought me one for five shillings (25p).

Our home near *The Green Dragon* backed on to tennis courts, which were bounded by Sherbrook Gardens – where we lived – then Myddelton Gardens and sections of Green Lanes and Green Dragon Lane. This square, home of Vicars Moor Lawn Tennis Club, was virtually a village in itself, as many of us were members or honorary members of the club, of which my sister Nan was a rising star junior player. Names that occur to me are the Hookers (leading lights), the Curries, Dabbses, Stubbingses, Pearsons, Holdgates and Barlows.

Two local teenagers, Hamish Currie and June Pearson, cleverly organised a unique little re-enactment by local children of King George VI's Coronation in 1937, with themselves in the roles of King and Queen (the jewels in their gilded cardboard crowns were wine-gums!), and Peter Rowley as the Archbishop of Canterbury. Everyone managed to wear costume, including me as a soldier – uniformed, thanks to my mother's handiwork, and equipped with a ceremonial sword off our dining room wall. (See Plate 30.)

Many of my happiest childhood days were spent in Grovelands Park – and still are. My companions now, though, are my younger son Jonathan, his wife Carol, and grandsons Jack and Carlo. All credit to the Council for shifting the children's playground nearer the refreshment pavilion than it used to be – but how sad that that modern curse, vandalism, has put paid to the fascinating aviary and the flotilla of shilling-an-hour rowing boats. (Note 4)

I never forget an appreciative glance for the stylish house of Grovelands which, famously designed by John Nash and landscaped by Repton, overlooks the lake. It belonged to the brewer, John Donnithorne Taylor, in the 1800s, but I knew it during the Second World War when it was a military hospital. The glow of the building and the green of the grass contrasted with the crimson blankets of the wartime wounded as they lay on their beds in the outdoor sunshine.

Just days before the Second World War started I was evacuated to a chicken farm in Cambridgeshire with my brother and sister. It was while I was there, when playing in the garden one day, that I heard Prime Minister Neville Chamberlain declare, on the radio, that we were at war with Germany. Life on the farm was quite pleasant, but we were home sick, and after only two weeks we returned to our home in Winchmore Hill.

Later in the war I was near to the carnage caused by a German bombing raid. I went to the cinema at Palmers Green when the air raid siren went off. I got a little worried and so I left to get the bus, which never came. I walked home, and next morning found that an area about half a mile from where I had been sitting had seen the worst raid of the War to date. Forty three people were killed and a bus blown up! I feel I was pretty lucky that day.

Like all families, ours played its part - a useful contribution, we hoped – during the war. My father (Leslie Lucas), was a Home Guard officer whose platoon was based in Rowantree House on Winchmore Hill Green, and my mother (Winifred) was a Red Cross nurse attached to a unit at Keble House School in Wades Hill. (See Plate 31.)

Many children – the Scouts anyway – collected old pots and pans to be melted down for weaponry. Three of us lived in Winchmore Hill and went to Southgate County School in Palmers Green – the other two were Rex Knight and Peter Morris – organised a little exhibition of First and Second World War relics in our respective front gardens on three Saturdays in 1941. The relics consisted of things like shell cases, and maps and medals from the Great War. Passers by contributed £7. 13s. 6d to the Spitfire Fund – worth well over £200 today. A Spitfire would have cost £5,000. At Plate 32 is a photograph of me (centre) selling the relics. This made the national press at the time, and is being shown at 'The Children's War Exhibition' at the Imperial War Museum, London for three years from 2004.

Well, Winchmore Hill regularly contributes to my fund, too – of happy moments in looking back.

<u>*Author's Notes*</u>

1. *John's story first came to my attention with the article on his war-time experiences featured in The Gazette of 10th March 2005. I approached Simon Jones, the Editor, for permission to reproduce the article, which he kindly granted so long as I acknowledged my source. However, I managed to track John down and met him to discuss a possible contribution. As he has spent much of his working life as a sub-editor and feature writer for the national Telegraph group we agreed that he should write things up in his own words. My thanks to both John and The Gazette for their co-operation. It is also interesting to note, incidentally, that John and Norman Last know each other from their respective youths, thus perpetuating the impression that even now the area sometimes seems to resemble some sort of 'giant village'.*

2. *Among the papers I have consulted over the years at the Local History Unit is the Programme for the Visit of Prince George on Saturday 30th September 1933 to commemorate Southgate's Charter Day. It includes the following,*

'The grant by His Majesty the King of a Charter of Incorporation to Southgate is the official recognition of the fact that Southgate has grown up. The scattered hamlets of a century ago became the small but vigorous Urban District of 1881, when Southgate was separated from Edmonton, and this in turn is now being transformed into an important Municipal Borough. After the Census of 1931 Southgate, with its 55,000 inhabitants, was included in the Registrar General's list of the 118 Great Towns of England, and now that His Majesty has conferred the Charter of Incorporation it assumes the rank and status of a Municipal Borough.....

.....A new chapter thus opens in the civic history of Southgate. On November 1st next it will exchange its governing body of 16 Urban District Councillors for

a Borough Council consisting of the Mayor, seven Aldermen and 21 Councillors........ The Charter Mayor will call the elected representatives together for their first meeting at the Town Hall at noon on the 9th November. At that hour the Southgate Council will..... elect the Mayor, who will hold office for one year....and is a Justice of the Peace for the term of his office.....The Aldermen are elected by the Council....The Borough Council will exercise all the powers of their predecessors, the District Council, and in addition certain powers which are now carried out in Southgate by the County Council.....Bye-laws "for the Good Rule and Government" of the Borough will in future be made by the Borough Council, and not by the County Council........A.E. Lauder, Charter Town Clerk.' (See Plate 33.)

3. *In December 2004 I received a letter dated 30th November from Anthony Farrant, in which he says, "A month ago, I purchased a copy of your latest book – 'More Winchmore Hill Lives' – and very interesting it is too. About the same time I realised that I have far too many records and magazines for a 2 bedroom maisonette! In my attempt to cull 50 years history, I started with the quarterly Newsletters of Vicars Moor Lawn Tennis Club. Among these was the enclosed item."*

The item enclosed by Mr. Farrant was a copy of an article in the Club's Newsletter for April 1976 by Pam Bowden. That article ran as follows:-

"As we are celebrating our 50th anniversary, some of our present members of the Club may be interested to learn what the Club was like fifty years ago. I believe that I am the only member still playing tennis who formed the Club when it first opened, although I hasten to add that I was then a Junior! Before Vicarsmoor (stet) LTC came into being, the area consisted of a few allotments and the rest was waste ground. This was a wonderful playground for the local kids. The Sherbrook was a muddy stream which ran where the path now is at the back of the houses in Sherbrook Gardens. There were trees whose branches stretched across the brook and we had great fun monkey crawling along the branches. My mother was not amused when a bough broke one day and I fell into the muddy water below.

In those days our house, number 16, Sherbrook Gardens, was the last house in the road and from there fields stretched all the way to Grovelands Park. Subsequently Sherbrook Gardens was extended and Myddelton Gardens was built to complete the boundaries of the Club. Just over 50 years ago a number of the local residents got together and decided to start a tennis club. The Ground Landlords – The New River Company – were sympathetic and with their help and a certain amount of toil and sweat, the Club came into being. Primarily it was intended for the use of those families living adjacent to the Club and a high proportion of them became members.

I think there were about eight Junior members, of whom, as I have said, I was one. We were very much pushed into the background and dashed onto the courts whenever we had the chance – which wasn't often enough for our liking. There were four red courts – those numbered 1,2,4 and 5 now. There were also three grass courts – the present court 3, the old all-weather court and another court alongside 4 and 5 where the Clubhouse now stands. The shed which was nearly burnt down a while ago was the pavilion, and there were no cloakrooms, but there was really little need for them as so many of the members lived within a stone's throw. On reflection it may be that my father had a 'loo' built at the back of 16, Sherbrook Gardens for more than our own convenience!

At weekends teas were served from trestle tables alongside the pavilion and I always remember the enormous tea-urn which we had. Irene Vernon and Peter Stubbings joined the Club in its early days and between us we have a frightening number of years of membership. My father was the Secretary of the Club for the first ten years and when he retired from that office the members presented him with a handsome card table in recognition of his services.

As I remember it, Vicarsmoor (stet) was a very happy club in those distant days. Times and the Club, have changed – but I like to think that it is still a happy club and that in the next fifty years many people will enjoy it facilities. As for me, I hope to be still playing when the Centenary comes round, though probably not at Vicarsmoor (stet)! - Pam Bowden."

Mr. Farrant continues, "Although I was a member of the club for some 26 years – mid 50s to early 80s, I do not remember this item, which has got me thinking. Hopefully, you can shed some light on the mystery 'Sher Brook'...."

Unfortunately I had to reply to Mr. Farrant at that time that I was stumped, and I have not met anyone since, including John Lucas, who has been able to shed much light on the stream.

4. *Another of the letters readers have been kind enough to write to me over the years was from Mr. Geering on 11th August 2004. It read,*

'Thank you very much for forwarding copies of your two books on Winchmore Hill, which I have loaned to my father, a resident since 1956, who has taken great pleasure reading them.

I have read the earlier book and would like to correct an error which I see has been repeated in the second book. This concerns boating on Grovelands Park lake. On P33 of the first book you say that you believe boating on the lake ceased about the time of WW2. Dr. James Curley, my former family GP, repeats this misapprehension in the second book.

As a resident of Winchmore Hill since 1956 I can assure you that boating continued on the lake until well into the 1960s, possibly early 1970s. I can well remember my brother and I rowing on the lake. I hope you do not consider this nit – picking. The books are an important chronicle of a well-loved area. Keep up the good work."

In the section on local poet Stevie Smith I quote from her children's book Allsorts, which appears to have been from the latter part of the 1960s. She says of Grovelands Park, 'Often I take a boat out and have a picnic lunch, first tying my boat up carefully to one of the trees that drop into the water from the lake's island, which is also where the swans have their house.'

I moved to the area in late November 1972 and very soon found myself walking in Grovelands Park. I must admit I have no recollection of boating from this time (or subsequently), though that is not to say that it wasn't still carried on.

5. *I'm sorry to record that on 29th December 2010 The Daily Telegraph reported John's death that Christmas Eve, aged 83. The obituary told us that he entered journalism after National Service in Palestine with the Royal Army Service Corp.. He initially worked on the Barnet Press and trade papers before joining The Telegraph, where he became a features writer and sub editor, helping to launch the Sunday version of*

the paper in 1961. He retired in 1995.

Jim Marriage - Interview 28th August & Letters September & November 2005

One of the other accounts in this volume is of the Downes Brothers taken at the family get-together organised by Val Darvell in Bounds Green, late summer 2005. Joan is the granddaughter of James Downes, being the daughter of Jessie, who was the sister of Val Darvell's mother Elsie. Joan married Jim Marriage and so I was able to talk to Mr. Marriage about his own family's association with the old village. His account is as follows:

'Readers will see from Alan Dumayne's account in this book that he was born in Harringay in 1929 and moved to Farm Road with his family in 1933. In his *Fond Memories of Winchmore Hill* he says of Highfield Road in his childhood years, "Nearly opposite the school, at the turn of the road, was the entrance to the old gravel pits, next to the row of red brick council houses built in 1899, but of sweeter memory were the two shops, Davies' and Gandy's. Davies' (previously Marriage's) was opposite *The Orange Tree*. Oh, the delights of the shop with all those glass jars on the shelves filled with brightly coloured confections...."

Ganderson's, or Gandy's as it was known, was on the corner of Cedar Road and Highfield Road nearest Green Lanes, but our family shop, as Mr. Dumayne says, was opposite the pub. My father Frederick ran it as a General Stores and it was his grandfather who, in about 1880, had built the shop with its living accommodation, now all converted into maisonettes. (See Plate 34.) He also built and rented out some of the nearby cottages, including those occupied by the Everett Sisters featured in *More Winchmore Hill Lives* (between Gandy's and Cedar's Hall). The Marriages, incidentally, were actually originally a family of millers from France. My father served in the Great War in the East Kent Regiment, at one stage being a stretcher-bearer.

I was born in the old shop in 1921, being one of two sons and six daughters. My father sold the shop when I was about twelve and we moved to the first house on the east side of Cedars Road. Dennis Woods is a neighbour who was born about the same time as me and who is still there! After four or five years we moved to nearby Carpenter Gardens and I lived there until I started serving my National Service in 1940. As a boy the roads were so free of traffic that we were able to use them as a playground. We would roller skate up and down them, ride on trolleys over them, play cricket, marbles, games using cigarette cards, whipping tops - everything! When my father bought a Standard car in about 1930 it stood out, as having a car was such a rarity.

I attended school in Highfield Road and knew the Everett sisters. The buildings in that neck of the woods haven't changed much, the main alteration probably being 'infilling'. Two features that have gone are Solomon's nurseries, which I think was still there in 1939, and the old tin mission (at Plate 12), which I believe went soon after the War.

Whilst I was at school Barrow Close was built nearby and it became home to many families from the East End. (Note 1) Some of the children were so poor that they came to class in bare feet. It hardly seems possible today! I don't know how these youngsters fared in the longer term. I was fortunate enough to have the ability, along with three other siblings, to go to Southgate County grammar school in Fox Lane. The old school buildings there are now flats of course, but the school itself moved to Cockfosters and became a Comprehensive.

I served in the RAF, in Coastal Command, as a Wireless Operator/Gunner in Sri Lanka, then still called Ceylon, in the flying boats - Catalinas and Sunderlands. Initially I was based at Vavuniya, about 20 miles inland from Trincomalee on the East coast, on the twin engined Beaufort torpedo bombers. (Note 2) The Squadron was sent out to Ceylon following the sinking of two of our Battleships by the Japanese Navy. By the time we arrived in May 1943, however, the Japanese had bombed Pearl Harbour and brought the Americans into the War. They therefore redeployed their Navy from the Indian to the Pacific Ocean and so, fortunately for me, the dangerous job of attacking their Fleet did not materialise. I was transferred to the less dangerous job of patrols in the Indian Ocean, first in Catalinas, and finally on Sunderlands.

Just prior to going abroad I was given leave, and Joan told me that her cousin, Reg Downes, was based in Gibraltar with the Commandos. Our first leg of the journey to Ceylon was from Portreath to Gibraltar, as it happened, and we landed about midday. I went to a local cafe with my pal and asked some soldiers there if they knew Reg Downes, whereupon one of them produced a small group photo' which included Reg. They took us a short distance up the road and I was able to say hello, before returning to the aerodrome for our next leg to Tripoli.

Sergeant Mills lived in the houses opposite the tin mission in Highfield Road and his eldest son Bert married my sister Joan.

I was demobbed in April 1946 and I married my own Joan that July. Newlyweds have always found it difficult to find housing and we were pleased to move to Finchley, where her parents were living. They gave us accommodation in the upstairs portion of their house. After about two years we moved to the borders of Wood Green and Palmers Green, where we stayed for approximately eight years, before moving to our current house in Potters Bar.'

<u>*Author's Notes*</u>

1. *At P. 57-8 of the 1991 Winchmore Hill Lives Mr. Love comments on the East End children who came to Barrow Close when it was developed between the wars. He too indicates a high degree of poverty amongst the newcomers. However, in their account in the 2004 sequel, More Winchmore Hill Lives, the Everett sisters say that their lifelong friend Gladys Fisher, a long term inhabitant of Barrow Close, felt that Mr. Love's remarks were not well founded.*

2. *As it happens, earlier in August 2005 we had spent a couple of days at Eastbourne with our niece Aneesha, and we so enjoyed the RAF air show that Aneesha bought me an Encyclopaedia of Military Aircraft when we got home. From that lovely book I am able to give a few details about two of the aircraft Mr. Marriage mentions.*

The twin engined Bristol Beaufort was the RAF's standard torpedo bomber from 1940 to 1943. It operated mainly in the North Sea and Atlantic, but when deployed to Malta in 1942 caused great damage to enemy conveys to North Africa. The aircraft had a crew of four, with a maximum speed of 265 m.p.h. It had a service ceiling of 16,500 feet and a maximum range of 1,600 miles. Its dimensions were - 44' 7" long, 12' 5" high and a 57' 10" wingspan. It weighed 21,228 lbs. with two .303 inch Vickers guns in the dorsal turret, one in the port wing, and one rearwards firing machine gun under the nose. It carried up to 1,000 lbs worth of bombs internally and 500 lbs externally, or one 1,605lb. torpedo.

The design of the Short Sunderland was based on that of a passenger aircraft that flew with Imperial Airways in the 1930s. Various versions were produced by Short and another Company, named Blackburn. It was used by the Military as a long-range maritime patrol aircraft with a crew of ten. It had a maximum speed of 217 mph at 5,000 feet and a service ceiling of 17,900 feet. Its maximum range was 2,980 miles and it dimensions were - 85' 3" long, 34' 6" high and a 112'9" wingspan. It weighed 60,000 lbs. loaded. It boasted ten .303-inch machine guns and could carry up to 4,960 lbs. of bombs, mines or depth charges.

Bill Parkinson - Interview 23rd August 2000

I was born in Glasgow in 1917 and joined the Royal Navy in 1937 as an apprentice engineer. I was lucky enough to be involved in the sinking of the Bismarck in 1941 and my ship, HMS Rodney, was re-fitted in Boston, USA, where they feted us.

One weekend when on shore leave I met my wife in Torquay. She was from Woodland Way in Winchmore Hill. We married in Gibraltar Cathedral in 1947 and I continued to serve with the Navy in various overseas locations. These included Malta, and my three sons went to the Naval school out there.

I was involved in the Suez crisis of 1956, but in 1958 I took early retirement at a time when the forces were being cut. We lived in Meadowcroft Road before moving, soon after, to my home in Arundel Gardens. My two youngest boys attended the schools in Highfield Road, but the eldest went to St Paul's School. This was then situated in Church Hill, and soon to move to Ringwood Way (after a short sojourn at St Paul's Institute in Station Road from 1958 to March 1961).

When we first moved to the area I worked at Regents Palace Hotel as an Engineer, before moving to Enfield Cables for 3-4 years. Upon being made redundant by them in the early 1970s I secured an Engineer's position with the Co-Op Bakeries. I covered all the London branches from their premises in Oakthorpe Road.

When my wife was alive we used to enjoy driving out into the Hertfordshire countryside. I have also enjoyed bowling in Grovelands Park, and used to walk my dog in the Park regularly. In my experience Winchmore Hill has always been a pleasant place to live, and, like Mrs. Doncaster, am happy to attend Reardon Court regularly.

Author's Note

My thanks to Reardon Court for putting me in touch with Mr. Parkinson, and allowing me to interview him on their premises at the same time as Phyllis Doncaster (nee Ives), featured in the 2004 More Winchmore Hill Lives. Mr. Parkinson is pictured at Plate 35.

The Pettengell Family

The following is a summary of family recollections collected for us by my friend Derek Norman, who now lives in Huntingdon. He knows the area because he was brought up in Edmonton and his cousins lived at 46, Carpenter Gardens, in nearby Winchmore Hill. They called Derek 'Little Arthur', and his father 'Big Arthur'. The eldest cousin was Peggy Pettengell (90 on 9th May 2011), whose daughter Kathleen has contributed a few lines on her behalf. Peggy's brothers Brian and Joe, and sister Ann, mainly remember events of the Second World War. The three remaining brothers were Raymond, Derek and Norman. Let's take Brian's account first,

'My name is Brian Charles Michael Pettengell, my father being Frederick H. Pettengell, who was totally blinded when serving in the First World War. Mum's sight was little better! She had only 10% vision and was also registered as blind. Her Christian names were Florence May, and we lived at 46, Carpenter Gardens at the time of the V1 'Doodlebug' attack on 7th July 1944, covered in *More Winchmore Hill Lives.*

Unfortunately my earliest memories are of this wartime era. I remember the searchlights and the sound of the air raid sirens and ack ack guns at night time. My sister Peggy ended up marrying Dennis, one of the soldiers who fired the ack acks! (See Plate 38.) I used to carry round a Mickey Mouse gas mask, whilst my younger sister, who was born in June 1942, was placed in what looked like a long tube with a gas proof flap secured over it. When we went out we could see lots of white lines in the sky, and I came to learn that these marked where aircraft had been. I could see the glow of the night sky when London was being bombed.

Sometime in the Spring of 1943 one of our aunts came to 46 with one of those wicker baskets with a lid, which she opened, and then pulled out a very small duckling, which she said would make a good Christmas dinner. The duckling was given the name of Minnie, and she soon settled in with Ginger the cat, and Bob the dog. Ginger and Bob used to sleep curled up with one another, and it didn't take Minnie long before she joined them. We had an Anderson shelter in our back garden, but it was never used because it became flooded, which suited Minnie, because she used to go and swim around in it. If she went for a walk our neighbours, who were good people, would bring her back to us. Needless to say, by the time Christmas came Minnie was such a firm part of our family that we couldn't do away with her!

I started at nearby Highfield Road School in 1943. When the air raid sirens were sounded we children took our writing slates and chalk into what were called 'strong rooms' at the back of the school, three or four classes to each strong room. The windows had brown paper stuck to them in diagonal crosses, with fine wire mesh on the inside. The senior pupils went into deep shelters.

On the night of 6th/7th July 1944 a flying bomb came over, its engine shut off, and I believe it bounced off the roof of the school and landed in the front garden of one of the nearby families – the Chamberlains I think. My ceiling came down, as did some roof tiles, plaster from the side walls, and the front door was blown to the top of the stairs. One of my brothers, Raymond or Joe, went to hospital with glass in his head. I don't know who got me out of my bed, but I was taken to the kitchen where Mum had some washing in soak in a galvanised bucket, and I was cleaned up with the washing water! My brother Derek, who was in the merchant navy, was home and just out of hospital after an operation, but he still went out to dig out people trapped in the rubble.

Someone must have told Mum and Dad that there was a WVS van in Highfield Road because we were given two empty milk bottles and sent to get some tea from it. As I walked down the road the block of three houses next to us had lost their roofs and windows, and had suffered a lot of damage to the walls. The next six houses, built in two blocks of three, were flattened, and you could see the furniture and beds. One bedroom still had a light bulb shining. There was a big hole near these houses which the fire brigade had filled with water, with gas bubbling up in it. I think thirteen people were killed in all. (Note: There is a photograph of the damage at P54 of *More Winchmore Hill Lives.*) Our cat and dog disappeared, the cat returning the following day, the dog after 18 months.

We were taken to a rest centre at the Congregational Church (now the United Reformed Church) at the top of Compton Road, where some years later I joined the cubs and scouts. I was given a small package with a tooth brush and a tin of Gibbs tooth cleaner, which was a solid block in the tin. I wasn't at the rest centre very long, because the next day I went into hospital with an infection of some kind. When I came out I was taken to 81, Selbourne Road in Palmers Green, where the family had been moved to. We were then moved up north to a suburb of Leeds called Middleton, where we went on trams a lot, but we soon moved back to 46, Carpenter Gardens.

We used to have a collection at school once a year for Iris Chamberlain, who had lost both her legs in the V1 incident. There was a bonfire on the nearby green to celebrate VE day in May 1945, and another one a few months later when Japan surrendered.'

'Hello there. I'm Brian's brother Joe, and I'd like to add a few words about life in Carpenter Gardens during the war.

My father, Frederick Pettengell, was blinded when he and a friend were taking ammunition by horse and cart to a boat in the docks during the First World War. For some reason the horses bolted, the cart overturned, and there was an explosion as the ammunition was thrown out of the cart onto the ground. My dad's friend was killed in the explosion.

Towards the end of 1940, well before the 'doodlebug' incident, I was leaving the house to go to the nearby school at about 8.45 a.m. I could see what looked like flies in the sky. These were German bombers flying roughly north. One of the bombs they released dropped about 200 yards north of Palmers Green Station, but because it landed in the railway cutting there was very little damage. Another time a bomb dropped in the playing fields next to Winchmore Hill Police Station, where the large Sainsbury's now is. There was some damage to nearby properties, but not as much as there would have been if it had landed on the Haslemere Road side of the fields. (Note: Presumably, the same incident recalled by Mr. Arnold in *Winchmore Hill Lives* of 1991.)

I remember a stick of bombs straddled the allotments near Highfield Road School, and another bomb fell in the school field near to the footpath to Firs Lane. The school suffered considerable damage due to the blast, and there was a large bomb crater, about 40 feet in diameter and about 20 feet deep, not far from the footpath.

We used to go down the back garden to the Anderson shelter when the air raid siren sounded. It was so cold down there that one night my dad said, "May, let's get out of this shelter and die in our own beds". We never used the shelter again, and eventually it flooded and our pet duck used to swim in it. The duck was given to our Uncle Arthur as a Christmas present for his son Little Arthur, who lived in Edmonton. The duck used to follow us to school, and it did the same thing when Little Arthur went to school. None of us could stand the thought of eating it, even though there was very little food due to the meagre rations.

I too remember the V1 doodlebug strike of 7th July 1944. I was woken up by a large explosion, coughing and spitting and unable to open my eyes. This was because of the dirt, dust and plaster mixed with blood covering all of my face. Dad came into the bedroom almost immediately to see if my brothers, Raymond and Brian, or I had been injured. The windows, doors and a wall were blown out. Dad, who was blind, had, I think, been sleeping with my mother and younger sister, Ann. The blast had thrown the front door up to the top of the stairs near the toilet. We all managed to get out of our house and join other people in the road.

Looking towards Highfield Road we could see that the blast from the doodlebug had demolished four houses on either side of our road, and had broken a gas main, which was on fire. There was considerable damage in Carpenter Gardens, and some houses in Highfield Road were severely damaged. In fact there was damage to property virtually everywhere you looked.

It was about 1.20 a.m. and the house the Pretlove family lived in was now a pile of rubble. I believe that there were two survivors. Dennis Pretlove survived the explosion, but his elder brother who was going to catch the last bus along Green Lanes, missed it, returned home and was killed. Mrs. Pretlove also survived. It was said that the V1 hit the chimney of the Dickenson's house on the East (Edmonton) side of the road and spun into the road. I don't remember what happened then until I arrived at the Rest Centre.

We thought our dog, Bob, was dead, but 18 months later a scruffy looking dog was sitting on our doorstep. I tried to shoo it away several times and then I realised it was our lost dog, Bobby. We don't know where he went during the time he was missing, but we were glad to get him back!'

Sister Ann writes, 'My first remembrance, aged about three, is of being in bed with my mother, lying on her left side away from the windows. I woke to a loud noise which came nearer and nearer, becoming almost deafening, before being replaced by silence. My mother rolled over on top of me and I struggled hard to get out, as I couldn't breathe. Then there was an enormous explosion. Next thing was my father coming in, asking, "Are you all alright in here May?" to which my mother replied, "Yes". Mum asked after the boys, and was told they were alright, but my brother Joey had glass all over him from the window at the front of the house. He added that the front door was now in the toilet – which was at the top of the stairs.

Our house was just four doors from where the bomb impacted. It was a direct hit, and the parents and son were killed and the daughter, my age, was in a very bad way, having lost her legs in the blast. Fortunately she made a good recovery, and I am pleased that she was featured in Stuart's *More Winchmore Hill Lives*, along with the account of our neighbour Phyllis Doncaster, nee Ives.

I also remember our dog Bobby disappeared, and everyone was looking for him before we left what remained of our house, but at that time we never found him. The strange thing about this was that he turned up 18 months later! Anyway, the next thing I can remember of the attack is arriving at the Congregational Church Hall at the top of Compton Road, where we were given hot drinks. I had never seen so many people in one place before. They had blankets around them and some were sitting on the floor, others on what looked like boxes.

The next thing I knew we were in Leeds, and in the big glass market with my parents and my brothers Norman and Joey. It was my birthday, I was going to be four, and Norman bought me a collie dog as a present. I remember little else on this short period of evacuation.

I recall a street party, which must have been to celebrate the end of the War. I presume it would have been VE Day. It was a big party, and the tables must have stretched the length of the street, laden with food and drink. I expect the benches and tables must have come from the school.'

Peggy's daughter, Kathleen, has selected a few facets of her mother's life for us as follows, 'My Mother has always been known as Peggy, but her full name at baptism was Margaret Kathleen Joan Pettengell. She was born on 9th May 1921 at the North Middlesex Hospital, Edmonton, and was the first of seven children born to Frederick Horace and Florence May Pettengell, nee Norman. Frederick was listed as a General Draper and the couple lived with his parents at 222, Victoria Road, Edmonton (otherwise known as 'The 2s'). The family moved to rooms at Miss Bellows' cottage on the corner of Green Lanes and Firs Lane in Winchmore Hill, then on to Hood Avenue in Southgate, before settling at 46, Carpenter Gardens.

Peggy went to school in Highfield Road and joined the Girl Guides. She worked at the counter at Baines Bakery, later on the till at Buttery's butchers on The Broadway, before moving on to Klinger's, who manufactured stockings in their Edmonton factory. Here she received a rather Maoist like document under the Stars of Industry Scheme, which said she had been, "adjudged Victory Worker Number 2 in the special drive for increased production held at The Klinger Manfg. Co. Ltd. Edmonton during the week ending 10th February 1943 thus setting an example for those who are working for the Victory of the United Nations". (Note 2.)

During 1940 - 1 Peggy's brother Raymond used to deliver newspapers to the nearby army camp and his mother told him to invite one or two soldiers home for tea. One of the soldiers was Gunner Dennis William Shepherd, whose visits became more frequent, culminating in marriage at Holy Trinity Church near The Broadway on 26th May 1942. (See Plate 38.) They lived at 17, Endymion Road, opposite Finsbury Park, until 1944, when a bomb landed nearby and shattered all the windows, spraying her bed with glass. So it was that she moved back to 46, Carpenter Gardens, occasionally sleeping over at her friend Bessie's house. This was where she was on the night that the V1 devastated the family's roof.

The family was, as we have seen, evacuated to Leeds, where she worked in the Stationery section of a large Department Store. At the end of the war, her husband having been absent for most of the time in Sicily and Italy, she moved to a flat at 17, Oakfield Road, Finsbury Park. Dennis was discharged from the Army in February 1946 and secured a permanent job at the GPO as a telephone engineer. The couple had children, and eventually in 1966 the family moved to Kent. Kathleen rates her a top class Mum!'

Having co-ordinated the collecting of the Pettengell accounts for me Derek, who lived in Edmonton at the time, volunteered his own wartime recollection as follows,

'I had an experience relating to a doodlebug when playing with a friend in Edmonton. I was playing with my friend Dennis Taber in an alleyway behind Huxley Road, running into Bromley Road, where I lived with my dad. There was suddenly a noise that got louder and louder and Dennis and I saw this doodlebug approaching from the direction of Pymmes Park. We were petrified and it was too late to get to the Anderson shelter in Dennis's back garden. We just gazed in amazement as the doodlebug passed almost over the top of us at what looked like about 300 to 400 feet. The V1 passed over us and as it got over Tatem Park or that vicinity the engine cut out. We watched it disappear and after several seconds heard a distant explosion. I believe it fell on Barnet or Friern Barnet, but cannot be sure. We had been frightened out of our lives.

I have since checked with a foot ruler on a Greater London Atlas, and Huxley Road is roughly parallel with, and on a direct line from East to West with, Friern Barnet.'

<u>*Author's Notes:*</u>

1. *I have consulted the Street Directories at the Local Studies Unit and the nearest I can find to 'the incident' are those dated 1938 (for before) and 1951 (for after). I have put the 1951 listings for this part of Carpenter Gardens in brackets after the 1938 ones:-*

North/West Side of Carpenter Gardens = (M.W.B Cottage, Ansell, Harry, W.) 62. Payne, Alfd. Jsph.(Draper, Frederick) ; 60. Swanborough Edgar G.(Edwards, Leonard. A.) ; 58. Hurt, Edmund (Hurt, Edmund); 56. Cook, Geo. Edwd.(Cook, George E.) ; 54. Shearing, Edwd. Rt.(Coulson, Francis H.) ; 52. Plaston, Harry (Kirby, Herbert W.) ; 50. Shepherd, Leo (Shepherd, Leo); 48. Elliott, Jn. (Elliott, John); 46. Pettengell, Fredk. Horace (Pettengell, Frederick H.) ; 44. Strutt Jn. Guy (Bullock, George H.); 42. Duke Mrs. (Chapman, Reginald H.); 40. Swanborough, Mrs. Helen K. (Swanborough, Francis S.H.) ; 38. Partridge, Leslie Danl. (Partridge, Leslie D.); 36. Pretlove Jn. Wm. (Diggins, Charles); 34. Chamberlain, Harry. (Finch, Sydney G.); 32. Larkins, Albert. (Cole, Leslie W.).

South/East Side: 2. Sutton, Mrs. R. (Woonton, Alfred G.); 4. Ginn, Bertram Chas. (Pretlove, Chas. S.); 6. Press, Albert (Westbrook, Arthur W.); 8. Gentry, Alfd.(Gentry, Alfrd. H.B.); 10. Holman, Chas. Hy. (Holman Charles H.) ; 12. Arnold, Jn. R. (Goddard, Sidney W.); 14. Budd, Charles Hugh (Budd, Charles H.) ; 16. Findley, Mrs. M (Moody, Herbert S.); 18. Morri, Herbt. Jn. (Wood, William E.) ; 20. Withers, Allen (Byrne, Thomas C.); 22. Minors, Rd. (Hill George T.); 24. Hopson, Hy. (Hopson, Henry E.) , 26. Withers, Thos.(Withers, Thomas A.) ; 28. Ives, Alfd. Albt. (Ives, Mrs. Amy E.) ; 30. Solomon, Joseph (Dickinson, John T.)

It is a little confusing, because the two sides are numbered in a different manner. In More Winchmore Hill Lives of 2004 Phyllis Doncaster, nee Ives, describes the effects of the V1 attack on her family at No. 28.

2. *Derek Norman and I were intrigued by this Stars of Industry wording, which seemed more reminiscent of a Workers' Revolutionary Co-operative than a British company, and he obtained a photocopy of the certificate, which is worded exactly as quoted. The other thing that had intrigued us is the reference to the United Nations. At P42 of their book on the European Union entitled The Great Deception, Christopher Booker and Richard North tell us that, 'The first UN General Assembly was held in London in January 1946, under the presidency of Belgium's foreign minister Paul - Henri Spaak.'*
   Perhaps, even in 1943, the politicians were already working on something behind the scenes?

Pat Sinclair - Southgate Village Life

'Dear Mr. Delvin, Tuesday 7th September 2004

I am enjoying your latest publication of *More Winchmore Hill Lives*, as I am always interested in other people's memories of time past in our lovely district.

I thought you might be interested in the enclosed (no need to return same) – A little account of my early childhood. As you see, I wrote this at age 77 years – I am now 81(!) so – another 4 years on and the only changes I've noticed since then have been the growth of eating houses in Chase Side, Southgate. I wonder how they all survive?!

With all good wishes. Sincerely – Pat Sinclair (Mrs.)'

Southgate Village Life - c. 1925-30. Written in June 2000

I am 77 years of age and have lived in Southgate since I was 5 years old. So my recollections of Southgate as a village are as of a child aged 8 years.

Early in 1931 whilst walking with my mother along Crown Lane, which was indeed a lane then, some workmen were cutting down the trees and hedges to make way for the building of the Underground Station. They called me over to view some baby birds in a nest, which they were reluctant to destroy, but had to. Then came the Piccadilly Line, extended from Wood Green to Cockfosters, and also the 'mushrooming' of suburbia, with houses, new shops, whilst the Odeon Cinema in Bourne Hill soon materialised.

I can still view from my childhood's mind both sides of Chase Side, with the open topped double decker 29 bus journeying through to Hadley Wood, Cockfosters, ending at the *Cock Inn*. I can clearly recall some of the old shops and cottages.

On the corner of Chase Road/Chase Side was *The Bell* public house. Next came the men's barber's shop, and rumour had it that the customers took their lives in their hands upon entering, as the barber's habit was to nip into *The Bell* for a 'refresher' between haircutting! Next was Lee's grocery stores - a double fronted shop including the Post Office. Then Wheeler's the Newsagent for whom my brother did a paper round, and I used to help him on a Sunday morning. Old Mrs. Biggs kept the little toy shop next door, which had a real Dickensian flavour, until her son took over as Mrs. B. advanced in age. Next was a haberdashery shop run, as I recall, by two maiden ladies, the Misses Draper – but perhaps that wasn't their real name and they were labelled this due to the nature of the merchandise. (I actually never thought of the matter until now!)

Other shops included another grocer where they used to grind coffee – and then other houses and cottages through to the Baptist Church, which had an elevated pulpit, which much impressed me as a youngster, as the parson appeared to tower above his congregation from a great height. The recreation ground with a roundabout and a swing, plus the allotments (now an Asda store) were behind St. Andrew's Church of England.

Then on to the Cockfosters Road with farmland, farm and an orchard at Cat Hill and Bramley Road. At Cockfosters just further on from the Underground Station is the old school house (still standing) where the boys were educated and I attended the Girls' Church School at the back of Christchurch. The cricket ground opposite Trent

Park was used by the Girls' School every year to celebrate May Day, when the chosen Queen and the attendants were enthroned, and the rest of us took turns in dancing round the Maypole. (I get such pleasure today to watch today's youngsters re-enacting those times with the Maypole at The Green, Winchmore Hill on May Day.)

Chase Side from the left, going towards Cat Hill, I remember *The Rising Sun* public house, Southgate Club (still in existence); the Police Station; old Mrs. Groves newsagent. I remember my brother and I carol singing in Bourne Hill and my brother (now 80) recalls that one house owner came out and asked him to stop singing and to let his sister carry on as she was much more in tune! However, somebody else gave us a bag of farthings, which we took into old Mrs. Groves' shop to spend on Christmas cards for our parents and friends. I recall the old lady being very disgruntled at having to accept all those farthings! (Incidentally, I guess at our tender age we thought of all adults as "Old"!)

Collins the butcher next and then the Crown Hotel, further on, *The Waggon and Horses*. Three pubs in that small village! (plus of course *The Bell*). Then to Sir Thomas Lipton's house and Estate, covering Osidge Lane and through to Cat Hill, with the Theological College between and at the end of Chase Side, the Boys' headmaster Mr. Bovey had his house on the corner of Cat Hill.

The 29 bus pursued its way towards Cockfosters in a truly rural setting. We children knew the names of all the wild flowers, knew where to blackberry pick, find chestnuts, hazel nuts and beech nuts – and collected frog's spawn, frogs, newts and the boys sometimes hunted for birds' eggs. We walked everywhere. On the rare occasions that we went to school on the bus it was a great excitement to go upstairs on the open deck and sit with the tarpaulin covers pulled up to our necks to keep the rain off.

So indeed came the end of village and country life as I knew it as a small child in Southgate. I guess life became easier for our parents with the modern transport and facilities which became available. My father became the proud owner of an old Morris Cowley car – a two seater, with a "dickie Seat" at the back exposed to the elements, where my brother and I were deposited – aged 8-10, no seat belt or helmets – my mother must have died a thousand deaths wondering if she would lose us en route. But we loved it. Perhaps we were in no great danger as the car probably only went at about 5 miles an hour. Anyway, we are still alive to tell the tale.
Note: I know that Mrs. Sinclair's account is mainly about Southgate, but it was 'the next village along', and I thought it would resonate with readers. I'm unaware of any local oral histories of Southgate, so it seems better to include it here rather than not have it published at all!

Harry Skinner - Interview 10th March 2005

My father was a builder, but not in any way related to the firm of the same name which was based in Station Road. My parents and three older brothers moved to Sunnyside Cottages in Green Lanes in 1907. These were on the site of what became Ironside's Garage. (Plate 39.) I was born in Hornsey on 31st October 1912 and remained there with my grandparents until I joined my immediate family in 1917. As you can see from the photograph at Plate 37, Michael Lawrence and family occupied one side of the cottages, and my family the other. We lived there until Ironside bought us out, though the transaction turned rather messy and ended up in the courts. I think my family was eventually paid £500 and given accommodation in the area. This would have been in the 1930s as I recall. (Note 1)

I did all my schooling in Highfield Road and attended at the same time as Harry Finch, who is featured in your original *Winchmore Hill Lives*, and his family. He was as fiery as myself and there was something of a clash of personalities between us. I also knew two of his brothers and Jack Maynard, who I presume must have been a brother of Lucy.

At this time Winchmore Hill was still a lovely country place with fields all the way to Enfield. It was a joy to be a child in such surroundings. One of the fields that stands out in my memory was one that was at the foot of what is now Sherbrook Gardens, though I can't recall any brook running in the vicinity. Occasionally I used to go to Firs Hall, which is where my daughter had her marriage reception. I can remember scrumpying as a boy in the grounds of Southwell farms, between the Hall and the New River, and climbing up an oak tree in Paulin's grounds to watch the cricket. What a good service the family did when they left the grounds to the Club. (See the Paulin family account later in this book.)

I did not frequent Grovelands Park much. For many years, of course, the Mansion was used as a hospital. (See Plate 94.) I did play in the area of Broad Walk as it was gradually built up. One grand mansion that I particularly remember was Dodeodata.

There were quite a few poorer people in the area in those days, alongside the rich of Broad Walk. I remember one man used to come up into our area from the old Workhouse situated where the North Middlesex Hospital currently stands.

At the age of 15 I joined J. & F. Stone, who were an electrical, radio and television company based about 100 yards south of *The Fox,* but on the other side. I was made manager of their first shop in Bedford, but I fell out with the Directors and was asked to leave. I returned to London. About this time I was offered a job by Jules Verne, the driving force behind Thorne's, but I turned it down and I have often wondered if I did the right thing. I know he was rumoured to be a little on the temperamental side, but if you were hard working and honest he was said to look after you.

Just before the War I married and moved to my wife's family home at 489, Green Lanes, which is one of the large mansions just south of St. John's Church (which is captured at Plate 67).

On 29th July 1940 I started my 5 ½ years service with the Royal Navy. Extracts from my official papers can be found at Plates 40 and 41. My seven brothers also served in the forces during the conflict - a record for England in that war we believe. I have a cutting of a *London Evening News* article of 29th January 1945 which featured the Skinners. It listed the family in service at that time as Bert (35) - Grenadier Guards, Frank (34) - Corporal in an AA battery, Fred (32) - REME (i.e. Engineers), Harry himself (30) - Minesweepers, Reg (23) - Marines, Ron (19) - air gunner, Victor (18) - Navy, Stan (21) - Armoured Corps, Vera - made gun parts, Marjorie - porter at Kings Cross, Dennis (15) - munitions worker. They were all captured in a photograph. Of the brothers Reg currently resides in Barnet, one is in Welwyn Garden City, one in Canada and one lives in Australia.

I was on minesweeping duties and was responsible for laying the 100-yard long lines that had wires dropping below them so that electronic impulses could be sent down to blow up the enemy's mines. The long lines were kept afloat by the sort of artificial foam you find in modern suspended ceilings. The most dangerous mines were the delayed action ones, which could go off as you were returning to sweep over an area.

I served in various locations, the first being Liverpool, where I spent two years. Plate 42 shows me in a group shot there from 1941-2. We did 4 days on and then 2 days off. One of my postings was to Nova Scotia, Canada in 1944 when I was part of an advanced party of three charged with investigating the possibility of building wooden ships. As it turned out, the yard where the ships were being constructed ran out of wood, and we had to wait two or three months for a fresh supply. This effectively took me out of the war for that period of time. My last tour of duty was on MMS 257, sweeping up and down the east coast of England, before I was discharged with the princely sum of £70. You will see from Plate 41 that my service record was quite good and before I left I had been promoted to Leading Wireman. Although it was a dangerous time I think I possibly enjoyed my time in the Navy more than any other period of my life.

On leaving there was something of a 'dog eat dog' atmosphere in an attempt to find work. I returned to J. and F. Stone and my pay was £3 - 10s - 0d, which was no great fortune, but I stayed with them for 31 years. I was Supervisor at their shops in London and Bedford.

I remember all the fuss when Cliff Richard moved into the house at the corner of Colne Road in the early 1960s. He had a fence erected to keep the girls out, but this was not enough and he soon had to move. (See Plate 63.)

About 1967 my wife's family sold 489, Green Lanes and we moved to my current address not far from The Broadway. Unfortunately my wife passed away in 1972.

I was raised in a lovely village where people had reasonable standards of behaviour. Now violent crime is so prevalent you are frightened to even open your front door. And then there is the terrorist threat. The world seems a more hateful place, and it doesn't look likely to improve in the foreseeable future. Despite the dangers of the Second World War, and the increased material wealth of today, I feel I was born at the right time.

<u>Author's Notes</u>

1. *The earliest Kelly's Directory I have where there is a listing by streets is the 1899-1900 edition. This shows Nos. 1 & 2 Sunnyside Cottages just to the east of The Green Dragon. There are no further premises between these Cottages and the name of the next road, which is Bush Hill. The 1909-10 Directory shows the situation unchanged. The next edition I have is the one for 1923, now at last showing 'Skinner Herbt. Wm. buildr' in occupancy at No. 2, and 'Lawrence Michael rustic worker' at No.1 Sunnyside Cottages, but by now there is a Green Dragon Garage between The Green Dragon Hotel and No.1. There is still an absence of further premises before Green Dragon Lane. The 1935 Directory shows 'Patterson Phillip Chas. Motor engnr.' at 891 Green Lanes, next door to '893 Lawrence E.J. rustic worker' and '895 Skinner Hrbt. Wm. bldr.' There is no mention of the cottages, but I presume that they had merely been renamed. There were now numerous premises before Green Dragon Lane was reached.*

The Teer Brothers - Interview 21st June 2008

I spoke with brothers Alf and Terry Teer at the Enfield home of Terry's daughter Beverley. Terry still lived in Carpenter Gardens, with his wife Vi. A number of months later their sister Myrtle added to their comments in a letter from America.

The Teer family had been in the old village some years when elder brother Alf was born in the family's fish shop called 'A. Teer's Fishmongers' at the top of Wades Hill in 1920. In the early years of his childhood his Dad ran a pony and trap, and the family often went out in it on Sunday evenings in the better months of the year. The pony, named Polly, was kept in Nix's dairy stables off of The Green, down the alley now known as Wades Mews. Uncles Will and Charlie ran a greengrocer's shop nearby.

Uncle Bob (see Plate 36) and Aunt Bea lived in the cottage that stood in the grounds of St. Paul's Church, just to the right as you entered from Church Hill. Alf attended the old school that was on the grounds just north of the Church itself. He owned a King Charles cocker spaniel, of which he was so fond that he asked the headmaster, Mr. Johnson, and his teacher, Mr. Hallam, if he could bring it to school with him. They agreed to the request and two or three times a week Alf would bring the dog into class to sit next to him. As a child he knew 'Chum' Wackett, featured elsewhere in this volume.

Alf recalled the fine livestock in Paulin's fields as you walked south alongside the Broadfields estate on Wades Hill. In his childhood he would help with the haymaking on Paulin's farm. All this was done using only horse and cart. Similarly Nix, in this era, ran his dairy business entirely with that mode of transport. At the bottom of Wades Hill, near the junction with Houndsden Road, was a stream that you could get to Church Hill by if you walked along its banks. There was another path that took you out to the hospitals in Worlds End Lane, one of which was for isolation cases. (See Plates 69 & 70.)

When Alf was a child Broad Walk had not been made up, and he remembered the pot holes in the road inhabited by the richest people in the neighbourhood! When it rained there were always puddles. At this time he would sometimes help Frank Smith deliver milk to the Mc Whirter household for Nix's dairy, and he could remember that the horse would stop outside the premises until someone from inside came and gave him some sugar. Frank's wife helped the Mc Whirters with their housework. Alf could also remember one of the Finch family pushing Nix's three wheeled handcart.

Alf recalled the shops on the east side of Wades Hill from his childhood. Starting from the houses to the north, the first shop coming south was his Dad's fish shop, then Hutchinson's café (where he met a former girlfriend), then there were two shops, one of which was electrical, next came Tancock's florist, Mr. Marlow's sweetshop and, on the corner, Aldridge's the greengrocers (selling only fruit). (Note 1) On the opposite corner *The King's Head* was run by the Booth family.

Around the corner, on The Green, Alf remembered Paterson and Young's, who ran a grocer's and Post Office, Grout's the drapers (who survived into the 21st century in Palmers Green), Bolton's the chemist, Salmon the plumber, followed by Nix's dairy outlet, then Dunnett's the Gents outfitters on the corner with Station Road. This listing tallied exactly with that from the 1930 Kelly's Directory at Pages 106/7 in my 1991 *Winchmore Hill Lives.* Alf recalled having the back of his head stitched up further down Station Road, by Dr. Goble at Grove Lodge, next to the Station.

Alf also recalled the shops on the Upper Green. Tidey's sweet shop was on the corner of Hoppers Road, Chalkley's Bakery being on the opposite (eastern) corner. Going west from Tidey's, towards Broad Walk, was Mr. Reeve's the boot repairer, then Aldridge's greengrocer (selling only veg.), a further shop, then Maynard the builder. Alf couldn't remember the old cottages that occupied the site of Maynard's before he built Cookley House in the late 1920s. The greengrocers on Wades Hill and The Green were run by two brothers, a third managing the Aldridge removals company on Winchmore Hill Road (See Plate 1 of the 1991 *Winchmore Hill Lives*).

It was a few years before brother Terry was born that Alf's father was plagued by a fishbone that lodged in his right hand. It turned sceptic and he was kept in a hospital by Bounds Green station for some weeks with the hand immersed in iodine. Unfortunately they had to remove his little finger, and a thin section of the wrist and arm just above it. In those days insurance was not so common as today, and so the incident led to Mr. Teer selling the business to a Mr. Robinson, and the family moved out from the flat over the shop, initially only over the road in Wades Hill. That new flat was over The Gift Shop, and it was where Alf's sister Myrtle was born on 10th June 1926. Like brother Alf she attended the old St. Paul's school in Church Hill, and recalled that each December her mother would buy Christmas cakes, which the family would take to their Grandfather's farm in Ongar, Essex. Myrtle looked back on her visits to Grovelands Park with great affection.

Terry was born in the old Salisbury Cottages, Hoppers Road, when his family was living there on 14th November 1933, and like Alf and Myrtle before him, he was delivered by Dr. Goble. The brothers remember Mr. Chamberlain, the sweep who was living there at the time. The Cottages had been condemned, just as the land was needed for the rebuilding of *The Salisbury Arms*, and so when only 18 months old Terry moved to his current address in Carpenter Gardens. He attended the school in Highfield Road, and was friends with Iris Chamberlain, Brian Cook, Nesta Rowe and Phyllis Ives, as well as Ron Pretlove, a child who survived the V1 attack of 1944. He also knew Bill Marriage, and a Bill Phillips.

In about 1936 the youngest of the four siblings, Shirley, was born at the family home at 95, Carpenter Gardens. The ten year old Myrtle took two buses to get a midwife from Southgate to deliver Shirley, although she didn't actually talk to the midwife, but left a message on the slate in front of her home.

Both brothers spoke of Fred Pavey, the builder who had his yard down by the skew bridge on the west side of Hoppers Road. They both also knew Charlie Finch, a one time neighbour in Wades Hill , who worked for 'Uncle Fred' as a decorator. They believed that Charlie worked on the 1951 Exhibition on the South Bank. They presumed he was a relation of Harry Finch, featured in *Winchmore Hill Lives* of 1991.

In about 1940 Alf and his pal Freddie Downes went up to London to try and enlist with the RAF, but were surprised to be told that the RAF was not taking any more recruits. So it was that he joined the Royal Navy, and was designated to serve on Motor Torpedo Boats (MTBs). He was posted to Portsmouth, Dover, Lowestoft, and even went out to Ceylon (now Sri Lanka), but never saw action. Whilst at Lowestoft he visited Terry and sister Shirley, who by then had been evacuated to Smallborough in Norfolk. Both brothers remembered the occasion. Alf also remembered walking across central London at night, when home on leave, without any fear of being mugged.

Myrtle had remained behind during the hostilities, and worked at Reid's

Chemist in Palmers Green. During this period she met the American soldier Peter De Santis, finally marrying him at Holy Trinity Church, just round the corner from the family home, on 28th June 1945.

Terry remembered a land mine being dropped by a German plane on St. Bart's playing fields (now Sainsbury's), but he didn't think it had gone off. (Note 2.) He was fairly sure that another one was dropped on the Highfield Road School fields.

Terry spoke of his friend Frank Hill living in cottages at the side of the school in Highfield Road. These were set back from the road, where the alleyway currently runs up to Farm Road. He remembered the old tin chapel further along the north side of the road (see Plate 12), and the derelict old white cottage at the eastern end of the school grounds, known for years as Solomon's Cottage, though by Terry's childhood 'old ma Solomon' had moved to a house at the foot of Carpenter Gardens. In fact the cottage had become so run down that it was demolished, and an air raid shelter constructed in its place. However, Terry says he never went in it as he used the Anderson shelter in the family's back yard at night, whilst by day he went to the shelter at the entrance to St. Bart's Playing fields (now Sainsbury's). His daughter Beverley remembered playing around the shelter as a child in the1960s. (Note 2.)

Terry informed me that the ramping for the searchlights for the AA battery in Firs Farm fields, was still there. He could, like elder brother Alf, remember the fountain in The Green, but neither could remember when it was taken down – they suspected it was during the war.

Moving to the post War era, Alf, Terry and Beverley spoke of a now disappeared shop at the southern end of Compton Terrace, which had been next door to their Uncle Will's home. However, they had little to say of this period as the area had been urbanised, and was physically much as it is today.

Notes

1. *The Kelly's Directory for Wades Hill for 1925 lists the following, starting at The Green each time (1929 Directory in brackets where different) –*

East Side: 1. Lovelace W.S., boot maker; 3. Marlow, Miss Flora, confr.; 5. Tancock, William, florist; 7. Johnson Hy.(Silver, Miss Priscilla), tobacconist; 9. Harris Wm. C., greengrocer (Arnold, Herbert Alfred, electrician); 11. Davis, Bernard (Hitchins, Stanley), coffee rooms; 13. Leigh, Orlando, A, fishmonger; 17. Tancock, William; 19. Fielder, Edward (Durrant, Frederick William); 21. Teer, Charles Edward; 23. Finch, Charles, builder......

West Side: 2. Cross, Harry (Exton & Hewson, Misses, tea rooms); 4. Swanborough, Silas; 4. Thompson, Herbt. Victor (Reeve, C.A.) boot repr.; 6. Bryant, Arth. W., butcher; Mummery's House Furnishing Stores (gone 1929); 10. Knowles, Oscar S., motor & cycle engineer (also 8. in 1929); here is Wades Grove.

2. *In the original 1991 Winchmore Hill Lives, Mr. Arnold and Mrs. Bensted, nee Spicer, tell of a landmine dropping and exploding in St. Bart's (later Langham) playing fields. Mrs. Bensted also describes the deep air raid shelter there.*

Mr. & Mrs. Traigis - Letters 2010

I was born in Enfield in 1929 as Iris Riddle, but in 1935 we moved to 136, Hoppers Road, in the stretch between College Road and Woodberry Avenue, and stayed there until 1954. I have read your books on the area and have little to add to what others have told you, but I thought my wartime experiences might be of interest to readers if you produce another book.

I attended St. Paul's School, which was then, of course, in Church Hill adjoining the church. Initially the entrance to these two buildings was rough gravel, and we played there before classes. In the centre of the play area was a large smooth boulder on which we jumped frequently during games of tag. During one summer holiday this area was tarmaced. In the process of doing this the boulder was moved and a deep well was revealed underneath. Our other playgrounds were to the side and rear of the school, one for either sex.

When War came we had three months off from school while the buildings had baffle walls installed, and sandbags fitted at the windows. During that time a teacher would come to our house every Tuesday or Thursday morning and give what lessons she could to us of varying ages who lived in the area at our end of Hoppers Road.

Upon returning to school Mr. Gayler had succeeded Mr. Johnson as headmaster, and the long daylight raids had started. We were not allowed to leave school while a warning was on, so we all had to carry small cloth bags with "iron rations". Mine were usually a sandwich, biscuit, apple and ovaltine tablets! We sat on the floor in cramped class rooms, and when planes and gunfire started up Mr. Gayler would strike up on the piano and we'd all sing such hymns as *Onward Christian Soldiers* as loud as possible, to cover up the frightening noise. We ten and eleven year olds had to keep a stiff upper lip and comfort the infants, who were often reduced to tears. When there was a lull there were anxious little trips to the outside toilets on the far side of the playground. The infants were lucky in having two chemical toilets in a curtained off corner of the cloakroom, as they often couldn't wait!

Our lives otherwise seemed to go on as normal, though of course we were really too young to fully understand the dangers. The worry and responsibility lay with the parents, who seemed fit for any disaster. Certainly my childhood was very happy, and we accepted the barriers and boundaries which were put on us. I vividly remember, whilst on the way to school one morning, a policeman on a bicycle with a placard round his neck on which was written, "Take Cover". He came over the railway bridge pedalling so fast that before I could ask him anything, he was gone. I had two little ones by the hand who I regularly took to school – so should I go on or turn back for home? We hurried on to school, because in those days you went to school whatever .....

I have fond memories of the Brownies at Compton Road Congregational Church, and then I became a Guide at St. Paul's, when we met at The Institute in Station Road. We usually had a room there, but on certain occasions we were allowed to meet in the Drill Hall underneath. We were fascinated when we discovered the "rifles" the Home Guard practised with, and were greatly disappointed upon finding they were made entirely of wood. I presume they had the real things issued later.

A group of school friends ran a library in a flat above a shop near Green Dragon Lane. We charged 1/2d to borrow a book and the money went to the Spitfire fund. We certainly needed more funds to send parcels to members of local families fighting abroad.

My parents had to go for instruction on how to deal with incendiary bombs – stirrup pumps – buckets of water and sand. My father, who had fought in the 1914 – 18 War, was above conscription age, so he had to fire watch locally at night, sharing night hours (and a tin hat and whistle) with other men in the road. He also had to fire watch one night each fortnight at his office in London. The threat of the small incendiary bombs was very real – they so quickly started fires.

Most people had air raid shelters, either an Anderson out in the garden or, like us, a Morrison which resided in our dining room, under which we all squeezed when the raids were bad. When the night bombing raids were at their height in 1940-1 the noise of the barrage which our guns put up was deafening. To make matters worse the soldiers used to drive a 'bofors' gun on a mobile mounting and park in College Road, where they would fire off for a while, and then move on. The other mobile gun was driven along the railway line which lay behind the houses opposite us in Hoppers Road. They would stop at different places and fire their shells. I can remember my mother saying 'don't stop – don't stop here!'. She was afraid that the German planes would mark the flashes and then drop bombs.

The only one of two public shelters which I can remember was the one dug on The Green, just down a bit from the horse water trough (opposite *The King's Head*). The door to this shelter was nearly always locked, but when possible we would peer in. It was dark, damp and smelly, so we never ventured in!

The other shelter was opposite Palmers Green Library in Green Lanes, a brick built affair, which again was often locked. We badly needed it one afternoon on the way home from school. We had heard a rumour that the fish shop at Bowes Road was 'frying', so instead of going straight home, four of us made a detour. This was later in the war, about 1944-5, when daylight raids by plane had stopped, but we still had the menace of 'doodlebugs', and later rockets. We were still in the fish shop when the siren went, so we dashed up the hill to the library to find the shelter locked. We rushed on, hearing the approach of a doodlebug, and reached Woolworths shop, by The Triangle, Palmers Green. There we heard a bomb's engine stop, so we lay down in the recessed doorway. We saw the bomb dip over the shops opposite, and it landed in a turning just up Alderman's Hill. We scooted along the shops at Palmers Green to the safe haven of Hoppers Road, where a good telling off awaited me. Of course I should have been home earlier.

There was a searchlight and gun placement in Grovelands Park which was eventually hit, but I can't remember whether it was by a 'plane, doodlebug or rocket. I could go on, but I don't think those memories would be interesting for your book, so I'll hand over to my husband Bill, who was born and bred in Scotland.

I began work at Winchmore Hill Police Station (see Plate 43) in September 1952, a newly qualified police constable, and newly wed. I had served my probation period at Kings Cross - a rough, tough area still suffering from the aftermath of the wartime air raids. I was immediately told by my wife that I had to address the public in a much nicer manner at Winchmore Hill, or there would be complaints. Point taken! However, crime was very low and my duties were of every day happenings – lost property, lost animals, disturbances outside public houses etc.

I did experience, though, my one and only unexplained event. One night duty I was operating the wireless in the police car as my colleague was driving up Green Dragon Lane. It was 2 a.m. and we were just thinking we would take our break as we had been on duty since 10 p.m. the previous day. At the same moment we both spotted, in the gloom, a lady who appeared to be walking her dog, but we both said at the same time that she had no legs, and neither did the dog! We drew up behind her quietly, but she turned a corner into Landra Gardens. We followed about five seconds later, but she had vanished. There was no sign of life at all – no lights, nothing! Neither of us believed in ghosts, and thus had no explanation, so we decided not to mention anything at the police station because of all the teasing we would get! It is so fresh in my mind even today. (Note 1.)

We also had all the excitement when Cliff Richard became known. He was living with his family in a house off Firs Lane – Kent or Colne Road I think. (See Plate 63.) It was besieged by girls. Cliff's Mum had given out some signed photos of him – the word got round and more and more girls arrived. Cliff heightened his garden fence for more privacy, but in the end he had to move out to Essex to ensure greater privacy. (See elsewhere in this book for more on Cliff and his time in the area.)

Author's Notes

1. *At Page 23 of my A Look at Old Winchmore Hill I reproduce a sketch by Dr. Cresswell of The Retreat Inn sometime in the period 1865-70. The Inn stood at the NE junction of Green Dragon Lane and the ancient Hagfields footpath, which followed a similar course to today's Green Moor Link. Dr. Cresswell's daughter, Henrietta, tells us, in her Memories of a Lost Village, that, 'The footpath was said to be haunted by the apparition of an old hag, ….'*

2. *Although this account was given by post, I should like to record that Yasmin and I were pleased to meet the Traigis family at their home in Seaford, Sussex, in the summer of 2010.*

3. *I sent my 'final write up' of what Bill and Iris Traigis had written for approval in December 2010, along with some comments about my researches in the Local Studies Unit, in relation to the account. I received the following in reply,*

'There doesn't seem to be anything to be altered but we were surprised that there is apparently no record of the gun and searchlight emplacement in Grovelands Park. We understood at the time that the soldiers operating there had just been brought up from Dover for a bit of a rest and quiet and then, I'm sure it was a V1 (doodlebug) dropped on their huts. On enquiries about casualties my parents were told by an army officer that he was not allowed to divulge any information. Maybe some of your older readers may remember something.'

Mrs. Doreen Van Der Sanden (nee Grover)
Letters 10th Sept. 2001 and 2nd Oct. 2002 from Rotorua, New Zealand

A friend of mine who lives in Palmers Green has sent me a press cutting from *The Enfield Independent* dated 15th August 2001 concerning the history of *The Green Dragon*, Winchmore Hill. I was most interested in this as I used to live in Fords Grove for about 14 years as a child from 1924. I can remember the playing fields opposite our house (No. 48) and used to watch the cricket during the summer months. I used to attend Highfield Road School. I can recall walking up to the top of Fords Grove, cutting through a garage to Farm Road, and across the nursery along a country lane to the school playground. Mr. Ling was the Headmaster in those days. The Capitol Cinema used to be at the top of Fords Grove but I suppose that is long gone. I used to attend Sunday School at Holy Trinity Church, and then visit my cousins who lived in Compton Road.

When we lived in Winchmore Hill my father used to travel each day on the tram to Stoke Newington where he was employed as a cashier in the branch of the Midland Bank. In 1938 we moved to Old Southgate after my father received promotion as Manager of the Midland Bank at Enfield Highway and from there he was transferred to the branch in Enfield Town. My father, Mr. Reginald Grover, lived to the great age of 86.

During the war I was in the W.R.N.S. stationed at Falmouth, Cornwall where I met my future husband Gerard, who was serving in the Royal Netherlands Navy. We emigrated to New Zealand in 1964, with our two daughters Anna and Lorraine, and we lived in Wellington for 24 years before moving to Rotorua on my husband's retirement. On 28th January 2000 we celebrated our 50th Golden Wedding Anniversary surrounded by our family and friends. (See Plate 44.) Sadly Gerard passed away in November 2001, but I have many cherished memories of the happy times we have shared together over the years.

Colin Wackett - Interview 11th March 2005

I was born at 1, Wades Grove in 1945 and so was a neighbour of Mrs. Wood and Mrs. Pettifer, who were both featured in the original *Winchmore Hill Lives*, and Jean Bilton, whose current home we are talking in. I have very fond memories of the area as a child even though we were not rich. Wades Grove was a small community of less well off people. There was another in Highfield Road, as well as a part of Vicars Moor Lane. It was still a society, locally, where you 'knew your place' when dealing with the people from the larger houses. (See Plates 46 & 48.)

I initially attended St. Paul's School at the old Institute in Station Road, where the Sorting Office is now. (See Plates 57 & 58.) I remember you accessed its basement drill hall from the classrooms on the ground floor by way of a spiral staircase, which was quite dangerous as it was not lit in any way. On the top floor was the very impressive Bird Room, which stood at the end of a long corridor. It housed a multitude of cases containing stuffed birds. There were more poor people in the area then and a Loan Club was run from the Institute, where you saved about half a crown a week in order to meet the expenses of Christmas or a summer holiday. If the Institute was closed for some reason collections were made in *The Queen's Head*. The Christmas bazaars there were wonderful, as were the regular jumble sales.

For some reason at playtimes we were only allowed to play on the footpaths in the grounds surrounding the building. There was a nearby drop of about 6' to the basement windows – something that I'm sure would breach all the current Health and Safety regulations! Perhaps the thing that stands out most about my school days there is the fact that I was forever coming home with splinters from the wooden floors of the drill hall! After a couple of years attending school there I continued at the schoolhouse adjoining the Church itself in Church Hill.

At the age of around eleven or twelve I received my first pair of roller skates. These, like all the others of the time, were strapped onto the shoes that you were wearing and came with steel wheels. The only smooth piece of road available to skate on without 'jarring' loose all of my teeth was a band of plain tarmac about 8 feet wide across the width of Wades Grove from Wades Hill. Once I became skilled enough to skate from one side of the road to the other without falling over I quickly became bored, and looked for more of a skating challenge.

I was skating, if I recall correctly, with Peter Haines at the time and we decided that it would be an acceptable challenge to skate down Wades Hill to the bottom! We saw little danger at the time as cars were so 'few and far between' and pedestrians never seemed to walk in the road, so where could the danger be? It went well to start with, but once past the entrance to Harwood's Yard and gathering speed, the vibrations through the skates became quite violent and unpleasant and I thought, 'Hey! How are we going to stop?' Neither of us had given any consideration to this factor and as we hurtled down the hill, virtually side-by-side, the reality of an unpleasant 'spill' began to dawn on us and, far too late, the stupidity of our actions became quite apparent. However, we were fortunate enough not to meet any vehicle moving or stationery, or pedestrian either. Successfully negotiating the 'S' bend past the Alms Houses we finally slowed enough to once again take control of our actions around the junction with Houndsden Road, both fully determined never to repeat that performance.

When I was about thirteen I used to attend a youth club at the Institute that was run by Peter Jay and his sister. I also used to visit the Institute when I was about 18 years old, when I paid around 4/- to see the up and coming pop groups in the classier upper hall. I moved to Barnet in 1968 and the Institute was still there, but it couldn't have lasted long though. Incidentally, I had never heard of the ghost Percy, who you say is rumoured to haunt the premises.

Coming up Station Road, but on the other side, I remember that where Milton Lodge flats now are, were two shops. The lower (more easterly one) sold electrical goods and then became a hairdresser's. Then, to their west, was an ivy covered house set back about 3', bounded by railings, with thistles in the grounds. West of the house was an alley, just before Carter Page's shop, which led to a line of about four cottages positioned at right angles to the road. (See Plates 4 & 5 and Note 1).

Just the other side of the Station was the foreboding Grove Lodge, which in the 1950s was occupied by Dr. Saar. I say it was foreboding, but perhaps my view was influenced by the fact that I was sent at night to fetch the doctor when my grandfather had his blackouts. Could you imagine such a night call by a local GP today?!

More or less opposite was the imposing Roseville, though I never went in. It was still called Dr. Simpson's house, even though he had long gone. It shows you what a personality he must have had. (See Plate 103.)

I remember getting stuck in the base of the fountain on the Lower Green in the early 1950s and had to be rescued by the local Newsagent Charlie Guy. So don't believe any book that tells you that the entire fountain had gone by then! The upper part had been removed it is true, as had the surrounding railings.

On the Upper Green itself I well remember Nix's Dairy because my father worked for George Nix, though I can only remember his son Reg – a man with a small physique but large personality. The actual dairy was on the right as you went down Wades Mews. The business was sold to Express dairy in the mid 1960s, but they brought their milk in rather than process it on site. Near the entrance to the Mews was Strangwick's fish shop.

Crossing over the Upper Green in the 1950s, the Red Cross was resident in the house on the corner with Broad Walk. I presume this was The Limes. They cleaned many a wound suffered by myself and friends. When it was being demolished we played 'war games' in it.

Turning down Hoppers Road, I remember in the early 1950s going down the little alleyway by Chalkley's to get free rolls freshly baked in the old ovens.

I went to Saturday Morning Pictures at the Capitol, where Capitol House now is. (See Plate 64.) It was 6d to get in and we all sang 'The Minors' Song'. We often used to play out the films we had just seen at the grounds of the Institute on our way home. We were given an apple and orange at Christmas.

You ask when money went furthest. I would have to say, most definitely, now! I bought a Phillips radio for £18 in the early 1960s – a lot of money in those days. The papers are currently warning of a gallon of petrol costing £4. When I started driving in 1967 it was 4/3d (21p) a gallon at a time when I was earning about £8 a week, making it more about £20 a gallon in today's terms. Then I think back to the 1950s and remember how the poorer folk would make a point of returning their Tizer and other soft drink bottles to the shop to claim the 3d deposit on each bottle. No one would do a thing like that today. Back then a poorer child might even raid a park or roadside rubbish bin!

You also ask when the area was at its best as far as I'm concerned. I would opt for the late 1950s. After that it changed quite suddenly. Up until about 1960 there was a real family centred community feeling and all the children were able to get into their homes without a key because the front doors had been left on the latch. In the main the streets or The Green were our playground. You could also play unsupervised in Grovelands Park, including the wooded stretch where we made 'camp' under the holly bushes, and damned the stream for our 'lolly stick' boat races. People didn't drop litter in the streets, they took it home in their pockets or put it in the rubbish bins. Why did it change? Perhaps it was partly due to the more extensive use of the motorcar. Instead of people walking around, and staying mainly within their community, they would have started to travel further afield, and thus never had the opportunity to meet the neighbours, or to become friends.

Author's Notes

1. *This part of Station Road is considered in detail in the Chalkley family account.*

2. *Colin volunteered to let me have the excellent account which he had taken on his mother 'Molly' that is featured next.*

Mary Jane ('Molly') Wackett, nee Fretwell - 'The Memories of a Country Girl'

The following obviously reflects a considerable amount of work by Colin and is published with his consent. I have mainly restricted the content to that pertaining to Winchmore Hill, but it is still far longer than most accounts I have published. I was reluctant to edit it because much of the interest comes from the small detail and the 'warts and all' flavour. Most people, in their accounts, have understandably omitted any internal frictions within their families, but Molly doesn't pull any punches and so, perhaps, gives us a slightly greater insight into life in days gone by. I have followed Colin's idea of breaking things up with sub headings. There are photos of 'Molly' at Plates 45, 46 and 47.

Background

I was born on the 10th December 1911, the eldest daughter of Tom and Mable Fretwell and had 2 sisters, Muriel and Dot, and a brother Tom. There was five years between Muriel and me and 1½ - 2 years between the others. We all lived together with my granddad Howlett in the small three bedroom Victorian terrace of no. 3 Kings Dyke at Whittlesey in Cambridgeshire.......I suppose that in a way we were lucky to live here, as it was the only terrace that had front gardens. They were about 20-30 feet long....

....My father, Tom Fretwell, was born on a farm at Stuntney near Ely, with four brothers and a sister. My dad worked on the land (labouring) until he was married, before coming to Kings Dyke to work on the brickfields, which paid more money and guaranteed a house to live in. Working in the brickyards he was getting up at 4 am in the morning. He used to get one day paid holiday each year. If he had more holidays he wouldn't be paid for them. His job was to help load the bricks into the wagons that were on the siding at the bottom of our garden. Then he'd have to push them around to where they had to be, ready for the engine coming to take the full wagons away.

His wages were poor and, in an effort to support all of us, he kept pigs and chickens and grew vegetables in the garden. He always said that there would come a time when we would not know the passing of winter into summer except by the rising and falling of the leaves on the trees.

My mother was born Mable Howlett, also in Stuntney. She had two elder brothers with whom she lived along with her father. Her mother died in childbirth so that there was no other woman in the house. Consequently she grew up being looked after and raised by her brothers, never knowing the love or presence of a mother, nor anyone to advise her properly about those 'women's things'.

I can't recall what date they were married. (It was October 1911.) I know Mum was only about 20,21 or so, and she was already pregnant with me, but it was early enough that it didn't show in the photographs. Perhaps my very earliest memories are in these years. Sometimes of an evening time a man used to walk round Kings Dyke calling out, "Lights out. Zeppelins coming!" Not that we ever saw any Zeppelins, but Mum always put the lights out anyway!.....

Work and Winchmore Hill

.....I went out to work when I was about 14.....I was 19 when I took my... job....going to work as a cook at a Boarding School in Taskers Lane, Brentwood, Essex.... In all I probably worked at the school for about 5-7 years......When I wanted a change from the boarding school I came to work at Winchmore Hill, in Branscombe Gardens, for a person named Mrs. Allen. I liked working for Mrs. Allen; she had two children and a dog called Mac. What was nice of her was that she asked if I would like my Mum and Dad to come and stop with me for a few days, and they did, Dad coming once and mother a couple of times. It pleased Mum as it was somewhere to spend time with me, but she did not stop long because of leaving Dad alone so long. I remember Dad used to sit on the seat near the horse trough on The Green talking to a retired policeman from Harwoods Yard, off Wades Hill.

It was while I was working here that my sister Dot came to work, and live in, close by for a family living in Cresswell Way. I would never have recommended them to Dot they were so mean. The husband and wife were always quarrelling, which upset poor ole' Dot. They even kept her short of food by locking the pantry door up. When I saw her, or she came to me in Branscombe Gardens where I was working, I always had to give her plenty of grub. They really kept her starving. It's funny though; the husband was always so full of booze and rowing when he came home. We spent as much time as we could together, taking walks up the park and that. Dot only stayed there a short time before going home and, much as I loved Dot, we were very close, I was not sorry to see her leave them rotten people and go back home.

Romance with "Chum"

It was while I was working for Mrs. Allen I met "Chum", christened Jack, my husband to be. I was actually already seeing a chap that I wasn't very keen on and my friend, Lucy Bass, said that she knew someone nice that she could introduce me to. Lucy arranged for me to meet "Chum" in a café, No. 1 Wades Hill – later to be Aldridge's the green grocer. When I saw "Chum" I was a little surprised for I'd already seen him as he had served me on a number of occasions in Aldridge's shop in Station Road. Anyway, he seemed nice enough and that's how we started going out. I was to find out that poor ole' "Chum" suffered with his nerves and why. I can't remember when we went out on our first "date", but often we caught a train to Gordon Hill that was in the countryside....

.....Mrs. Allen's dog would follow me everywhere and, every evening, I would ask Mrs. Allen if I could take the dog for a walk while I posted my letter. The letterbox was on the corner of Seaforth Gardens and Broad Walk. Of course I had arranged to meet "Chum" there. Sometimes I had a letter, sometimes I did not. I expect that Mrs. Allen knew what I was up to, but the old dog got a walk anyway.

After a short courtship of 17 months, well that WAS short then, "Chum" asked me to marry him. To contemplate marriage after such a "short" time in those days was considered too shocking to think about. I was so surprised and said, "What do you want to get married so soon for? We've only been seeing each other 17 months, you're an only child and must be spoilt at home."

Chum replied, "That's what you think. If you were in my shoes you'd feel the same." "Why?" I asked. "Well," he replied, "every time I go in through the front door I never know what to expect. Is she in a good mood or a bad one? There's nearly always a bad atmosphere in there. I can't wait to get out." We were married soon afterwards. I was to find out later that old Mrs. Wackett just could not take a joke and was so self righteous and strict that it defied belief. I hardly ever saw her smile or able to see the funny side of things.

At the outbreak of war Mrs. Allen went down to the country with her two children to get away from the bombing. She left her husband at home though. But it was the end of my working there.

Returning to the subject of "Chum" (Jack), he was the only child of John

William Wackett (Note 1), known as Jek to the other men of his age - why I don't know - and Ethel Emily Wackett, nee Hack. Not much is known of them prior to their marriage, and even this date is unknown to me. John is believed to have been born and lived over a shop in Windmill Hill, Enfield, next to the station (now the site of the Jobcentre), while Ethel is believed to have been born and raised on High Leigh Farm, Hoddesdon........I soon found out that "Chum's" life had been little better than mine, and in some ways worse. His own mother told me that when they first got married they lived in a flat in Wood Green. It could have been Wightman Road, but I'm not sure. Because she was afraid to let "Chum" walk about and play, in case he went down the stairs, she used to regularly tie him to the end of their bed. What sort of life was that for a child?

When they moved to no. 1 Wades Grove, Winchmore Hill there was a stable next door. I think it was the coalman who kept his horses there. (Note 2) Well anyway, Ethel told me that one day when "Chum" was about 4-5 she dressed him in a little sailor suit, little white collar and everything. She said that she felt so pleased with the way he looked. However, he went out in the back garden, through the back gate, to play in the stables amongst all the dirt and hay. She gave him a 'damn good whipping', as she put it, when he came back. What ever was the matter with her? The clothes were washable and it was only childlike to play.

Not only could "Chum" remember this occasion, but he also told me of another that seemed quite brutal and horrific, even for those days. He told me that Thursday when his Aunt Sarah come - she always came to pay a visit on a Thursday afternoon - he told her that he had a 'zebra's back' and did she want to see it? "Well, what ever do you mean?" she asked, whereupon he pulled up his shirt to show her his back. "That," he said, "is where Mum hit me with a coiled up clothes' line." That's how wicked she was. This happened because he protested when his mother was bathing him in a long tin bath and washing his hair. He hated his hair being washed 'cos the soap stung his eyes. Of course, being a kid he screamed and cried out. "If you don't shut up I'll leather you one" she threatened, and with that she grabbed hold of the wash line hanging coiled up and leathered him leaving those stripe marks. Do you know that it makes me cry even now to think of it? I couldn't do it. She really was cruel and should have been hit herself. If she didn't want children why did she have them? I know she was 36 before she had "Chum" and she was alone and on her own a long while with little or no patience, but it's still no excuse.

Marriage

I married at St. Paul's Church on 22nd October 1939 (see Plate 45), borrowing a wedding dress from one of Muriel's friends, as we couldn't afford one, and wearing a blue garter. The reception, for what it was, was held back at the in-laws (John and Ethels'). We were lucky to even have a piece of cake. Mum didn't travel down for my wedding. I wasn't too surprised, but I suppose I was a bit disappointed. She hated travelling. She would get all worked up and agitated about it, sometimes going to the toilet umpteen times before leaving home. She suffered with heart problems, a blockage to the heart as well, and used to always carry a small bottle of brandy with her least she should feel ill or faint. Dad came, though, and I know that Muriel and her husband Jack did, with Jack's sister Elsie. I am unable to recall if Dot came or of any other guests, but again I cannot remember. I had two bridesmaids, one an Irish girl called Molly Kylie, a good looking girl, and I forget the other, but our best man was Reg Cox.

I can't remember now, but we were getting married, or shortly after that, one Easter, "Chum" brought me an Easter egg in a jug from Marlow's at 3, Wades Hill. It was ever so nice and I said so. "Oh, that's lovely," I said, "what a pity there's not a pair." With that "Chum" went out and brought me another. I've still got one of those jugs, a pale orange colour it is, and I wouldn't part with it for the world.....

....I always loved flowers and, whenever he could afford them, "Chum" would buy me some or, if it were possible, he would pick me some, even wild flowers. He knew how much I liked them. He tended our gardens at Wades Grove carefully, and there always seemed to be something in flower for me to pick or look at. His father, John, was a quiet and meek person, totally dominated by his wife, and would do anything for a quiet life. However, it seemed that he could never be left in peace. If he were sitting in a chair it wasn't right. If he were reading a newspaper it wasn't right, and he usually went to bed early for a little peace. Mind you, going to bed early might have had something to do with him working at the local coal yard in Vicars Moor Lane. He had to be up early to start work, but I firmly believe that if this were the case then he was secretly pleased for an unarguable excuse to go to bed and out of her way.

Our first home was a flat in Eaton Park Road, where we stayed quite happily until the onset of World War 2. After commencement of hostilities, "Chum" being called up with all the other men, Mother-in-law kept on at me, saying it would be better for us all if I stayed with her, "safer with a war on, and you'd be on your own anyway". I didn't really want to, and probably did so at the time to keep the peace. I wondered if I should have?

The Second World War

War was bad, too 'orrible to describe, we were frightened to death when the raids started and the bombs started falling, we'd run anywhere for cover. It was all that noise, guns going off, bombs exploding, windows breaking, people screaming in the street, sirens blaring and the drone of the bombers overhead, and the darkness with all the lights out made it all the worse. Of course daft things happened in the war. Frightened and scared as I was they (the local government) chose me to be a "fire watcher" 'cos I had no children or anyone to look after. I told them that it was a laugh as I'd run away. I don't know about putting fires out. I was stationed in a small wooden hut outside no. 27 Wades Hill with Dick Simpson. (Note 3.) We were supposed to watch for incendiaries falling, and go and put the fires out. I didn't know Dick very well then but I told him, straight an' all, that if any fires wanted putting out I'd be running the other way. We had some fun though, and used to spend hours talking and playing cards. Dick got to be a good ole pal.

All through the war life was miserable. There was no pleasing Ethel. We always seemed to be having rows just because from time to time I went out with some of my pals. She used to accuse me of being unfaithful to "Chum". I was glad to go out in the Blitz to do my part in the war works just to get away from her. It seems impossible to believe, but Ethel was so jealous. On one occasion that "Chum" came home on leave she wanted to come with us to see a show that was on at either the Wood Green Empire or the Finsbury Park Empire. We both wanted to spend time together alone and to enjoy what we could as we never knew if there was going to be a tomorrow, and so we wouldn't let her come with us. She called us "a pair of mean gutted buggers!" Can you believe it?

Probably the only time she was nice was when we were in the Morrison shelter, and then she could be as sweet as honey. The Morrison shelter was in the kitchen in the corner. I suppose that she was nice as she thought that it might be we were at death's door with the bombing all around us. It never seemed to worry Pop; he slept all through it in his own bed. There was also a big communal shelter built on The

Green. It was underground and, being built quickly, was always swimming in water. We never went there very often.

"Chum" was in the Royal Artillery on a searchlight battery, as I don't think he had been passed as "A1" fit. I remember "Chum" coming home on a week's leave, I think it was, saying, "I've got to go abroad. I can't tell you where, as we're not allowed to tell anybody. He wasn't even allowed to say if it were the next morning or the next day. They all had to promise so as not to endanger us at home, or those on the other side of the water. He was on his way to Germany, but it had to be kept a secret, as there were spies everywhere ready to give us away. Part of his service was in England, and some in France and Germany. It didn't seem to matter where he was stationed, but whenever he came home on leave he couldn't wait to get back to Germany, or wherever, as they were bombing us in London harder. I recall that towards the end of the war 'Chum" had got friendly with a German couple over there.

I had to leave domestic service, as the government didn't think that it was important enough, and sent me to work at a spectacle factory in Clerkenwell. I had to get the 7.32 a.m. train from Winchmore Hill station every morning, getting home again about 7 p.m. In the winter the trains were dark and unlit in case any of the enemy planes saw the lights and bombed us. It was the same up in town, and for light we carried torches that we had to shine down on the pavement to see where we were going. We worked in the top of a building, right up in the roof. At first, when there was an air raid, we all went down into the basement, but it soon got that the air raids were so frequent that they said we should stay where we were and carry on working. It was frightening, I can tell you, with bombs dropping all around. The first job they put me on was grinding the lenses for the spectacles. What a blooming mess I made of that. They soon took me off there and on to the assembly side.

I had made friends with a couple who worked with me there and lived in Wightman Road, Hornsey. Sometimes on Saturday afternoon I would go and visit them, once staying the night because there were so many bombs dropping, and they insisted as they had a spare bed. Ma Wackett was furious, insisting that I had stayed out 'merely to enjoy myself while her son was fighting with the services.' Couldn't she see, or didn't she want to see, that it was as dangerous for me to stay at Hornsey as it was Winchmore Hill. Wasn't it even more dangerous to be travelling and walking home during the blitz that night?

The War Ends

After the cessation of hostilities, and "Chum' was again a civilian, we quickly moved out of Ethel's in Wades Grove, to share a house in Barrowell Green with a man who was either separated, or divorced. Unfortunately we had no privacy there and within months, when I was pregnant with Colin, we moved back with the in-laws. Unfortunately, even the birth of either Colin, or later Jennifer, was not to draw Ethel and myself any closer. She found and took every opportunity to "bad mouth" me. Colin used to like to get down from his high chair from the table when he had finished eating and I used to make him stay until we had all finished. Unfortunately, in his 'paddy' to get down he screamed and kicked the table to be let down. Of course Ethel comes in and accuses me of being a bad mother to them, and mistreating my children.

We got so fed up with her coming in, sticking her nose in, that I got "Chum" to fit a bolt on the door so as to keep her out. She made sure that everyone knew what she "believed to be true" and lost no time in going round our street of 14 houses telling everyone what a bad mother I was, and how I abused and mistreated my children. I don't think that anyone believed her, for later Mrs. Reynolds from number 6 told me that when she heard the accusation she told Ethel "not to be silly and that Molly was a good woman, her children were always well turned out, presentable and well fed, considering how much she had to live on". I thought a lot of Mrs. Reynolds for what she had said.

"Chum" was working at George Nix's milk yard, and he used to push a hand cart of milk up and down the hills round about us, that was damned hard work for him. Times were still hard and to help ourselves we had an allotment, first just over the bridge in Hoppers Road, and later, when we lost that one, another over the bridge in Vicars Moor Lane, both on the railway embankment. We had an allotment up to about 1955.

John, known affectionately as "Pop" by the children, often took Jenny to a small café at the bottom of Eaton Park Road. It was by a big tree that grew out on the pavement, said that he was glad to get out of the way of Ethel. Ethel died in April 1951 and "Pop" continued to live with us. He was very helpful and while I was out at work he did various chores about the house, dusting and whatever shopping that I needed. He took Jennifer out a lot in her pushchair. He would also spend hours reading to Colin and Jennifer from their comics, Beano, Dandy and such like.

Pop was never any trouble to me until he started having his "funny turns" – falling down and having blackouts. Near the end I remember sitting on the edge of "Pop's" bed. He knew that he'd got to go into hospital (St. Michael's of Chase Side, Enfield) and this was on the recommendation of the doctor. Well we was both shattered, as we had to take it in turns to look out for him. I said to him, "It's only for a few days to give "Chum" and me a break, to get a night's rest. I know you don't like the idea, but it's just to give "Chum" and I a few nights rest, then you'll come back again. You're not forced to go if you don't want to Pop. Please don't think that we don't want you." With that he took my hand between both of his. "Don't worry Molly", he said, "I know you don't want me to go, but I don't mind going as long as I know I'm coming back again."

Well, that was his peace of mind. He went off to the hospital quite happy, but I never saw him again. "Chum" did. He went to visit on the afternoon of the next day. "You'd better take a packet of tobacco for him and a bottle of orange drink for him" I said, but he never got them. He died while Chum was there. The saddest part was I felt I'd turned him out. I supposed it may have happened anyway, but I still felt bad.

After he died Mr. Nicholson, who was the pharmacist in Bolton's the Chemists on The Green, told me that some time after Ethel had died "Pop" had told him something in confidence. "I can tell you something that you might like to hear," he said, "Pop's gone now, I know, but he told me that the happiest times he had was while he was living with you after his wife died. How you looked after him and how kind you was." Well, I thought, that was nice to know, wasn't it!

I'll always remember one holiday we had in Herne Bay about 1955. We were out in Herne Bay and "Chum" thought that he had lost his wallet, so he went to the police station with Colin to report his loss. Well, it turned out, when he got back to where he was staying, that instead of putting it in his inside coat pocket, as he thought, he had pushed it down his coat sleeve. When he took his coat off it fell onto the floor. We were lucky in that way to get it back 'cos it had all our holiday money in it.

The Children - Colin and Jennifer

From the start my children Colin and Jennifer (see Plate 46) were always arguing. If Jenny had the rocking horse or the little 3 – wheeler bike then Colin would want it. It was only when Colin started going out with his mates that things got better around the house, and I had a little peace.

As I have said, "Chum" was working for Nix's Dairy delivering the milk, and when Colin was old enough to behave himself, "Chum" used to take him with him. Colin used to sit on the seat and hold the reigns, thinking that he was driving the horse. Of course that old horse knew exactly where to go and where to stop, without being told.

One winter, when Colin was still quite small, about 4 or 5, his Dad and "Pop" took him and Jennifer over to Broomfield Park, Palmers Green. As they went through the park gate Colin could see the ducks walking on the ice that covered the little boating pond. I suppose that he thought that he could do the same, because he ran to the edge of the pond and stepped out onto the thin ice. Well, of course he went right through. It's a good job that it wasn't deep, only 18 inches or so. His Dad fished him out and ran all the way home with him in Jenny's push chair, leaving "Pop" to bring Jennifer home on the bus or train. I don't suppose he ever tried that again.

Once, when she was about 5 or 6, Jenny came in and asked me if she could have the money to buy an ice cream. I told her to go to my purse and to take out the 3d or 4d that she wanted. Well, when she got my purse there was barely enough in coppers to pay for the ice cream. "Oh Mum, you've got hardly any money" Jenny said, "If I take the money for an ice cream what are we going to buy any food with?" "Take it," I told her, "something will come up and I don't suppose we'll starve." Yes, she was concerned, even at that age.

When my two children were at school they would often act the fool. Sometimes they'd push me into the pantry and shut the door so that I couldn't get out, as there was no catch on the inside. "Chum" would lose his temper and get ever so annoyed. It was so cold one night that the washing had frozen on the line, and when I went out to get it in my children locked me out, even in that cold, again making "Chum" furious. Even at the meal table if Colin or Jenny started giggling over something, I couldn't help it but I had to join in with them. This again would get "Chum" annoyed and ended with him going in to the kitchen to stand and finish his meal; my we did have some laughs.

When Colin was small and "Chum" was decorating Colin's bedroom, Colin wanted to help, so I gave him a jam jar of water and a brush to pretend paint. However, that wasn't good enough. He wanted real paint, and when he started dabbling around and trying to paint with the real thing "Chum" got so cross. He opened the bedroom window and threw the tin of paint down to the bottom of the garden. I remember saying, "That'll do a lot of good. You say we're hard up, we bought the paint and now you've slung it down the garden."

When we went to the seaside Jennifer, instead of playing on the sand, was up and away, we'd lost her, she'd be where the roundabouts were looking at the little horses and little cars going round. The number of times that her Dad had to fetch her back to the beach but, when our backs were turned, off she'd be again; we'd thought we'd lost her more than once.

When we stayed at Ramsgate Jenny was not very old; we were having our dinner when Jenny said that she wanted to go to the toilet and knew which way to go. So off she went. She was a long time gone, so her father went to look for her. Hearing a banging on the door, found that she had bolted herself in, and was now unable to unlock the door. The man who owned the hotel had to climb through a window from one room, through another window, into the toilet. The toilet window was ever so small and the man wasn't pleased at all. When we got back to the table the others seated there did give us some "black" looks. What an experience, when I think about it now I can laugh, but it was embarrassing at the time.

When both Colin and Jennifer were under ten we saw an advert for some kittens being given away free. We went to see them, the intention being to have one, but when we saw them playing together we had to have both of them. We decided to call them both "Tibby" so that by calling one they would both come. They were "good old" cats.

When Colin and Jennifer were about 9 and 11 they went to Evans & Davies store in Palmers Green, where there was a section especially devoted to pet mice. The mice were running around in a large open tank of model houses called "Mouse town". Colin was so taken with the mice that he bought one, and only told Jennifer as they were on the bus on their way home. I don't know how, but he was going to try and keep it a secret, but he ended up buying a special cage with a little wheel for the mouse to run round in. It used to quite make me laugh to see it running in the wheel and going nowhere.

Often on a Sunday Jenny and "Chum" would take bicycle rides out into the country. It was many years later that I learned that they went out way past Cuffley. She used to like going out with her father, as there wasn't the traffic on the roads to make you feel nervous.

When Colin was about 11 or 12 he stayed with Muriel at Kings Dyke for 2 or 3 weeks of his summer holidays. He did this for a couple of years. He told me, many years later, that he didn't really like staying there as his first week there he was totally on his own, all the other children still being at school. Apparently he used to stand by the playground wire wondering why the other children couldn't be out playing with him. By the time that they were on holiday, of course, he had only enough time to make friends and then he was coming home. I know that he spent a considerable amount of his time down the knothole behind Mum and Dad's house with Herbert, a rather simple fellow. Herbert used to let Colin operate the levers, from Herbert's little hut, that pulled the little trolleys of clay from the bottom of the knothole up in to the brickworks. Sometimes when Colin went over to the club Herbert would be there and would buy him a Vimto fizzy drink.

It was about this time, too, that we went to Walton-on-the-Naze by coach on a day trip. Colin was splashing about in the sea and shouting out and we thought that he was splashing and playing, enjoying himself. Pity of it was he was stung by a jellyfish over his stomach and legs. Poor old "Chum" took him to the first aid post, a wooden horse drawn van, and had to wait with him. The first aid man just sat there and did nothing. "Chum" asked, "What are you waiting for? Aren't you going to do anything?" "Sorry," replied the ambulance man, "I've to wait and see what colour he turns!" Anyway, it turned out all right in as much as it wasn't a dangerous jellyfish sting. It took a number of days before Colin could walk properly and go about normally though, and for many years he couldn't bear his legs and tummy to be in the sun. This was an upsetting occasion for us all.

The Children Marry

Years later Colin got a motorbike and I still remember laying awake for him to come home. When I heard his bike as he turned into the road I knew that everything was all right and I could go to sleep. He's got a couple of motorbikes again now, and often pops over to see me on one.

Colin had one or two girlfriends before he got married to Jean Tinworth in 1968, and that was after eight months courting himself. "Chum" was still alive then, but was taken queer at the wedding and the ambulance took him to hospital during the wedding service. After the service was over Colin, Jean and Jenny, who was one of the bridesmaids, went up to the hospital - Barnet General – to see him. Reg took them in his car and I thought that was nice of them.

In about 1964 Jenny met a young man named Heinz Widler from Switzerland. He was in England working at Rochford's nurseries, Turnford, learning about plants and flowers. She met him in a dance hall in Enfield Town, which was over what is now Bradford and Bingley's by the market square. Colin met his wife there and all. Jenny liked him so much that when he went back home to Switzerland she took a job as an au-pair just to be near him. They must have got on all right as they got married in 1970 and I went over there for the wedding, as did Colin and Jean.

My Husband Dies

"Chum" passed away on 18th October 1969. It's funny how things work out, as on the day he died Colin, Jean and her mother, Marie, came to see us on the Saturday afternoon. We were sitting chatting and "Chum", as always, was watching the wrestling on the TV. He used to get all worked up over it. I said, on many occasions, that it would be the death of him, and it was! The doctor said it was his heart and it could have happened at any time, so I suppose that it was nice having family around. Colin 'phoned Jenny in Switzerland, and she came home for the funeral. Even after he had "passed on" flowers still bloomed in profusion in my garden, and I always felt that my "Chum" was still there tending especially for me. Every time a flower bloomed it was as if he said, "Here you are Molly, I grew this just for you. I know how much you love your flowers."

More than once after he died I would be dusting or cleaning upstairs and I thought I heard his "coo-ee" whistle that he used to make when he came in. I remember that on one occasion it seemed like he called out to say that he'd made a cup of tea and that it was ready for me to drink. I even called back saying that I would be down in a minute, but of course it was just my mind playing tricks, he wasn't there. Of course I miss him, who wouldn't miss their husband? I often think that now I've got some money saved. What's it all for, as I have no one to share it with for holidays or anything. We could have used that money when poor ole "Chum" was still alive, 'cos we never had much at all then. Not even two 'appenies to rub together!

Old Age

Colin and Jean never moved too far away from me, and I'm grateful for that as they've always done jobs for me, so I've got dependent on them. Colin's very good with his hands, mending the car, about the house, making things and that. They always come to see me regularly and take me for rides or to spend the day at their place. It's got so that I'm so dependent on them that I hate them going away on holiday, seems like I'm all on my own.

When I was able I used to spend a few week's holiday with Jenny and Heinz in Switzerland each year, and took a friend once, Mrs. Scopie, but I got sains' I was too bad to go. Still, Jenny and Heinz always came to stay with me at Wades Grove a couple of times a year. It was nice having them over as I used to go for rides with them in the country, often stopping at a tea room in Broughing, Much Haddam, or garden centres somewhere, for a cup of tea and a cream cake. Now I'm in my little sheltered accommodation flat in Southgate they still come over, but 'cos they can't stay with me any more they stop at a hotel in Chase Side, Enfield. I still get my little rides out an' that, so it can't be all that bad.

As I've said, I love my flowers, and even today I always have flowers in my little flat, my son and daughter-in-law see to that. They even fitted up a window box and hanging basket for me to enjoy, until my arthritis got so bad that I couldn't water the window box, so they took it down. I've still got my hanging basket that Jean does for me, but I still do so miss my garden.

I like the warmer weather, not too bright though, 'cos of my eyes, so I can get out for a little ride somewhere; I do so like to see the trees an' flowers and peoples' nice gardens. I'm 90 years old now an' sometimes my arthritis plays me up so much or I get so muddle headed that I can't remember what I'm doing or what I've done that I wish I was dead 'an in me wooden box. Still, when I look back there are happy times and worrying times as well. Never mind, one makes up for the other I suppose - life can't always be sweet!'

Molly died on 17th April 2003.

<u>*Author's Notes*</u>

1. *Part of Colin's account included an Appendix which draws on Census and other data that looked back to the history of the various strands of his family. The family could not be traced back in Winchmore Hill, and so I have not sought to reproduce much of Colin's research here. However, the family did have a longstanding presence in the Enfield area. The reader might be interested in the following snippets, taken from his research -*

'It may be deduced that the Wacketts arrived in Windmill Hill c1846 and Enfield pre 1827....' However, the first Census showing the family is the 1851 one, which lists Isaac Wackett, aged 46, as living in Windmill Hill. He was a hurdle maker and was born in 1804/5 in Hertford. Mary (presumably his wife) was aged 49 and also listed as a Hurdle Maker. She is indicated as being born in 1801/2 in New South Wales, Australia – quite an unusual origin for a Middlesex resident in those days!

The Wackett family are still shown at Windmill Hill in the 1901 Census, with the 76 year old William earning his living as a grocer. However, Colin tells us that, "Kelly's records for 1913 show that he (John William Wackett) and Ethel Emily Wackett (nee Hack) moved into Wades Grove, Winchmore Hill, late in 1912 or early 1913."

Ethel Emily Hack, then aged 14, was shown in the 1891 Census as working as a 'general domestic' servant in Hornsey. In the Census of 1901, by now aged 24, she is indicated as working as a Household Domestic at The Isolation Hospital, Old Green Dragon Lane, Winchmore Hill. She was born in 1876/7 at Tilsworth, Woburn, Bedfordshire.

2. *Colin has established that the stable later became a garage for a long time (Ossie*

Knowles), then a shop fitters' workshop (Balfe), next a vegetable store and afterwards a wholesale electrical store.

3. *Mr. Simpson contributed to 'More Winchmore Hill Lives' (2004) and was also a long term friend and neighbour of Lucy Pettifer, who contributed to the original 'Winchmore Hill Lives' (1991).*

A.E.E. Westoby

Many longer term residents will be familiar with the name of Westoby, whose family ran an Estate Agent's business in Winchmore Hill for most of the 20th century. In August 1986 Mr. A. E. E. Westoby, when he knew of my developing interest in local history, was kind enough to see me in his office at 22, The Green one Saturday morning, to pass on some of his knowledge, including various papers. I took notes, which I still have on file.

He told me that the houses on the north side at the foot of Station Road were built in the 1880s, as were the few houses on the western arm of Radcliffe Road, shown on the 1895 OS Map. He held an old map which indicated that the first house built was on the corner of Radcliffe and Station Roads in 1886. The main stretch of Radcliffe Road, parallel to Station Road, was, he said, built in about 1908, with Edgar J. Westoby, estate agents, at No. 55 on the northern corner with Green Lanes. (Note 1) That was where Mr. A.E.E. Westoby was born in 1909. The Trustees of the Radcliffe School Estate of Steeple Aston, which had owned land in that vicinity for centuries, still owned a few of the houses in that area.

Mr. Westoby said that when he was young Station Road and Compton Road were 'posh'. He remembered the Gillingwater family in the old cottages that stood where Cookley House now stands next to Repton Court, on the Upper Green. However, he said that there was no split between the better off newcomers and the old villagers. He went to the Collegiate School at the top of Farm Road, which later became a synagogue, until he was 13, whence he attended a school in Surrey. After leaving school he joined his father's business and did his Surveyor's qualifications by studying two hours a night at Lincoln's Inn Fields. In 1931 Mr. Westoby became a Fellow of the Surveyors' Institute.

His father, Edgar J. Westoby, started his business where King Easton had their plot just west of the railway line in Station Road, in 1903, though the building was later pulled down. There weren't any telephones in Winchmore Hill then. He remembered visiting 'the lanes' of Farm Road and Fords Grove when the latter was known as Mortiboys Lane, after the farmer not far down on the right, who wore an Australian hat. The family moved from Radcliffe Road to Vicars Moor Lane in about 1917. He remembered visiting his cousin in Houndsden Road, and since then Houndsden Gutter had been diverted in that vicinity.

Before the corner shop on The Green was Westoby's it was Dunnett's the tailor's. He remembered Mr. Dunnett from his youth, with long whiskers and a tape around his neck. He was a bit of a character, and his grandson lived in the upstairs of the premises until his death in 1985. He also remembered Horace Regnart as a bit of an eccentric, with a loud stuttering voice.

There was a definite house building boom from 1900 to 1910, then another in about 1922-3, and the large houses fostered a growing service industry with regard to employment, but he felt as he was growing up that the increasing urbanisation helped spoil the area's character. The prices from his younger day sound very low in today's money. In about 1928 a house in Compton Road would have cost around £750! In the 1930s a semi detached house with a garage would cost about £950 to £1,000.

The Westoby family had played a prominent role locally. For example, Edgar had helped form Winchmore Hill Bowling Club in Radcliffe Road, whilst the family had had a hand in the sale of the Marchioness of Ely's Eversley Park Estate in 1921, and in 1931, Roseneath and Broadfields following the death of Sir William Paulin.

The above was what I believe Mr. Westoby told me in 1986, *though I can't vouch for the accuracy of the account in my usual manner,* as he never saw the write up and so didn't have the chance to correct it. However, I can vouch for the accuracy of the following bit, as he wrote to me on 4th December 1989, following the publication of *A History of Winchmore Hill*. He kindly said, 'I like your book very much,' and he hoped his enclosed notes would help me.

These notes tell us that *Avondale*, with its 6¼ acres of land on the northern corner of Vicars Moor Lane and Wades Hill, was auctioned in about 1929, and purchased by Arthur Ingram Junior, who demolished the house and built Hillcrest and on the frontage to Wades Hill and Vicars Moor Lane. (Note 2)

In 1931 Arthur Ingram Senior bought Broadfields, putting in the roads Paulin Drive, Broadfields Avenue and Cresswell Way. He then sold off plots to other builders, and it was Readers of Chingford who put in the attractive houses in Broadfields Avenue. So it would seem that a small detail on Page 100 of my *A History of Winchmore Hill* is slightly in error if Mr. Westoby is correct.

Mr. Westoby wrote that he lived with his parents at Moors Lea from 1917 to 1935. Moors Lea is shown just to the west of the railway and footpath to Station Road on the 1895 OS map. In or about 1930, he informed, the old building was demolished, along with nearby Percy Lodge on the southern corner with Wades Hill, and the land was developed. H & GW Rowley of Tottenham put in housing on this land around 1932. E.J. Westoby built the new Moors Lea, set back behind new houses fronting onto Vicars Moor Lane, in 1932, using most of the materials from the old house, and A.E.E. Westoby lived there until 1935.

Mr. Westoby wrote that the Rowleys built houses along the frontage of Wades Hill as far as the tennis courts which ran behind the rear gardens of Wilson Street. He says that these were leased to Vicars Moor Tennis Club when they left the courts in *Roseneath* in about 1932. He says that these were replaced by Council Housing when Barber Close was developed in the 1950s.

At Page 104 of *A History of Winchmore Hill* I quoted the late Lucy Pettifer as saying that she remembered German POWs demolishing Percy Lodge and Avondale during the Second World War, but Mr. Westoby wrote, 'Apologies to Mrs. Pettifer but all this happened before 1939 and German POWs!' It was clear that he considered Lucy's recollection of Barber Close being built by the German POWs was also in error.

Mr. Westoby had put his written doubts to me over the telephone first. I have kept the notes I made when I visited Lucy on 2nd December 1989, when I challenged her recollection of events. She remained adamant about the wartime demolition of Percy Lodge and the replacement of the tennis club by Barber Close. Lucy said that she was manageress of The Button Box on The Green during the war, and the shop rented tea rooms from the tennis club whilst it was still there.

In August 2010 I was working my way through the David Hicks Archives at the Local Studies Unit when I came upon a few snippets that relate to the foregoing. One item was a photograph which shows celebrations at a VE Day Party at the Tennis Club in Wades Hill, so it was clearly still there in mid 1945. Two of the attendees listed are Lucy Pettifer and her daughter Shirley. Bella Hemington, a grand daughter of Rat Hemington (pictured at P29 of *More Winchmore Hill Lives*) is also listed as an attendee. The subjects of the photograph are all children, bar one adult woman, who must, I suspect, be Lucy in her younger days.

The Hicks Archives also includes a note by David saying that Barber Close was built in the 1940s. A Mrs. Betty Smith of 16, Barber Close had told him that there was an inscription near the entrance to the Close which stated that it was 'opened' in 1947 by former Mayor Alderman J.T. Barber (pictured at Plate 33), for people with TB and chest infections. (Note 3) Apparently prospective inhabitants had to be vetted! This opening date would be quite consistent with the POWs having made a start on Barber Close in 1945, so it quite likely that Lucy was right on this issue, though inexplicably wrong about Avondale and Percy Lodge.

<u>*Author's Notes*</u>

1. *The 1905-6 Kelly's Directory listing for Radcliffe Road shows only 1 – 25 on the west side of the road and five houses on the east side. The listing for the south side of Station Road starts, 'New Wharncliffe Coal Co. Limited; Westoby Edgar J. house & estate agent. Clarke Herbt. Lim. Coal mers. Station Parade 1. Ebben William, baker ….' The next Kelly's I could trace was for 1908-9, where there is now a full listing of 1 – 55 for the west/north side of Radcliffe Road, where the last entry, by Green Lanes, is, 'Westoby Edgar J. auctioneer & estate agent'.*

2. *A Palmers Green and Southgate Gazette article of 13th May 1932 tells us of Beaumont Lodge, 'ultimately it became Avondale Ladies' College; kept by Miss Steele, who relinquished it about three years ago; it was demolished and new villas built on the ground …' The 1929 Kelly's Directory features Percy Lodge, but not Avondale. In the 1930 edition there is no Percy Lodge either.*

3. *When out leafleting Barber Close on 30th November 2010 I looked for the said inscription, but could not find it. It may have been on a small cement edifice by the wall of one of the first houses on the north face of the Close, but washed away by the rain.*

4. *I spoke to a Mrs. Westoby at The Wool Shop on the southern corner of Green Lanes and Shrubbery Gardens on 4th September 1990. She said that she had been there for 31 years, but was now aged 88 and in failing health. She said that the previous two years had been disastrous, as people had lost interest in knitting, or buying woollen goods. She was selling up within a week!*

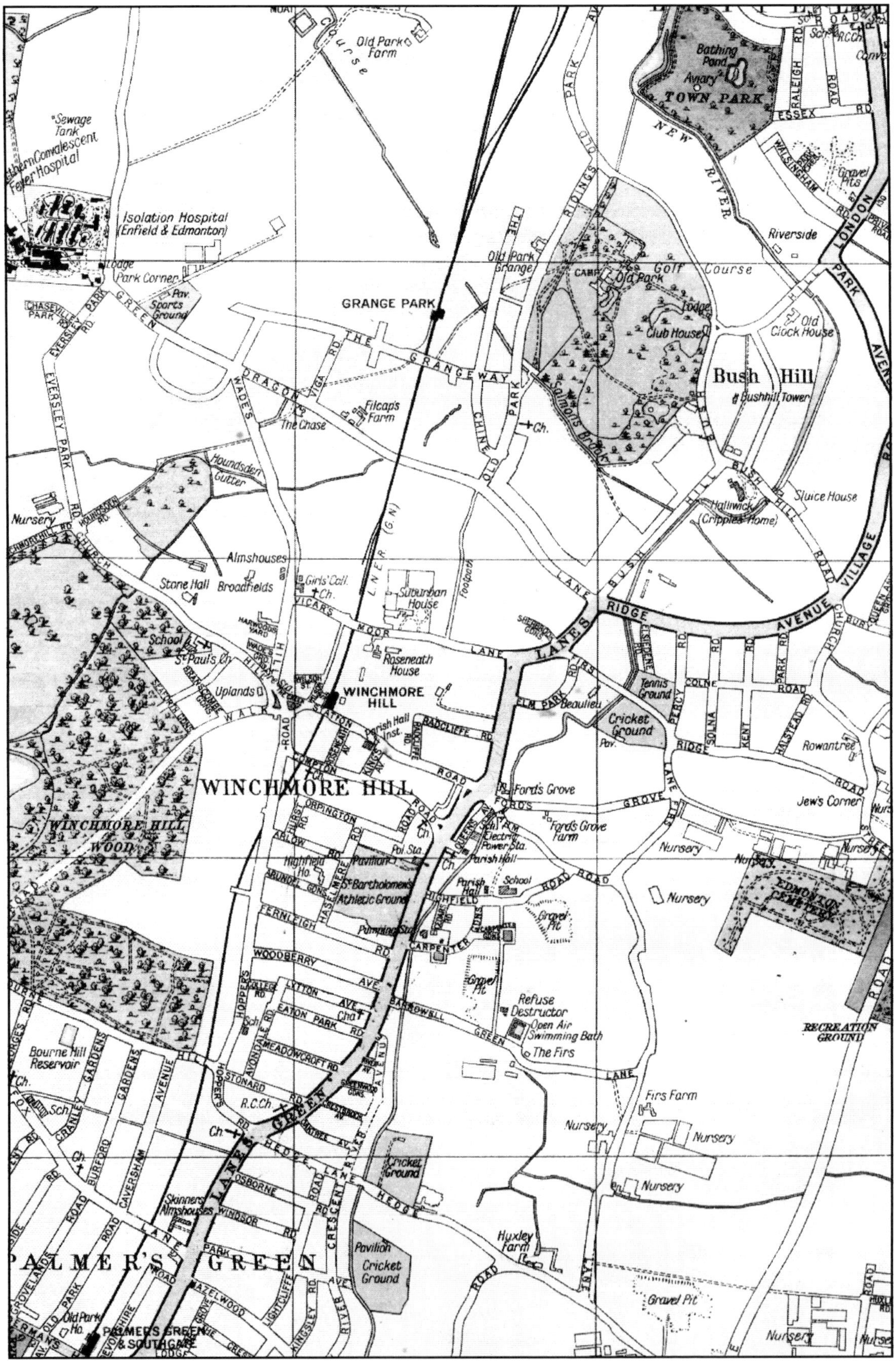

Figure 1. Winchmore Hill in 1923.
We have Broad Walk being laid out through the Wood, but apart from the infill between Hoppers Road and Green Lanes, Winchmore Hill is still very much a village.

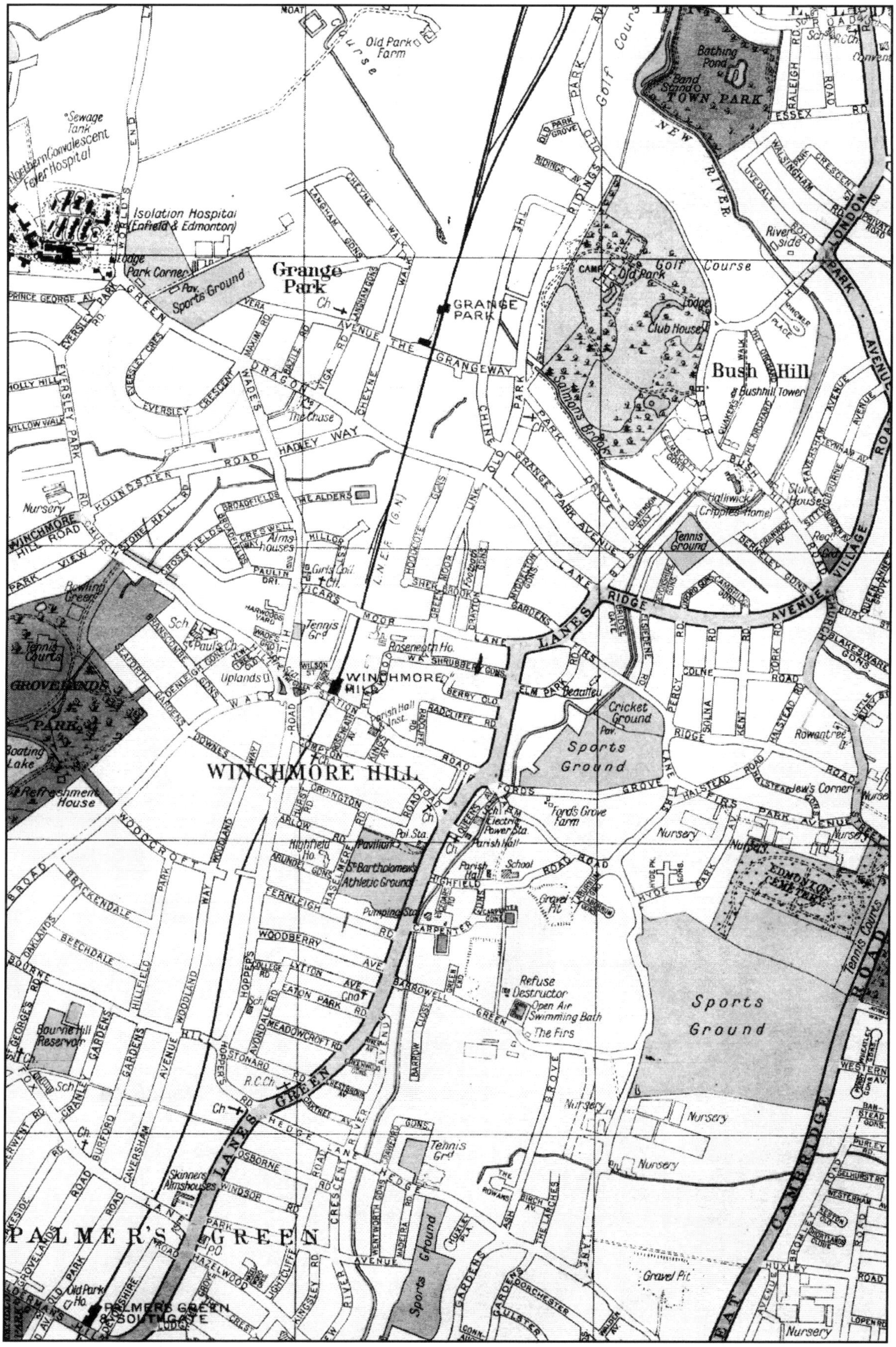

Figure 2. Winchmore Hill in 1936.
In just 13 years the old Middlesex village had become a suburb of London.

Plate 1. Jean Bilton's family, North Row, Vicars Moor Lane.
This photograph was given to me, with permission to publish, by contributor Jean Bilton. Her father, Joseph Henry Whitworth, is the taller boy in this snap, which also shows his brother Horace and their mother, who looked after Udall's Chapel, further west in Vicars Moor Lane. It was presumably taken outside the family home in the 1890s. North Row cottages are still there today, and are pictured at Plate 2.

Plate 2. North Row, Vicars Moor Lane.
I took this photograph on 14th July 2006. North Row is quite old and has been a familiar sight to locals for well over a hundred years. I hope to find out more about these four cottages.

Plate 3. Sergeant Walter C. Burch and the Herts Yeomanry in 1915
The front page of The Recorder for Palmers Green, Winchmore Hill and Southgate of 9th September 1915 bears the headline, '120 Degrees in the Shade. Warmer than "Dear Old Winchmore Hill"' for an article about the local Sergeant's service in Egypt. The article included, 'I enclose a photo of a fairly common occurrence in the camp. From left to right the photo shows Lance Corporal Schultz, Corporal Dykes, Lance Corporal Carroll, Lance – Sergeant Carroll, Sergeant Burch, and Corporal Eastwell.' This was copied from the L. B. Enfield Local Studies Unit.

Plate 4. Holly Cottage, Station Road, perhaps in Edwardian times.
My thanks to the L. B. Enfield Local Studies Unit for this snap. As I explain at the start of the Chalkley family account, the first building on your left past the station is what was known as Holly Cottage, and just past it was a shop that was once occupied by the Chalkleys, more latterly by the Waters.

Plate 5. Binste(a)d Cottages. This snap was kindly given to me for publication by the late local builder Ewan Lewis. A local paper of 10th August 1928 told us that Mr. W. Binstead ran the bakery shop described by Miss Cresswell in her Memories of a Lost Village, which was on the site of the current railway station. The shop was demolished in 1869 to allow the railway cutting, and the compensation Mr. Binste(a)d received enabled him to build these three cottages, which were named after him. The view is looking north from just off of Station Road, with the front doors facing towards the railway line. The cottages are looking rather forlorn, and Ewan must have taken this not long before their demolition, to make way for Milton Lodge, which I presume was probably in the winter of 1972-3, when the nearby Holly Cottage was knocked down.

Plate 6. 1905 wedding of Wilfred Fletcher Chalkley and Emily Morris.
This photograph has kindly been given for publication by Margaret Johnson (nee Chalkley), who has identified those in attendance as follows (left to viewer's right) – Top row (Chalkleys): Lillie (1876 – 1933), Percy (1882 – 1919), Eliza (1845 – 1914), Thomas (1844 – 1921), Doris aka Ethel (1880-1938), Reginald (1885-1934), unknown; Bottom row: Mother Morris, Polly Morris, Anna Morris, Emily Morris (1876-1966), Wilfred Fletcher Chalkley (1872-1941), Florence (1875-1834), Gertrude (1878-1955).

Plate 7. Wilfred Fletcher Chalkley and family c 1914/5.
This photograph, presumably taken at the stables in Compton Terrace, has kindly been supplied for publication by Margaret Johnson (nee Chalkley), who has identified her family's members as (left to viewer's right) – Wilfred Fletcher and children Gordon, Harold, and Wilfred Jnr., then W.F.'s brother Archibald. Gordon was Margaret's father. Harold married Doris Stockton and when Wilfred Fletcher died in 1941 they managed the family business, supported for some years by their son John.

Plate 8. Wilfred Fletcher Chalkley and car.
This photograph has kindly been supplied for publication by Margaret Johnson, although neither she nor I have been prepared to hazard a date.

Plate 9. Wilfred Fletcher Chalkley outside 21, The Green.
This photograph has kindly been supplied for publication by Margaret Johnson (nee Chalkley), although she is unable to date it. Thomas Chalkley died in August 1921, leaving his son Wilfred Fletcher (1872-1941) to take over the family business.

Plate 10. A traffic free view of Chalkley's in a narrow Hoppers Road.
This photograph has kindly been supplied for publication by Margaret Johnson (nee Chalkley), although she is unable to date it.

Plate 11. The old Hoppers Road bakery from The Green in June 1992.
This is a similar snap to the one of 1989 at Plate 27 in **Winchmore Hill Village 1780 – 1830**, *when the building fronting the Upper Green was occupied by Anthony Cope Ltd. This was taken in June 1992, with Yasmin returning to her car. Behind her is the ancient bakery, and a few yards along, on the corner, is the shop that, like the bakery, was once run by the Chalkley family*

Plate 12. James Gladwin (1838 – 1889) outside St. Paul's Mission, Highfield Row in 1887.
I am grateful to contributor Brian Cook for giving me this old photograph of his great grandfather for publication.

Plate 13. Eva and Lilian Gladwin at St. Paul's School c 1908
A second photograph supplied by Brian Cook for this book. His Aunt Lilian is in the middle of the second row up, whilst Aunt Eva is third from the right in the row above that. Miss Mellership is the teacher seated above her colleague Mrs. Fielder. Here they appear to be wearing the same clothes as in the photographs of St. Paul's children featured at P83 of A History of Winchmore Hill and P71 of the 1991 Winchmore Hill Lives. Perhaps they were all taken on the same day!?

Plate 14. Ernest and Albert Gladwin, Highfield Road.
Brian Cook has kindly supplied this picture of his mother's brothers taken in about 1923.
The brothers are outside No. 1, which was later renumbered 31. (Young Ernest is to your left.)

Plate 15. Shops on the Lower Green in Edwardian times.
This old postcard was franked 9th September 1905. Nearest, at No. 8 The Green, is Buckle and Vaughan, saddler F.G. Speight was at No. 10, Garrard the builder was at No. 12, Frederick Barker the ironmonger was at No. 14 and then, at No. 16 was William Gabriel the corn and seed merchant – later to become Downes's. The mansion of Uplands is in the distance.

Plate 16. Will and Harry Downes in the Stores at the Northern Hospital (Highlands).
Will and Harry were the sons of James Downes, who was the brother of J.T. (Plate 19.) and Charles Snr. (see Plate 25). Will had three sons, featured in the next Plate. One of Will's sisters was Elsie, whose daughter Val Darvell was featured in More Winchmore Hill Lives of 2004.

Plate 17. Don, Les and Eric Downes in August 2005.
I took this at a large Downes family gathering in Bounds Green, where I interviewed the brothers. Twins Don (far left as viewed) and Les were born in 1924. They sit and study More Winchmore Hill Lives as younger brother Eric, born in 1926, looks on. Their father, Will, was the brother of Val Darvell's mother Elsie.

Plate 18. Malcolm and Bob Hill at Trafalgar Square, August 1952
Photograph kindly supplied for publication by Bob Hill, who is on your right.

Plate 19. J.T. Downes aged c 55 in c. 1912.
Photograph kindly supplied for publication by Bob Hill.

Plate 20. J.T. Downes's eldest daughter Jane at 16, The Green c. 1912.
Photograph kindly supplied for publication by Bob Hill. In more recent years the shop has become a hairdresser, and many people are unaware that the rear part probably dates back to at least the late 18th century. If you look closely you can see that the upper window comes down to floor level.

Plate 21. Samuel Jeffs – Hall (b. 1901) aged about 50.
Bob Hill has kindly supplied this snap of his step father for publication. Bob says he was a decent sort of man.

Plate 22. 12, 14 & 16 The Green on 21st March 2005.
16 The Green had now become Show 11 Unisex salon. It saw off the competition from New York Hair and Beauty at No. 14, which has now become Treacle's Tea Shop.

Plate 23.
The shop, c. 1911, by The Dog and Duck in Hoppers Road (and a few doors down from the Fentum's) which was, for many years, run by Charles Downes's family. The 1903-4 Kelly's Street Directory lists for this part of Hoppers Road (going south) 'Downes John; Fricker George; Fentum Charles, theatrical scene painter; Fentum Fredk., tobacconist; Jackson Jas. Alex. beer retlr.; Downes Chas. general shop; Bennett Thomas', then six occupants of Arkley Terrace (which is still there). (Photograph kindly supplied for publication by Bob Hill.)

Plate 24. By the Dog and Duck, 26th May 2001.
This is a more recent view, looking north, of the area around The Dog and Duck. The cottage just south of the pub formerly housed the shop run by Charles Downes and family, shown at Plate 23. I believe that it has recently been refurbished.

Plate 25. The wedding of Charles Downes Jnr. and Evelyn Sudul, 6th July 1935

My thanks to Janet Palmer for supplying this wedding picture for publication. This Charles was the son of Charles Downes Senior (brother of James and J.T. Downes). For many years Charles Snr., and his wife Charlotte, ran the General Store immediately south of The Dog and Duck, featured at Plate 23. Janet Palmer believes that those captured are (viewer's left to right):- Back row: Miss Jean Geyelin (groom's niece), Mr. Arthur Sudul (bride's father), Miss Cassandra Downes (groom's sister), Mr. Clifford Humphrey (Miss Marjorie Sudul's fiancé), Mr. Charles Downes (groom), Evelyn Downes (bride), Mrs. Charlotte Geyelin (groom's sister), Charles Snr., Miss Dorothy Page (bride's cousin). Front row: Charlotte Downes (wife of Charles Snr. & groom's mother), Miss Ivy Downes (groom's cousin), Miss Marjorie Sudul (bride's sister), Mrs. Annie Sudul (bride's mother).

Plate 26. A very young Pauline Holstius outside 27, Hoppers Road.
I am grateful to Pauline for supplying this snap outside the house where she was born in 1916.

Plate 27. The Holstius Sisters – on 15th March 2008. (Pauline is on your left, Joan to your right.)
Just before I left, after interviewing the sisters, I got them to pose outside Pauline's Broadfield Cottage on Wades Hill. Somehow the snap has a rustic feel to it.

Plate 28. Olde Thatched Cottage, Palmers Green.
This lovely old cottage by the Triangle was built in about 1790 as a lodge to a mansion called 'The Lodge'. The Holstius sisters attended school nearby, and so remembered the old cottage. Pauline was good enough to give me the picture, from a postcard franked 23rd December 1904, for publication.

Plate 29. Top of Hoppers Road in 1935.
I am able to publish this photograph from the Hicks Collection by courtesy of LB Enfield Library Service. It shows the NW corner of the road just before the new Salisbury Arms, we know today, replaced the old pub, shown, just to its north. The old pub looks as though it might well have been built onto the front of older premises. Beyond is Stockton's the butcher, which hides Esther Cottages. The gap for Walker's Yard is clearly shown on what must be the side of Victoria Cottages. Norman Last lived opposite these premises as a boy, and there is more on this stretch with his first account in More Winchmore Hill Lives. There is also more on the history of the pub and Stockton's in **Winchmore Hill Village 1780 – 1830** *(e.g. Pages 161 – 164).*

Plate 30. Youngsters re - enact the 1937 Coronation of George VI at Vicars Moor Lawn Tennis Club. John Lucas kindly supplied this photograph for publication. Local teenagers Hamish Currie, as King George VI, and June Pearson, as the then Queen Elizabeth, in 1937. Peter Rowley, with the cross, was The Archbishop of Canterbury. John can be seen to the viewer's extreme right as he plays the part of a soldier.

Plate 31. The Lucas family in their back garden in the early 1930s.
John Lucas kindly supplied this photograph for publication. Leslie and Winifred Lucas enjoy tea in their back garden in Sherbrook Garden in the early 1930s with their children (l to r) Nanette, John and Ray.

Plate 32. John Lucas and pals raise money for Spitfires in Sherbroook Gardens, 1941.
John Lucas kindly supplied this photograph for publication. Here he shows off some War memorabilia to a passing lady in a fundraising drive to sponsor Spitfires in 1941. His pals Rex Knight and Peter Morris, who were also both involved in the enterprise, look on in his front garden in Sherbrook Gardens.

Plate 33. Thomas Barber, Southgate Charter Mayor, 30th September 1933.
This is a picture from an old postcard that I purchased. See John Lucas's account for more on the day that Southgate became a Municipal Borough. One presumes that Barber Close, at the top of Wades Hill, takes its name from this gentleman.

Plate 34. What had been Marriage's shop in Highfield Road, September 2005. The premises have been enlarged and converted into flats.

Plate 35. Bill Parkinson in 1997.
This photograph was kindly supplied for publication by Mr. Parkinson.

Plate 36. Alf & Terry Teers' Uncle Bob.
This old photograph was kindly supplied by the Teer family for publication. Uncle Bob and Aunt Bea lived in the cottage that stood in the grounds of St. Paul's Church, just to the right as you entered from Church Hill.

Plate 37. Sunnyside Cottages in Green Lanes c 1905 – latterly Ironside Motors.
Our thanks are due to Harry Skinner for supplying this photograph for publication. It is of Sunnyside Cottages in Green Lanes in about 1905. Michael Lawrence and family occupied one of the cottages and, from 1907, the other was home to Mr. Skinner's family

Plate 38. The marriage of Margaret 'Peggy' Pettengell and Dennis Shepherd.
This photograph was kindly supplied, with permission to publish, by the Pettengell family, via their cousin Derek Norman. Peggy married Dennis at Holy Trinity Church, Queens Avenue, on 26th May 1942, two years before the family was affected by the German V1 flying bomb attack on Carpenter Gardens.

There are too many people to label everyone, but some of those in attendance are as follows. In the front row, to the viewer's left, is contributor Joe as a boy (wearing a rosette), with his cousin Derek Norman to his left. Derek is hiding little Brian, who is next to bridesmaid Patricia Shepherd. Moving to the adults behind, the uniformed bridegroom Dennis is standing next to his sister, May. Bride 'Peggy' is standing next to Joyce Withers. Behind Joyce is Peggy's blind father Frederick. The white bundle to Joyce's left is baby Ann. Just in front of Ann, to her left, is Grandma Norman (hiding Peggy's mother May), then Grandma Pettengell, then Grandpa Norman (on the extreme right of the picture).

Plate 39. Ironside Motors, Green Lanes, 31st October 2000.
The premises of Ironside Motors mark the former site of Harry Skinner's Sunnyside Cottages.

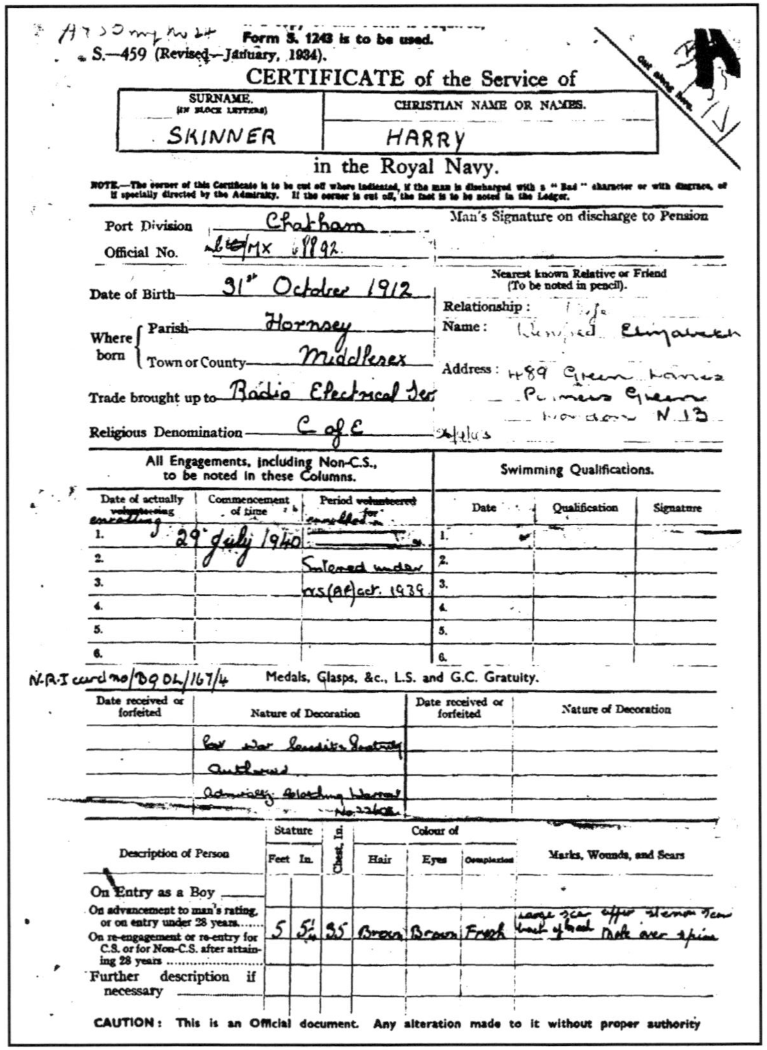

Form S. 1243 is to be used.
S.—459 (Revised—January, 1934).

CERTIFICATE of the Service of

SURNAME. (IN BLOCK LETTERS)	CHRISTIAN NAME OR NAMES.
SKINNER	HARRY

in the Royal Navy.

NOTE.—The corner of this Certificate is to be cut off where indicated, if the man is discharged with a "Bad" character or with disgrace, or if specially directed by the Admiralty. If the corner is cut off, the fact is to be noted in the Ledger.

Port Division Chatham

Official No. MX 69992

Date of Birth 31st October 1912

Where born: Parish Hornsey; Town or County Middlesex

Trade brought up to Radio Electrical Ser

Religious Denomination C of E

Man's Signature on discharge to Pension

Nearest known Relative or Friend (To be noted in pencil).
Relationship: Wife
Name: Winifred Engalwen
Address: 489 Green Lanes, Palmers Green, London N.13

All Engagements, including Non-C.S., to be noted in these Columns.

	Date of actually volunteering	Commencement of time	Period volunteered for
1.		29 July 1940	
2.			Entered under
3.			NS(AF)act. 1939
4.			
5.			
6.			

Swimming Qualifications.

	Date	Qualification	Signature
1.			
2.			
3.			
4.			
5.			
6.			

N.R.I card no/BQ OL/167/4

Medals, Clasps, &c., L.S. and G.C. Gratuity.

Date received or forfeited	Nature of Decoration	Date received or forfeited	Nature of Decoration
	[illegible]		
	[illegible]		
	Admiralty [illegible] No. 22608		

Description of Person	Stature Feet	Stature In.	Chest, in.	Hair	Eyes	Complexion	Marks, Wounds, and Scars
On Entry as a Boy							
On advancement to man's rating, or on entry under 28 years	5	5¼	35	Brown	Brown	Fresh	[illegible]
On re-engagement or re-entry for C.S. or for Non-C.S. after attaining 28 years							
Further description if necessary							

CAUTION: This is an Official document. Any alteration made to it without proper authority

Plate 40. Harry Skinner's Service Papers - Page 1.
Mr. Skinner kindly supplied copies of his service papers for publication, as they are now of historical interest.

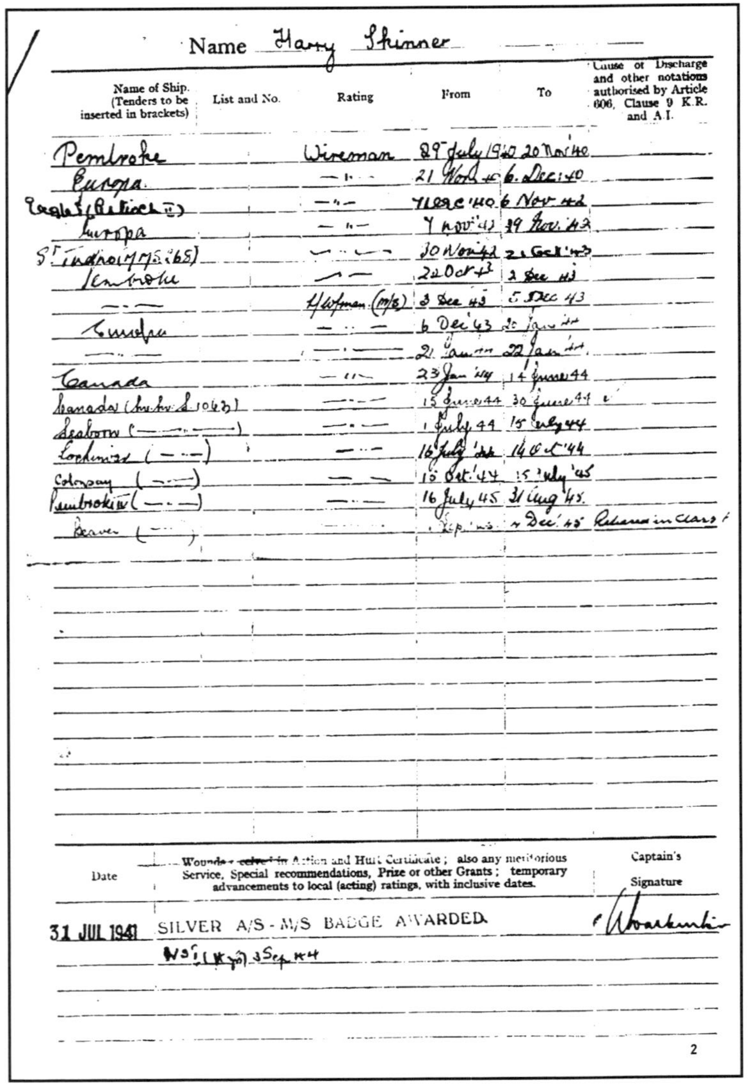

Name Harry Skinner

Name of Ship. (Tenders to be inserted in brackets)	List and No.	Rating	From	To	Cause of Discharge and other notations authorised by Article 606, Clause 9 K.R. and A.I.
Pembroke		Wireman	29 July 1940	20 Nov 40	
Europa		— " —	21 Nov 40	6 Dec 40	
Eaglet (Relief)		— " —	7 Dec 40	6 Nov 42	
Europa		— " —	7 Nov 42	29 Nov 42	
St Tudno (M/S 65)		— " —	30 Nov 42	21 Oct 43	
Pembroke		— " —	22 Oct 43	2 Dec 43	
— " —		L/Wireman (M/S)	3 Dec 43	5 Dec 43	
Europa		— " —	6 Dec 43	20 Jan 44	
— " —		— " —	21 Jan 44	22 Jan 44	
Canada		— " —	23 Jan 44	14 June 44	
Canada (Lucky Lad 1063)		— " —	15 June 44	30 June 44	
Seaborn (— " —)		— " —	1 July 44	15 July 44	
Corduroy (— " —)		— " —	16 July 44	14 Oct 44	
Colony (— " —)		— " —	15 Oct 44	15 July 45	
Pembroke IV (— " —)		— " —	16 July 45	31 Aug 45	
Beaver (— " —)			1 Sep 45	2 Dec 45	Released in Class A

Date	Wounds received in Action and Hurt Certificate; also any meritorious Service, Special recommendations, Prize or other Grants; temporary advancements to local (acting) ratings, with inclusive dates.	Captain's Signature
31 JUL 1941	SILVER A/S - M/S BADGE AWARDED.	[illegible]
	NS (K.) 3 Sep 44	

2

Plate 41. Harry Skinner's Service Papers - Page 2.
Harry saw a varied service.

Plate 42. Harry Skinner in the Royal Navy on Minesweeper duties.
Our thanks to Harry Skinner for this photograph of himself (front centre) amongst other members of the crew of minesweeper MMS 257 in Liverpool in 1941 or '42.

Plate 43. Winchmore Hill Police Station on 27th July 1986.
The Recorder of 13th January 1916 reported, 'A long felt want has been supplied by the opening of the smart new police station near St. Bartholomew's Hospital Athletic Ground (now Sainsbury's). The opening was a purely informal affair, the men stationed there taking up their new duties at six o'clock on the morning of December 13th (1915) as if nothing unusual had happened.' See the Traigis's account for a few words from Bill on what it was like to serve locally later in the century.

Plate 44. Doreen and Gerard Van Der Sanden on their 50th wedding anniversary. on 28th January 2000. Photo' kindly supplied for publication by Mrs. Van Der Sanden, nee Grover.

Plate 45. 'Molly' and 'Chum' Wackett marry at St. Paul's Church, 22nd October 1939. Photo' kindly supplied for publication by Colin Wackett.

Plate 46. 'Molly' Wackett with young Colin and Jennifer.
Photo' kindly supplied for publication by Colin Wackett.

Plate 47. 'Molly' Wackett in middle age.
Photo' kindly supplied for publication by Colin Wackett.

Plate 48. Young Colin Wackett at home in Wades Grove.
Photo' kindly supplied for publication by Colin Wackett.

Accounts of 'The Great and The Good'

Plate 49. Barclay tombstone in the Quaker Burial Ground.
The Church Hill burial ground contains a number of the Barclay clan. I took this photo', near the road, on 27th April 1987. The tombstone is inscribed, 'David Barclay of Cheapside. Son of Apologist. Born 1682. Died 1769' A similar photograph of his son David of Walthamstow's tombstone appears on the back cover of my 1989 A History of Winchmore Hill.

Plate 50. Thomas Hood (1799 – 1845).
There is a Blue Plaque at Poultry, near Bank Tube Station, commemorating Hood's birthplace, and another on the site of his old cottage in Vicars Moor Lane, showing where he lived from 1829 – 1832. A man with a huge literary output, his poem November still sounds fresh today.

Plate 51. The Paulin Family – probably in the late 1880s.
This is a photograph lodged with Enfield Local Studies Unit, who kindly allowed me to copy it. It shows William Thomas and his wife Fanny (nee Mann), with their daughters Fanny Ina (b.1879) and Mary Julia Irene (b. 1882).

Plate 52. Roseneath

The Mann brewing family moved to Roseneath in the mid 1850s. Regnart, who was a child in late Victorian Winchmore Hill, tells us that, 'After his mother's death in the middle nineties, Sir Edward (Mann) rebuilt his father's home, Roseneath, in Vicarsmoor Lane, and went to live there, but in a few years he left Winchmore Hill for good.' It would seem that when Sir Edward left the area he sold or gifted Roseneath to William Thomas Paulin . An article headed 'Future of Grovelands' in The Palmers Green and Southgate Gazette of 12th June 1920 ran, 'The winding up meeting of the Southgate branch of the Middlesex VAO was held .... last week .... The first auxiliary hospital effort in Southgate was made in August 1914, when by the benevolence of Mr. W.T. Paulin, Miss Paulin and their friends, Roseneath was equipped and always remained an independent unit ....' I presume, then, that Roseneath stopped functioning as a hospital in 1920, which would mean the photo' in this undated postcard would have been taken sometime between mid 1914 and mid 1920. The mansion became a Nursing Home and was still part of Paulin's estate when he died in 1931. It was demolished in 1936.

Plate 53. Broadfields (?)
This photograph was given to me for publication in the late 1980s as being a St Paul's Church fete at Suburban House in Vicars Moor Lane, but Lucy Pettifer, who worked at Broadfields for a spell, said that it is of that mansion during one of the annual summer hay parties. Irene Wood subsequently wrote, 'I cannot remember what Suburban House looked like, but the photo' does look like Broadfields taken from the side of the house, although Broadfields seemed to be a much larger house than that of the photo'. From other photos I have viewed it physically looks like Broadfields, though I agree with Mrs. Wood that it is not as large as I would have expected.

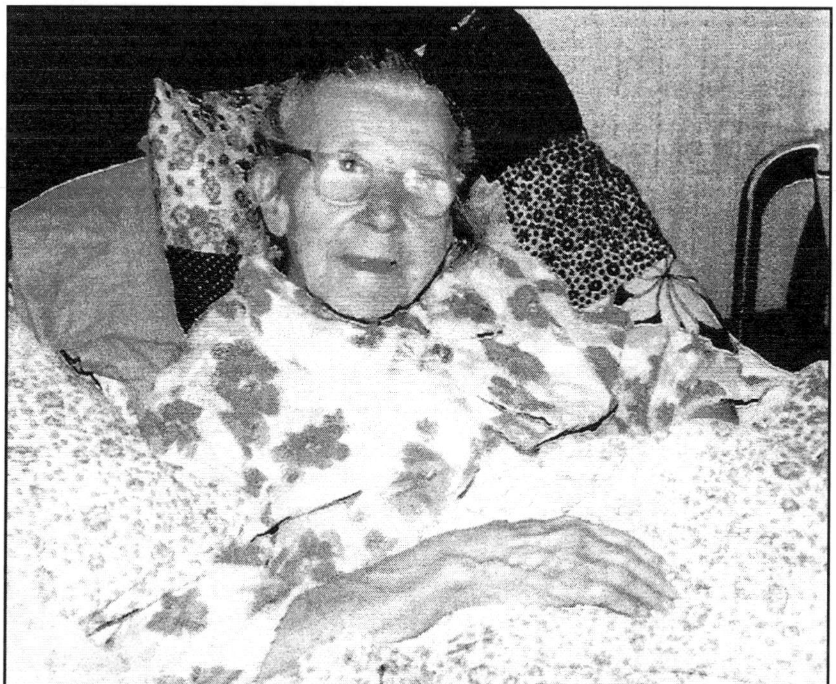

Plate 54. Miss Irene Paulin's maid Charlotte Wragg aged 105.
Taken on 18th August 1983, this photograph was given to me, with permission to publish, by contributor Pauline Holstius, who was almost certainly the photographer.

Plate 55. Paulin's chauffer William Martin

This is a photograph from the David Hicks Archives, lodged with Enfield's Local Studies Unit, who have kindly let me have a copy. David's caption to the snap reads, 'This splendid motor car belonged to the Paulin family. It was a Wolseley 30/40 h.p. with coupe de ville coachwork by Thrupp & Maberley. The chauffer was William Martin.' William developed health problems when serving in the trenches of the Great War. Regretfully he never got over these, and died in 1925 at the youthful age of 27.

Plate 56. The Paulin Cricket Ground.
I took this photo' on 27th July 1986. Winchmore Hill Cricket Club was founded on what we now call the Paulin Ground in 1880, when the land was owned by the Busk family. The Paulins purchased the acreage in 1920 and Irene Paulin, who died in 1960, left the ground for the Club's use on a 99 year lease. The old village team is still there today thanks to the benevolent Paulins.

Plate 57. Outside St. Paul's Institute in Edwardian times.
This is a photograph from a postcard franked 7th December 1910 which I bought. William Thomas Paulin's wife Fanny died at the early age of 49 in February 1901. Although it was demolished in the late 1960s to make way for the current Postal Delivery Office, the foundation stone still exists in the grounds of St. Paul's Church. It reads, 'To the Glory of God and In Memory of Fanny Paulin. This building was erected by William Thomas Paulin, Ina Dewdney, Irene Paulin. 1903. Arthur J.B. Dewdney, Vicar.' Fronting on to Kings Avenue, it cost the Paulins about £14,000 to build.

Plate 58. Inside St. Paul's Institute.
My thanks to the LB Enfield Library Services for this snap from the Hicks Archives, dated 6th October 1910. Everything looks so formal and grand.

Plate 59. The Mc Whirter Brothers.
Norris Mc Whirter in the garden at 10, Branscombe Gardens in the summer of 1926 with his elder brother Kennedy (centre) and twin Ross (probably on the left.) This photograph was kindly supplied for publication by Norris, and appeared in the original Winchmore Hill Lives of 1991.

Plate 60. Norris Mc Whirter's chauffer in 1929.
Norris's father was a senior man in Fleet Street, but served as a private in the Great War, and later employed his former NCO, Sergeant West, as his chauffer. Here he is pictured with the family Darracq in 1929. The snap was kindly supplied for publication by Norris Mc Whirter.

Plate 61. Chadwell Spring, Hertfordshire – source of Sir Hugh Myddelton's New River-on 3rd August 2000. The 'River' was constructed along the 100-foot contour over nearly 40 miles to its, then, final distribution point by Saddlers Wells in Islington. Incredibly, its fall over this distance was a mere 18 feet. The New River was opened on 29th September, 1613. Four hundred years on, it still starts at Chadwell, and runs through Winchmore Hill, now terminating at Stoke Newington.

Plate 62. Statue of Sir Hugh Myddelton at Islington Green.
I took this snap on 26th April 2010 on my way to research at the nearby London Metropolitan Archives. The statue is situated here because it is near to the original termination of Sir Hugh's remarkable engineering feat.

Plate 63. 2, Colne Road, October 2010.
For a few years in the early 1960s, at the height of his success, Cliff Richard chose to live at the corner house shown, until the over enthusiasm of some girl fans became too much for him (as contributor Bill Traigis recalls). See Plate 89 for how the area around Colne Road looked a century ago.

Plate 64. The Capitol Cinema, Green Lanes.
My thanks to Sheila Dumayne for this photograph from Alan's collection. The cinema is spoken of in glowing terms in this book by Alan and Brian Bennett of The Shadows. Prior to finding fame Cliff Richard performed in a talent show held here. The Cinema closed in December 1959, to be replaced by the Tax Offices bearing the same name.

Plate 65. The Collegiate School 1906 – 1963.
Although Paul Scott was not a long term resident of Winchmore Hill, he went to The Collegiate School, before achieving posthumous fame with his Raj Quartet. There is a brief history of the school at the end of the Scott account. This picture is from an undated postcard kindly given to me by Gordon Farrant of Putt's Estate Agents, with permission to publish. Queen's Avenue is to your right, Farm Road to your left.

Plate 66. Stevie Smith's former home at 1, Avondale Road.
I took this picture of the poet's former home on 5th April 1990. You can see the Enfield Council Blue Plaque by the door. In 2005 a further one was unveiled by Andrew Motion, then the Poet Laureate, reading, 'English Heritage. Stevie Smith 1902 – 1971 Poet lived here 1906 – 1971'.

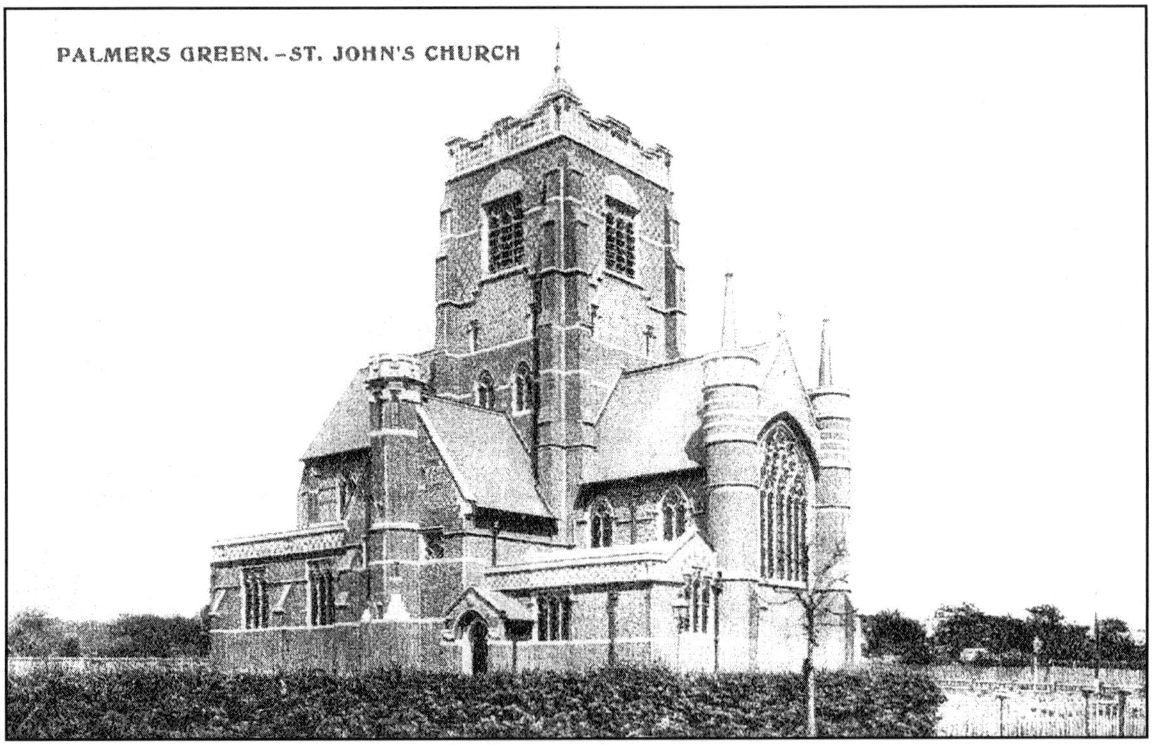

Plate 67. St. John's Church, Palmers Green.
On the fringes of our area, the church was important to Stevie Smith and her family - and no doubt many other families in Winchmore Hill. The architect was J. Oldrid Scott, and the foundation stone was laid by Vyell Edward Walker on 17th October 1903, although the building wasn't completed until 1908. This old undated photograph is striking because the church, which is hemmed in today, was then (literally) in acres of space.

Previous 'Lives' Books re visited

Plate 68. Arthur Pettifer (1898 – 1989).
Those who have read my 1991 Winchmore Hill Lives will remember Arthur's account of his younger days, which was reproduced by permission of The Southgate Civic Trust, who originally obtained it through the efforts of Pauline Holstius. In 2008 when the Holstius sisters were giving me their account, Pauline kindly gave me this photograph of her erstwhile neighbour for publication.

Plate 69. Staff of the Northern Hospital.
Miss Evelyn Spratley says in the 1991 Winchmore Hill Lives that, 'I was born (in 1904) in the part of Highlands then known as the Northern Hospital, used by child convalescents from the London hospitals. My father was the resident Chief Engineer.' There is a series of accounts in the 2004 follow up, More Winchmore Hill Lives, surrounding Highlands Hospital. I bought this blank postcard because it was labelled 'Northern Hospital, Winchmore Hill, N21' in pencil on the back, but there is no date.

*Plate 70. The Northern Hospital from Winchmore Hill Road in Edwardian times.
This is from a postcard franked 2nd October 1906, when Miss Spratley was a baby. There is a fairly similar view even today if you stand and look towards what was Highlands Hospital from The Vale. There is a section in my 2001 A Look at Old Winchmore Hill where I explain that the Northern was opened in 1887, and was later amalgamated into what became Highlands Hospital.*

*Plate 71. Ron Farrant (Mr. 'Another' in the 1991 Winchmore Hill Lives) in 1962.
This shot is taken from a document in the Hicks Archives, lodged with Enfield's Local Studies Unit. It shows Mr. Farrant presenting two armchairs as leaving gifts to the local Methodist Church's Rev. Ernest W. Odell and his wife in August 1962.*

Plate 72. Winchmore Hill Methodist Church 1912 – 1986 at Easter 1986.
Whilst on the subject of Mr. Farrant's Church I thought readers would be interested in this photograph of the previous building to occupy its Green Lanes site. It was kindly supplied for publication by Mr. D.J. Swinson who, on 20th January 2000, in the accompanying letter wrote: 'I was the steward responsible for the church buildings from 1981 until my retirement from that office last year .... Briefly, the original church, now the church hall, was built in 1880. In 1912 a new church was built, seating 750, in front of the old one. In 1932 a small hall was added to the rear of what is now the church hall i.e. the original 1880 church. In 1986 the 1912 church was remodelled, made smaller, with provision for a car park and reopened in its present form on 10th April 1987.' There is a picture of the original chapel in 1880 at P62 of my A Look at Old Winchmore Hill.

Plate 73. Charles Fentum as a young man. By The Dog and Duck, the other side to the pub from Charles Downes and family (see Plate 23), was the Fentum family, featured in More Winchmore Hill Lives. I didn't have the space to publish all the visuals that Dorothy Collins gave me for publication then, so I thought I'd include a few more now. This is the local carpenter, scenic artist and amateur actor who married Dorothy's grandma Emma Abery. (She was born in Hoppers Road in 1847, probably just a few doors down, in cottages that preceded Arkley Terrace).

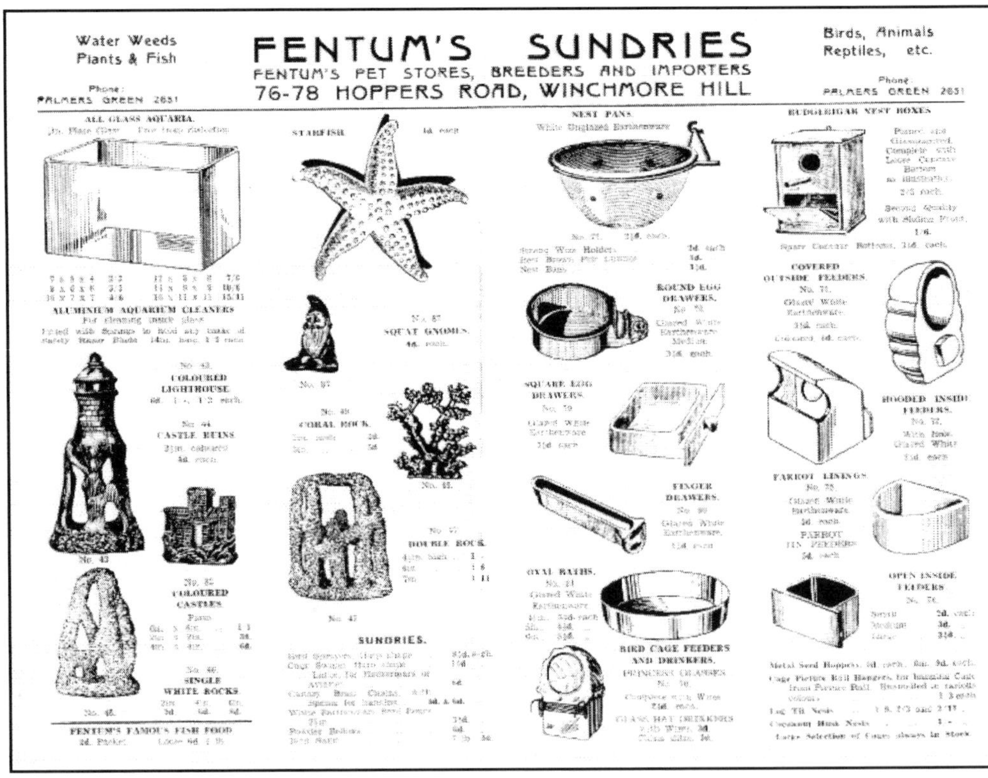

Plate 74. Advertisement for Fentum's shop in Hoppers Road.
This is a leaflet that Dorothy Collins gave me for publication which shows the Fentum stores had a surprisingly wide range of goods for a 'tobacconist'.

Plate 75. Henry 'Tiddles' Hemington and family.
Mrs. Gwen Webb's great uncle Alfred Walter 'Spurgeon' Hemington (1868 – 1937) was the driver of Aldridge's horse and cart at Plate 1 of Winchmore Hill Lives (1991). His brother William 'Rat' Hemington (1857 – 1945) was at Plate 16 of the 2004 follow up book. Mrs. Webb also supplied me with a picture of their brother – her grandfather - Henry 'Tiddles' Hemington (1859 – 1944) for publication. She told me that he is in the back row furthest to your left. His wife Eliza is holding baby Reginald (b. 1921) and their son Henry Charles is the man to the viewer's furthest right. Mabel, his wife, is the lady directly in front of 'Tiddles'.

Plate 76. Three Kings.
I bought this unused and undated postcard at a collectors' fair and, surprisingly, it is from 'Republica Oriental Del Uruguay'. Past contributors like Arthur and Lucy Pettifer would have had their childhood under King Edward VII. George V succeeded him in 1910 and the Prince of Wales, as he was for some while, was Edward VIII for a short time in 1936.

Plate 77. Herbert Henry Asquith (1852 – 1928).
When some of the contributors to my 'oral history' books were young H.H. Asquith was Primer Minister. From 1908 to 1915 he was leader of a Liberal administration, and then for a year he led a wartime coalition.

Plate 78. The Woodman, Bourne Hill
My thanks to Mr. Waring for giving this undated postcard picture for publication. In my **Winchmore Hill Village 1780 – 1830** *I suggest that The Woodman was not on the 1801- 2 Edmonton Enclosure Map. If that is correct then the building originated in the 19th century, probably for residential purposes. The premises became The Woodman in 1868, when retired police sergeant Henry Wale converted them from their former function. Henry Reed became the landlord in 1893, and remained as such until his death in 1924, whence his wife Caroline took over until her own demise in 1948, aged 96!*

Plate 79. Week's Fishmongers on Wades Hill before 1914.
This is another picture that Pauline Holstius kindly let me copy with a view to publication. It accompanied her original write up of Arthur Pettifer's life in Oakleaves 1 of 1987, and her caption enables me to tell you that Frank Weeks, in the white apron, smoked his own haddocks in oak sawdust. To his right is the cashier Miss Grace Moorhead, and to his left Mr. Tancock, whose family were the subject of Margaret Christie's account in More Winchmore Hill Lives of 2004. Tancock's florist shop is to the viewer's extreme left, the premises now being entirely residential. The fishmonger is now the Winchmore Tandoori Restaurant.

Plate 80. Winchmore Hill Road.
My thanks to Mr. Waring for giving this undated postcard picture for publication. At P110 of A History of Winchmore Hill I recorded that the Kelly's Directory for 1902-3 marks a change in various local road names. What had long been called Chase Side became Winchmore Hill Road, whilst what had been known as Winchmore Hill Road was re-titled Church Hill. This winding road doesn't look anything like Church Hill, so I presume it is a snap of the currently named Winchmore Hill Road. Such little traffic suggests that it is from Edwardian times.

Plate 81. Local railway cutting in Edwardian times.
This postcard is franked 9th September 1904. The line through Winchmore Hill was opened in 1871, and this was still very much in the age of steam.

Plate 82. The fountain on The Green in Edwardian times.
The old pump, which Mrs. Todd of Uplands funded, replaced the village well in 1850, and can be seen on the viewer's left hand side. The fence to Dr. Vivian's Roseville is on the opposite side of the photograph. I have two versions of this photograph. One is an old postcard franked 23rd July 1904, and the other, which I have used, was kindly supplied, with permission to publish, by Gordon Farrant of Putt's Estate Agents in Grange Park

Plate 83. Compton Road before the summer of 1913.
This is from a postcard without a franking, but it would be from before the summer of 1913 since the local Recorder of 5th June 1913 announced that Compton Road, amongst many others, was soon to be tar painted in order to abolish 'the dust terror' of unmade roads. There were only three houses shown in Compton Road in the 1899 – 1900 Kelly's Directory, thus narrowing the possible time range for this photograph.

Plate 84. A tram near The Green Dragon

An electric tramway from Finsbury Park to Wood Green was opened in 1904, being extended to The Green Dragon in August 1907, and Enfield in mid 1909. 'Topical Talk' in The Recorder for Palmers Green, Winchmore Hill and Southgate of November 1907 exclaimed, 'In this district all was peace and quietness after ten o' clock. The shops in Winchmore Hill are shut long before then, but for two hours and more afterwards these noisy, clattering cars race up and down, carrying driver and conductor, doing nothing but using up electrical energy, wearing out the wheels and rails, and, worse than all, keeping people awake'. This photograph was kindly supplied for publication by the Everett sisters.

Plate 85. Church Hill in Edwardian times.
This is from a postcard franked 24th July 1912. The old clapperboard cottages at the bottom of Church Hill are still there, but the pedestrians don't seem to be as concerned about walking in the road as we would be today.

Plate 86. Rural Fords Grove.
My thanks to The Gazette for letting me publish this snap from its archives. Only four residents are shown in Fords Grove in the 1899 – 1900 Kelly's Directory. The Enfield Gazette of 31st October 1924 reported that, 'More than half the southern side of Fords Grove has been recently covered with houses; the road is being widened and a footway constructed.'

Plate 87. Olde Bourne Hill.
My thanks to Mr. Waring for giving this undated postcard picture for publication. The local Recorder of 24th November 1910 noted that Bourne Hill (however it was then defined) was going to be straightened, tarred and have pavements laid down. The article said that, 'Those trees are coming down, and even the hawthorns will be out of place in a brand – new Bourne Hill'.

Plate 88. Pickering's Cottage in Farm Road.
Alan Dumayne moved, aged four, in 1933, to what had been the site of Pickering's Cottage at 83, Farm Road. This photograph, was given to me, with permission to publish, by the Everett Sisters, who featured in More Winchmore Hill Lives. They called it Hyams Cottage, and that is what it is listed as in the 1891 Census. Plate 90 portrays a member of the Pickering clan.

Plate 89. Ridge Road during the Great War. Ridge Road is on the fringes of our area. This picture is taken from an old postcard that is franked 1916, revealing how rural it all was. Colne Road was built over these fields, the first two houses being listed in the 1909-10 Kelly's Directory, a half century before Cliff Richard went to live there.

Plate 90. Mrs. 'Moss' Dudley (nee Pickering) during the Great War.

This photograph was kindly given to me, with permission to publish, by the Everett Sisters, who featured in More Winchmore Hill Lives. They gave it to me at the same time as the one of Pickerings', or Hyams, Cottage, and told me it was of Mrs.'Moss' Dudley, nee Pickering, as a Postwoman in the Great War (1914 – 18). The 1891 Census shows Hyams Cottage as occupied by Carpenter Joshua Pickering, 48, his wife Hannah, 48, and their eight children. These were Constance (21), Ernest (19), Sidney (19), Percival (14), Rosetta (12), Olive (9), Dora (6), and Mabel (3). Presumably this snap captures one of the daughters. Could Mrs. Dudley have been the post lady delivering to the Holstius household when Pauline was born in 1916!?

Plate 91. Station Road in 1914.
Note the old version of The Queen's Head. The new version of the Inn was built behind this older version in the mid 1930s, which allowed the road to be widened. The photograph is by kind courtesy of The Gazette.

LIEUT. WILLIAM LEEFE ROBINSON, V.C.,
Worcester Regiment and R.F.C.,
Who brought down the Zeppelin at Cuffley, near Enfield.

Plate 92.

Plate 93.

Plate 92. Lieut. William Leefe Robinson VC who brought down the Zeppelin at Cuffley on 3rd Sept. 1916. Various contributors to my 1991Winchmore Hill Lives mention this incident, even though it happened a few miles north of the village. For example, Harry Finch, born in the village in 1907, says,'One of my most vivid memories as a child was seeing the Zeppelin shot down near Cuffley in early September 1916. The craft seemed to pass over the Winchmore Hill skies before being picked out by searchlights. I saw a plane fly over the Zeppelin as it was travelling north and the next thing I knew the latter was coming down in flames. The following day my brother and I travelled to Cuffley and brought back some fragments of the airship but I don't know what has happened to them. A friend of mine remembers seeing the incident all the way from Bethnal Green, which shows you how bright the flames were! I learned later that the pilot of the plane that brought the Zeppelin down was Lt. W. Leefe Robinson. He was awarded the V.C. for the "kill". I also recall seeing another Zeppelin being shot down over Potters Bar by Captain Brown.'

William 'Billy' Leefe Robinson was featured in a supplement entitled Fifty Great heroes produced by The Sunday Telegraph *on 16th January 2011. It tells us that 'Billy' was born on his father's coffee estate in India, joining the Royal Flying Corps from the Worcestershire Regiment in 1915. It explained that at 1.10 a.m, having been in the sky for two hours already, he and an observer caught sight of a Zeppelin in two searchlight beams over Woolwich. It transpired that it was one of sixteen sent over in a raid. He chased after it but lost it in the clouds, however searchlights at Finsbury picked the Zeppelin up again. Despite being short of fuel, Robinson pursued it in his BE2c 2963 aircraft. The Zeppelin dropped its payload, after which Robinson released two drums of ammunition into the airship, to no effect. He then attacked the ship from its rear, releasing his last drum of ammunition into the ship's twin rudders, which seemed to do the trick, and its gas burst into flames. "Thousands of Londoners looked up and cheered as the airship plunged from the sky."*

Upon landing at Sutton Farm airfield in Essex, Robinson was lifted shoulder high to the edge of the airfield. His award of the Victoria Cross was announced just two days later, and he received over £4,000 from well wishers. Robinson was promoted to captain, but his plane was shot down over France early in 1917, and he was taken prisoner of war. Because of his achievement he was treated particularly badly, and upon his release at the end of the war his health was poor. He died in December 1918 aged just 23.

In the Local Studies Unit are articles dated 10th June 1921 from an unspecified newspaper, one of which starts, 'The following is the full speech delivered by the Rt. Hon. F.E. Guest, Secretary of State for Air, in unveiling the Cuffley memorial to Captain Leefe Robinson, V.C., yesterday;-

.... This young officer joined the Army at the age of nineteen and went to France as an observer. After a few months he was wounded and came home for treatment, but in eleven weeks he was back again at the front, not only cured of his wound, but with a pilot's certificate, a record I think I may say, which shows the quality and calibre of the boy. On September 3rd, 1916 ..... at three o'clock, when the guns were heard and the drone of the engines which brought terror to so many defenceless homes was heard in the sky. Shortly afterwards the searchlights' rays showed you the advance of that serpent of the air, coming along apparently undisturbed by shells, to drop its venom, its bombs, carrying death and destruction to all our humble homes. This boy received the orders to get up in the air and fight it. Those of you who are acquainted with the early difficulties of night flying will appreciate that that in itself was a very considerable act of daring, but when you add to that the intense difficulty of locating the enemy, you will perceive what a fine service he rendered to his country on that night. Suddenly flame was seen to come from the Zeppelin. Almost immediately it spread to a blaze, and lazily dropped from the sky in a molten ball of flame ....'

An allied article tells us that the 17' high memorial, built of silver-grey Cornish granite, which Mr. Guest was unveiling, was funded by readers of The Daily Express, being just off the Great North Road near Cuffley Station.

Plate 93. A postcard picture of the Zeppelin brought down at Potters Bar, 1st October 1916. This is presumably the other incident mentioned by Mr. Finch in Winchmore Hill Lives of 1991. The Robinson 'kill' must have looked similar. For example, Evelyn Spratley, born in our village in 1904, says in that same book, 'A vivid memory of my childhood was the night during the Great War that a Zeppelin was shot down over Cuffley. I recall that the light from the flames would have been sufficient to allow me to read a book without recourse to any other form of illumination.'

Plate 94. Grovelands Hospital, Christmas 1923, when some contributors were young.

Plate 95. Station Road after 1917.
Unfortunately I am unable to date this photograph, kindly supplied for publication by Sheila Dumayne. Notes in the Hicks archive tell us that The London and Provincial Bank in Station Road became Barclays (as it still is) in 1918. That bank's name seems to be visible, so it is presumably post 1917. The shop which for many years was run by James Waters is on the right. Some of this book's contributors will have remembered Station Road like this.

Plate 96. The Broadway in the 1920s.
When Harry Skinner was young he lived within a stone's throw of The Broadway, and he would recognise it as portrayed on this postcard, which I have seen stamped with a 1925 postmark.

Plate 97. The Broadway in the 1930s.
This is a similar postcard view of The Broadway, but this time the postmark is 6th May 1934.

Plate 98. Notice of opening of Barclays Bank in Green Lanes on 9th July 1928
Mr. A.P. Treharne also managed the Station Road branch. Reproduced thanks to the LB Enfield Library Service.

Plate 99. A later view of a tram near The Green Dragon.
This photograph was kindly supplied, with permission to publish, by Harold Pike & Co. The earlier photograph (at Plate 84) has only horse drawn traffic around the tram, whereas this one has motor vehicles, which I am unable to date. In 1938 all tram routes in Edmonton and Enfield were converted to trolleybus operation (except the Southbury Road route).

BOROUGH OF SOUTHGATE

EMERGENCY POWERS (DEFENCE) ACTS, 1939 AND 1940

REQUISITION OF UNNECESSARY RAILINGS

UNDER direction by the Minister of Supply all unnecessary iron or steel railings, posts, chains, bollards, gates, stiles, etc., in the Borough of Southgate will shortly be removed and collected for use in the national war effort in iron and steel works and foundries.

Notice is hereby given that on or before the 24th November, 1941, the work of removal will commence with the railings, etc., in the following streets and places:

ALDERS, THE
ARLOW ROAD
ARUNDEL GARDENS
ASH GROVE
AVONDALE ROAD
BARROW CLOSE
BARROWELL GREEN
BEAULIEU GARDENS
BEECHDALE
BERRY CLOSE
BIRCHES, THE
BOURNE HILL (PART OF)
BRACKENDALE
BRANSCOMBE GARDENS
BROADFIELDS AVENUE
BROAD WALK
BUSH HILL GOLF COURSE (THAT PART WITHIN THE BOROUGH OF SOUTHGATE)
CARPENTER GARDENS
CEDARS ROAD
CHINE, THE
CHURCH HILL
COLLEGE ROAD
COMPTON ROAD
COOMBE CORNER
CRESTBROOK AVENUE
DOWNES COURT
DRAYTON GARDENS
EATON PARK ROAD
ELMSCOTT GARDENS
EVERSLEY CRESCENT
EVERSLEY PARK ROAD
FARM ROAD
FERNLEIGH ROAD
FIRS LANE
GRANGE PARK AVENUE
GREEN DRAGON LANE
GREEN END
GREEN LANES (PART OF)
GREEN MOOR LINK
GREENWOOD GARDENS
HADLEY WAY
HASLEMERE ROAD
HEDGE LANE (PART OF)
HIGHFIELD ROAD
HILLCREST
HILLFIELD PARK
HOODCOTE GARDENS
HOPPERS ROAD
HOUNDSDEN ROAD
HURST ROAD
LARCHES, THE
LAUREL DRIVE
LYTTON AVENUE
MEADOWCROFT ROAD
MYDDLETON GARDENS
OAKLANDS
OAKWOOD CRESCENT
OLD PARK RIDINGS
ORPINGTON ROAD
PARK DRIVE
QUEENS AVENUE
RADCLIFFE ROAD
RINGWOOD WAY
RIVER AVENUE
ROSENEATH AVENUE
ROWANS, THE
SEAFORTH GARDENS
SHERBROOK GARDENS
SHRUBBERY GARDENS
SPINNEY, THE
STATION ROAD, N.21
STONARD ROAD
STONEHALL ROAD
VICARS MOOR LANE
WADES GROVE
WADES HILL
WOODCROFT
WOODLAND WAY
YEW TREE CLOSE

It is hoped that owners will be prepared to make a free gift of their railings, etc., to the nation, but property owners and others whose interests are affected by the removal and who desire to claim compensation may obtain the appropriate form from: The Borough Engineer and Surveyor, Mr. J. T. W. Peat, F.R.I.B.A., Southgate Town Hall, Green Lanes, N.13.

Under the provisions of the Compensation (Defence) Act, 1939, no claim for compensation ordinarily can be entertained unless notice of claim has been given to the appropriate authority within a period of six months from the date of removal of the railings, etc.

Under the provisions of Regulation 50, paragraph (3A) of the Emergency Powers (Defence) General Regulations no person shall be liable, by virtue of any obligation imposed by any lease or other instrument affecting the land or by or under any enactment or otherwise to replace or provide a substitute for the thing severed, or to pay any sum by way of damages or penalty or to suffer any forfeiture in consequence of a failure to perform any such obligation, and any person who has guaranteed the performance of any such obligation shall be correspondingly relieved of his liability under the guarantee.

GORDON H. TAYLOR,
Town Clerk

Southgate Town Hall,
Green Lanes, N.13.
10th November, 1941.

Plate 100. 1941 Notice to Remove Railings for the War Effort..
My thanks to the LB Enfield Library Service for this item from its archives. Various contributors mention the Second World War, and this notice perhaps gives us a feel for the era.

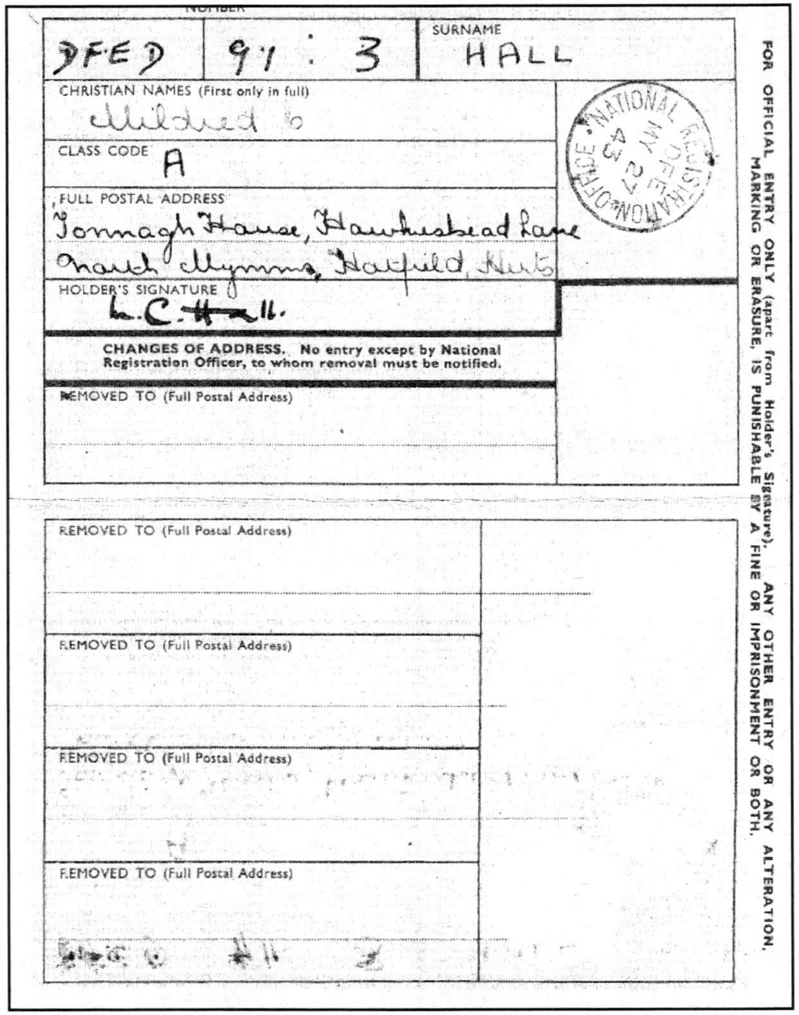

NUMBER		SURNAME
DFED	97 : 3	HALL

CHRISTIAN NAMES (First only in full) Mildred

CLASS CODE A

FULL POSTAL ADDRESS Tonnagh House, Hawkshead Lane North Mymms, Hatfield, Herts

HOLDER'S SIGNATURE L. C. Hall.

NATIONAL REGISTRATION OFFICE MY 27 43

CHANGES OF ADDRESS. No entry except by National Registration Officer, to whom removal must be notified.

REMOVED TO (Full Postal Address)

REMOVED TO (Full Postal Address)

REMOVED TO (Full Postal Address)

REMOVED TO (Full Postal Address)

REMOVED TO (Full Postal Address)

FOR OFFICIAL ENTRY ONLY (apart from Holder's Signature). ANY OTHER ENTRY OR ANY ALTERATION, MARKING OR ERASURE, IS PUNISHABLE BY A FINE OR IMPRISONMENT OR BOTH.

Plate 101. A Wartime ID Card

With the Pettengell and Traigis accounts being so linked to the war I thought it an idea to print a wartime ID card. Unfortunately I couldn't find one from this area, so I'm publishing this page from nearby Hertfordshire.

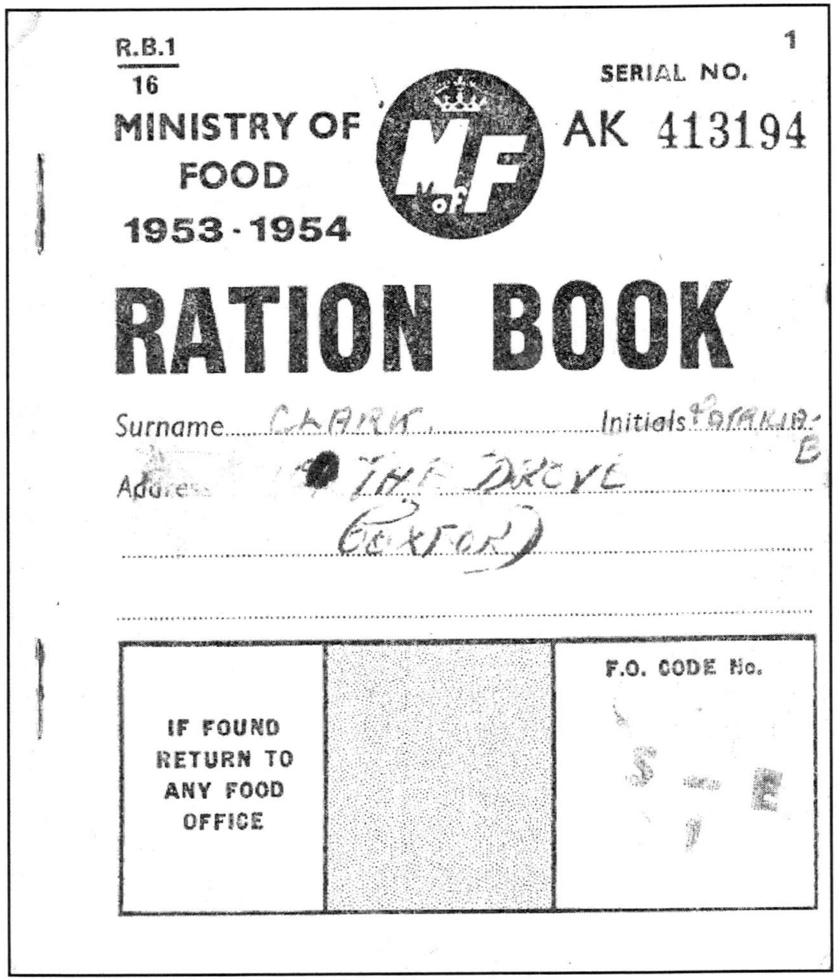

R.B.1
16

1

MINISTRY OF FOOD
1953-1954

SERIAL NO.
AK 413194

RATION BOOK

Surname CLARK Initials
Address THE DROVE OXFORD

IF FOUND RETURN TO ANY FOOD OFFICE

F.O. CODE No.

Plate 102. Cover to a 1953-4 Ration Book.

I don't have a ration book, either from my mother, or from Winchmore Hill contributors, so I bought this one from Oxford to demonstrate how rationing persisted long after the War finished. Youngsters like Colin Wackett and Bob Hill were brought up in an austere environment, where obesity was therefore not a problem.

Plate 103. Looking south over the Upper Green.
This slightly hazy photograph was kindly supplied for publication by the late Ewan Lewis. On the left is Roseville mansion, which was demolished in the late 1950s, and to your right is the terrace of Devonshire Place. The corner shop was, of course, for many years run by the Chalkley family.

Plate 104. Winchmore Hill Methodist Wedding of the Year for 1965. I was going through the Hicks Archives at Enfield's Local Studies Unit, in Thomas Hardy House, when I was pleasantly surprised to come across this photograph boldly labelled as the Winchmore Hill Methodist Church Wedding for 1965. Taken on 20th February 1965, it shows Miss Ann Shopland marrying John Lyon at the Green Lanes Church. I became friendly with John through attending UK Independence Party (UKIP) meetings, where I also became acquainted with Eddie Bolton, the subject of an account in this book. John was a sincere, decent sort of man but, unfortunately, he passed away in the Spring of 2009. Ann (as of April 2011) is still active within UKIP.

Part 2

The second part of this book is a collection of accounts of some (only) of the illustrious names associated with Winchmore Hill, taken from pre existing sources, and assembled here 'under one cover' for the first time.

DAVID BARCLAY OF WALTHAMSTOW AND YOUNGSBURY

AFTER ZOFFANY

Although the Barclays are not known to have lived in the village, they had country homes in nearby Bush Hill, and many of the banking dynasty are buried in the Quaker's Burial Ground in Church Hill. The back cover of my 'A History of Winchmore Hill' boasts a picture of the gravestone of this Barclay, who was known as David of Walthamstow and Youngsbury (1729 - 1809). He was David of Cheapside's second son by his second wife, Priscilla Freame.

Harold Abrahams

I moved from Radcliffe Road to Fernleigh Road in the scorching summer of 1976, and I went with my wife and mother to see *Chariots of Fire* in Wood Green in 1981. It was only many years later that Graham Dalling told me that Harold had been living at Orpington Road in the 1970s. I think it is proper that a man whose early life was a key part of such a huge world wide 'blockbuster' should appear in a book of this ilk. Surprisingly, though, given that great fame, I have not been able to track down a book on Abrahams, and for this summary I have relied on the local *Weekly Herald* of 20th January 1978, *The Enfield Gazette* of 21st May 1981, and an Oxford University Press website oxforddnb.com. article by Norris McWhirter (featured later in this book).

Harold Maurice Abrahams was born at 30, Rutland Road, Bedford on 15th December 1899, the son of Isaac and Esther, being the youngest of four sons and two daughters. At that time the family surname was Abrahams, but his father (1850 – 1921) was originally Isaac Klonimus, who escaped from Lithuania as a persecuted Jew, changing his surname to Abrahams by 1880 in recognition of his own father, Abraham Klonimus (b. 1810). Despite his poor English, Isaac set up the Bedfordshire Loan Company in 1885, becoming a naturalised citizen in 1902. Isaac's three other sons also proved to be exceptional, achieving high positions – consultant physician, chief justice of Tanganyika and Ceylon, and coroner for Huntingdonshire.

Harold's imagination became fired in the summer of 1908 when he watched his brother Solly compete in the fourth Olympic Games at the White City. He was sent to Bedford School, then briefly to St. Paul's, and then to Repton, where he won the public schools' 100 yards and long jump championships in 1918. He served briefly in the Army as a second lieutenant in 1919, before reading law at Gonville and Caius College, Cambridge. He stood a muscular 6' ½" tall, and swept all before him on the athletics field, being selected for the sixth Olympic Games in Antwerp. He won a unique eight victories in the Oxford versus Cambridge 100 yards, 440 yards, and long jump.

Abrahams won the 1924 British Amateur Athletic Association (AAA) 100 yards title in 9.9 seconds, and smashed the British long jump record with a leap of 24ft. 2 ½ ins., which remained unbeaten for 32 years. He prepared thoroughly for that year's Olympics, held at the stade de Colombes in Paris, with his French Arab coach Sam Mussabini developing the now common practice of dropping the torso onto the finishing tape.

Harold's defining moment arrived when he became the first European to win the 100 metres at an Olympics. His winning time was officially 10.6 seconds, and thus equalled the Olympic record, but the stopwatch apparently recorded 10.52 seconds, which was rounded up to 10.6, whereas in later years it would have been rounded down to 10.5 seconds. There were no flag waving victory ceremonies at the 1924 Olympics, and his Gold Medal – which was later stolen – was sent to him by post! At the Games he was one of the British team that won a Silver medal in a relay.

Unfortunately, the following year Harold broke a leg, complicated by severely torn muscles, whilst long jumping, and was forced to retire from active athletics at the age of only 25. However, he still remained involved with athletics, with roles in administration and journalism. In fact his son is quoted as saying that he only had his accident because he was showing off to journalists! He wrote for the *Sunday Times* from 1925 until 1967, and broadcast with the BBC from 1925 until 1974, possessing a wide vocabulary and a clear voice.

As an administrator Abrahams rewrote the AAA rules of competition, which formed the basis of a revision at international level. He was Honorary Treasurer (1948 – 1968) and Chairman (1948 – 1975) of the British Amateur Athletic Board and in November 1976 was elected President of the AAA. He was an unrivalled compiler of athletics statistics, and was founder of both the British and world associations in this field.

Apart from all this Harold also somehow found time to have other successful careers. He was called to the bar at the Inner Temple in 1924, where he practised as a barrister until 1940. He served from 1939 to 1944 with the Ministry of Economic Warfare, and then with the new Ministry of Town and Country Planning until 1963. He was also Secretary of the National Parks Commission from 1950 until 1963. Perhaps it is no surprise to learn that he was appointed a CBE in 1957.

Film producer David Puttnam attended Minchenden School in Southgate, where he had already succumbed to an obsession with the cinema. In the late 1970s and early 1980s the British film industry was going through a low point, owing much, as far as I recall, to the money of George Harrison. Things were so bad that David couldn't raise British money for his brainchild that became *Chariots of Fire.* Half the £2 ½ million that the film cost came from an Egyptian shipping magnate, and the other half from an American source.

Chariots of Fire told the story of Harold and Eric Liddell, two British sprinters who won gold at the 1924 Olympics. The film portrays undergraduate Abrahams overcoming prejudice shown to him by Cambridge dons, because of his Jewish background and his 'professional' attitude to the sport in an age of the 'gifted amateur'. However, there is some suspicion that this man, who did so well at Cambridge, was not subjected to the level of anti Semitism implied in the film. Liddell won the 400 metres, and there is a religious aspect to his story too, because he refused to race on Sunday as it is the Christian Sabbath.

Harold never actually practised the Jewish religion, and became a Christian in 1935. He was a very keen Gilbert and Sullivan fan, and through this interest met his Anglican wife Sybil Marjorie Evers, who was a D'Oyly Carte singer and producer of light opera. They married in 1936, but unfortunately she died suddenly in 1963. His son Alan, and daughter Susan, were both adopted.

Puttnam had met Abrahams once, and with the film in mind, arranged to meet him again in January 1978, but before then, tragically, Harold died of a stroke in Chase Farm Hospital, at the age of 78. He was then living in Orpington Road with his son Alan, and family, having moved in with them in about 1968. Alan, who worked as a security consultant, was thrilled by *Chariots of Fire*, and was a little surprised to see such driving ambition in his father as a young man. Alan said,

'In the film he's a non establishment, slightly anti authority figure, an outsider. But when I knew him he had become very much a part of the athletics establishment – one of the grand old men of the sport, sitting on all kinds of international committees, a member of all the right clubs and a man held in very high regard.'

Puttnam is reported to have said, 'Abrahams was an extraordinary and wonderful man; very good and very forceful although, as any of the athletes of the 50s and 60s will tell you, he did become rather reactionary in his later years.' At the time of his quote, in May 1981, he was living near the Royal Albert Hall in Kensington and spending much of his time in America, but he still visited his parents in Eversley Park Road, Winchmore Hill.

In 2007 English Heritage unveiled a Blue Plaque to Harold at Hodford Lodge, 2, Hodford Road, Golders Green, which was his London home at the time he won his Gold Medal.

The Barclays

As you enter the Burial Ground of The Friends Meeting House on Church Hill there are three tombstones near the pavement (see Plate 49). These are inscribed, 'David Barclay of Cheapside. Son of Apologist. Born 1682 Died 1769', 'John Barclay (Son of D. Barclay) Born 1728 Died 1787' and 'David Barclay Son of D. Barclay. Born 1729 Died 1809'. The Barclay family lived in the vicinity of today's Quakers Walk, Bush Hill, and were early players in the modern day Barclays Bank, with its branches in every part of Britain - and beyond - but their worship and burial at the heart of Winchmore Hill earns them a firm place in this book.

In researching this famous family with local connections I was lucky to come across, *A History of the Barclay Family with Pedigrees from 1067 to 1933 Part 3. The Barclays in Scotland and England from 1610 to 1933* by Lieut. – Colonel Hubert F. Barclay and Alice Wilson-Fox, published by The St. Catherine Press, Stamford Street in 1934. That forms a prime source for the following. Other useful sources were, *History of Barclays Bank Ltd.* by P.W. Matthews of 1926, *A History of Quakerism at Winchmore Hill* by A. David Olver, and minutes of Friends Meetings, whilst the Barclays bank archivist wrote to me on the subject in 1987. But before we concentrate on the Barclays, let's look at -

The Goulds and Freames

In 1888 two banks amalgamated into one. Those two were Barclay, Bevan, Tritton & Company, of 54, Lombard Street, and Ransom, Bouverie & Company of 1, Pall Mall East. Barclays Bank & Co. Ltd. was formed on 1st July 1896 from the amalgamation of this new bank with many others.

It is obviously therefore not possible to identify one single person or company as the originator of the massive public company we know today, but an early leading light who might lay claim to be a key player would be goldsmith John Freame (1665 – 1745). Professor Olver tells us that he was the banker for the London (Quaker) Lead Company. By 1698 he was a partner in the goldsmiths firm of Freame and Gould, based at *The Three Anchors* in Lombard Street. It is known to have still been there in 1702, and in 1728 John Freame bought the freehold to the premises in Lombard Street known as *The Black Spread Eagle*, remembered today in the Bank's logo.

On 19th August 1697 John Freame married Priscilla Gould, who was the daughter of his partner, the prominent Friend Thomas Gould, at Devonshire House, Bishopsgate. Presumably Thomas was part of the Gould family that administered Edmonton Manor from Fords Grove Mansion in the mid 18th century. In 1733 their daughter Sarah, known as Sally, married James Barclay, son of David Barclay of Cheapside. The notice in the *Gentleman's Magazine* described her as, 'daughter of Mr. John Freame, Banker & Deputy Governor of the Lead Corporation'. From at least 1714

John had a country house at Bush Hill.

John Freame died on 28th September 1745, but he had anyway been succeeded in the business by his son Joseph, who in 1736 took his brother in law James Barclay into partnership in place of Thomas Gould. Joseph Freame had a son named John, who died in 1766, and a daughter named Priscilla, who married David Barclay of Cheapside, after the latter's first wife had died. The Freame family had a somewhat complicated relationship with the Barclays, and I have tried to summarise it at Figure 3. But what of the Barclays themselves? The following is their history, summarised at Figure 4.

Figure 3. The Freames & Goulds

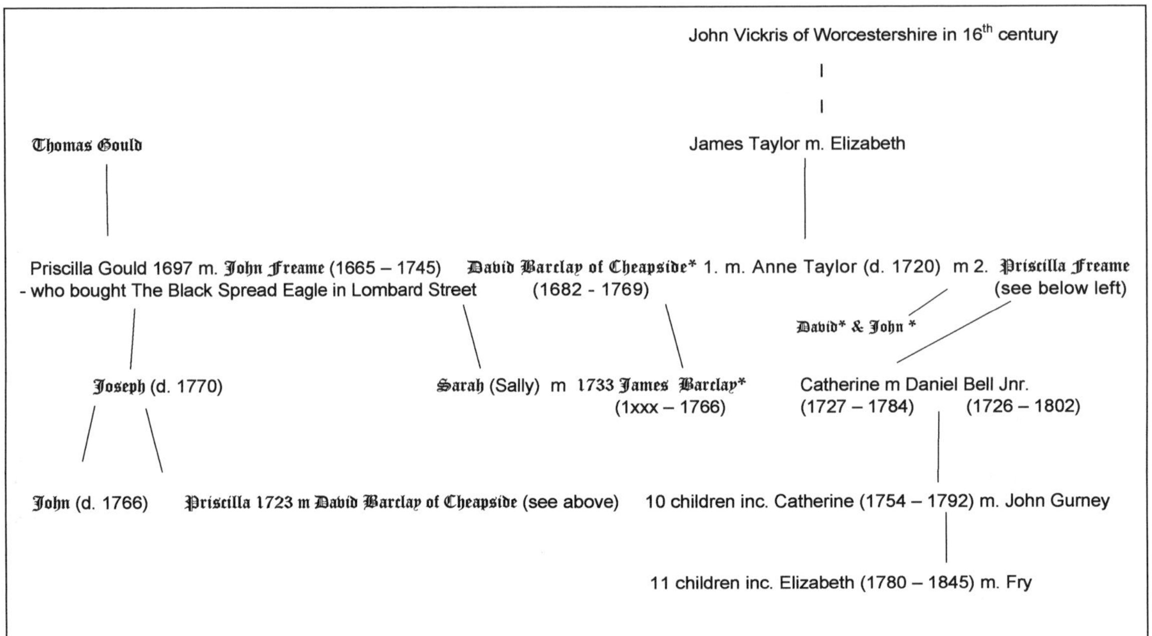

Notes: For both this family tree and the one for the Barclay family I have shown those individuals who went into the Barclays banking business in Old English typeface. Those who are known to be buried in the Quaker grounds of Church Hill are marked by an asterisk.

Colonel David Barclay (1610 - 1686)

Colonel David Barclay, third son of David Barclay, was born in 1610 at Kirktounhill, on the estate of Mathers in Scotland, which had been in the family's possession since 1351. On 2nd July 1644 he took part in the Civil War battle of Marston Moor, where Cromwell and his Ironsides won a decisive victory over the Royalist forces thanks in large part to a magnificent charge of the Scots horsemen, under David Leslie, with whom rode David Barclay and his troops. They were said to have scattered Prince Rupert's Cavaliers, 'like a little dust'. Thus the whole of the north of England fell into the hands of 'the godly party.' Barclay and Wilson-Fox say that David's, 'arresting personality set him above ordinary men, as did his great height and dignity of manner'.

On Christmas Day 1647 the Colonel married Katherine Gordon, daughter of Sir Robert Gordon, of Gordonstoun (who was a second cousin of King James VI), and his wife Lady Jean Gordon. Katherine was known as 'The White Rose of Gordonstoun', and was apparently greatly loved and respected. It has puzzled historians as to how Colonel Barclay, who had left Scotland as a lad and joined the Swedish Army as a soldier of fortune on poor pay, had returned home in a position to purchase the Urie Estate, build its mansion, and settle a large sum on his wife.

When the Colonel gave up the governorship of Strathbogie Castle, he returned to live at his wife's home, Gordonstoun, with her parents, and it is there that his son Robert was born on December 23rd 1648, and spent his childhood. David and Katherine also had two other sons – John and David – as well as two daughters, Lucy and Jean, but it is Robert who made a strong mark on the world, through his Quaker beliefs. It was in 1648 that George Fox began his sermons that started the sect, and their turning point seems to have been in 1652, after Fox had preached on the top of Pendle Hill in Lancashire. He wrote in his Journal, 'Justice Bennett of Derby was the first to call us Quakers, because I bade him quake and tremble at the Word of the Lord.'

Friends believe that there is something of God in all of us. They start their meetings in silence and are not led by an appointed person, but allow anyone present to do this. Quakers accept the life and teachings of Jesus, and that we should love one another. War is therefore frowned upon, and women viewed as the equal of men. Two hundred years ago the movement was a prime mover in the abolition of the slave trade. More details are available from local Quakers, or Friends House, Euston Road, London, NW1 2BJ.

Hard though it is to understand today, this teaching brought the pioneer George Fox into direct conflict with all the religious bodies in England and Scotland, who resented this claim to direct inspiration 'from within' without input from the clergy, and a furious opposition arose to the new doctrines. Thousands of enthusiastic people crowded to the meetings, and the Establishment became seriously alarmed.

In 1646 and 1648 ordinances had been passed by Parliament for the prevention of "Blasphemies and Heresies," which covered several of the Quaker doctrines, notably their denial of the sacraments and an ordained priesthood. Their refusal to pay tithes, used to support the Church of England, raised a legal point, which was placed in the hands of justices of the peace. In 1654 Cromwell declared in a speech in the House of Commons that liberty of conscience was a natural right, and the Quakers breathed more freely.

David Barclay thought deeply about religion, and considered Fox's teachings, but to begin with he did not embrace the then new philosophy. His first step, in 1653, was to make a frank admission that he was not convinced of the soundness of the doctrine of the Kirk of Scotland. In 1654 Oliver Cromwell was appointed Lord Protector of the Commonwealth of England,Wales, Scotland and Ireland. An Ordinance of April 12th fixed Scotland's representation in the United Parliament at thirty members, the first name on the list being Colonel David Barclay of Ury, representing Forfar and Kincardineshire. We learn from one of his grandsons that, "In the end he got the Government then in power to restore all the Nobility and Gentrey to their fortunes, which made him so popular in the Countrey that he was again in the year 1656 elected Member of Parliament for the two Shires ...... Although Cromwell had been so complaisant in the matter of the forfeited estates, David Barclay retained his independence of opinion, and was one of the four members who 'vigorously' opposed and voted against Cromwell's being made King."

In 1657 Parliament advised Cromwell to accept the title King, but he declined the advice and remained as the Lord Protector. Barclay's name does not appear in the House of Commons list for 1658, so it seems he gave up his Parliamentary work now that his objective had been achieved. He returned home to his family.

Shortly after the Restoration of 1660 David Barclay disentangled himself from all public affairs, travelling between his family homes in Edinburgh and Gordonstoun, until March 1663, when his dear wife, Katherine, died, aged only 43 years. Her last wish had been to bring home her eldest son, Robert, from Paris, where he was staying with his uncle, the Rector of the Scots Theological College there. David Barclay therefore took the long journey to Paris, and brought him home.

In 1665 Colonel David suffered a shock when he was, 'att the instigation of malicious persons, committed to the Castle of Edinburgh, by order of the Government.' He wasn't charged with any crime in the Committal Order, and his imprisonment has never been explained, though his grandson attributed it to 'mere jealousy'. This maltreatment was the more extraordinary in that the Royalist Government was actually in debt to him for a considerable sum he had advanced out of his own pocket, to pay his regiment.

In Edinburgh Castle he had to share a cell with a Member of Parliament, one John Swinton, of Swinton, who had been a judge of the Court of Session under the Commonwealth and, though originally a Royalist, had become one of Cromwell's most trusted and influential agents in Scotland. Swinton had joined the Society of Friends and it seems he converted David Barclay to the faith, which Barclay considered most resembled the teachings of Christ. We find in the Journal of the Society of Friends that 'David Barclay of Urie, in the Kingdome of Scotland, received the truth in 1666, being the fifty sixth year of his age, about the seventh month, and abode in it'.

The Colonel had sent his son Robert to live at Urie, and even at this early period of his life, he was already deeply engaged in writing his world famous '*The Apology for the True Christian Divinity, as the same is held forth and preached by the people called in scorn Quakers'.* David was at long last granted freedom on August 23, 1670, whereupon he set to work on building his house and restoring his property.

Colonel David also built a Meeting House in the grounds close to the mansion, in spite of having been expressly forbidden by the magistrates to "keep Quaiker Meetings". Henceforth Urie became the centre of the Quakers in the north even though the Synod of Aberdeen had issued a sentence of excommunication against 'Papists, Quakers, and other scandalous persons', and Christians were enjoined not to communicate with them. In September 1686 David Barclay, 'being past the 76th year of his age, took a fever, which kept him about a fortnight and then carried him off.'

Robert 'The Apologist' (1648 - 1690)

So now we continue the story with David's son Robert Barclay, 'The Apologist', who was born on 23rd December 1648. He spent his childhood at Gordonstoun, the home of his maternal grandfather, whose wife, Lady Gordon, brought him up after his mother's death in 1663. In 1666 he strongly turned to the beliefs of the Friends. It was in 1670 that a second Conventicle Act confirmed an Act of 1664 and sought to destroy non-conformity by outlawing all such meetings, forbidding trial by jury to any accused. The Friends were not only being persecuted in England and Scotland, but all over the Continent.

William Penn became a Quaker in 1668, whereupon he established a friendship with Robert. Penn wrote many fiery pamphlets that brought him into conflict with the authorities. In 1670, whilst imprisoned in Newgate Gaol for holding open-air meetings, he launched his 'The Great Case for Liberty of Conscience' which, alongside Robert's 'Apology', did much to educate the authorities on the teachings of the Quakers.

Robert's 'Apologia' was initially written in Latin 'for the information of strangers', and published in Amsterdam, but he then translated it into English, and it was published in London in 1676. It was a remarkable work for a 27 year old, and has always been accepted as the text book of Quaker theology. Macaulay says, 'It was a lucky chance for the Quakers that they got Robert Barclay and William Penn to make sense of the unintelligible jargon of George Fox and Nayler'. Whereas 'The Apology' became the standard book of Quaker theory, Penn's pamphlet 'No Cross, No Crown' illustrated their practice, and Fox's 'Journal' described their history and origins.

In 1672 King Charles 11 issued his Declaration of Indulgence, suspending the draconian laws of religious intolerance, but such was the public outcry that the following year The Test Act was passed, barring all but followers of the Established Church from public office.

George Fox had long been considering the formation of a Colony of Friends in what is now the USA, and had discussed the matter with William Penn and Robert Barclay. Penn was particularly sympathetic to the scheme, and through his leadership 230 Friends, mostly from Yorkshire and London, set sail for the New World in the ship *Kent* in the summer of 1677. Other ships soon followed, and within 18 months there were some 800 Friends in the Colony. They obtained a tract of land from the Native Americans, in exchange for a long list of various articles, including guns, kettles, garments of all kinds, tools, mirrors, glass ornaments, and miscellaneous other goods.

The Quakers settled on the Delaware river, and built a town called Burlington, on the site of what is now Philadelphia - 'The City of Brotherly Love'. In 1681 William Penn was the driving force behind the purchase and settlement of the tract of fertile land about 300 miles by 160 miles which Charles 11 insisted was called Pennsylvania. Penn envisaged it as a democratic State based on Quaker teachings.

In 1685 James 11 came to the throne and two years later he made his Declaration of Liberty of Conscience, professing tolerance of all religions. However, Robert realised that the previously overt hostility towards Quakers was now channelled into vexatious legal prosecutions and ruinous fines for non-payment of tithes. In March 1688 we find Robert again on the road. He spent the whole summer in London, 'writing and serving his friends to the utmost of his power.' His oldest son, Robert, accompanied him, and, after being presented to the King, spent much of his time at Court.

On April 27th 1688 James 11 issued his Declaration for Liberty of Conscience for the second time, without any concessions to public opinion, which considered it 'papist'. It met with considerable opposition within the nation, and the Archbishop of Canterbury, with six bishops, boldly declared it to be illegal. James was overthrown and, in 1689, William and Mary of Orange were installed in his place. One of William's first initiatives was the passing of the Toleration Act, which gave reign to free expression of belief. The Friends' passive resistance had helped convince the nation that it was unjust for the state to try and control a person's belief. Robert died on 3rd October 1690, being buried beside his father.

David Barclay of Cheapside (1682 - 1769)

Robert's son David, later known as 'of Cheapside', was born at Urie in 1682. He was one of Robert and Christian's seven children, three of whom were sons. He left home when quite young, having received a parental gift equivalent to about £500 sterling, which was then a very tidy sum. He went to London, where he became apprenticed to James Taylor, Citizen and Glover, whose daughter Anne he married in

1709. He joined his father-in-law in business and became an opulent export merchant.

On 21st March 1987 I visited the Taylor family estate in Oxfordshire and was allowed to peruse family papers. These revealed that Elizabeth Vickris was descended from the 16th century John Vickris of Worcestershire. She married a James Taylor, and they had two children. One of these was James Junior, who died young, and the other was David Barclay's first wife Anne, who died on 3rd December 1720. David and Anne had three sons and four daughters.

David and Anne's son James married Sarah Freame in 1733, and became a partner in the London bank in 1736. He died of consumption in 1766 and was buried at Winchmore Hill. James had two sons, Joseph (died 1797), and Alexander (died 1812), both of whom remained unmarried, and one daughter, Anne, who married James Allardice of Allardice, County Kincardine.

David and Anne's son, Alexander (1711 – 1771) went to live in Philadelphia. He married twice, one of his sons being Robert of Bury Hill (1751 – 1830), who married Rachel Gurney. Robert didn't come into the bank, but instead became the co-owner of the Anchor Brewery in Southwark, later to be known as Courage brewery. Robert was father to Charles Barclay, Chief of Mathers and Urie.

Although the *Pedigrees* book I have used as my main source says that David and Anne had only two sons, the Taylor family papers indicate a third son, by the name of Robert. David and Anne's daughter, Christiana, died unmarried; daughter Patience, married John Stedman (or Thomas Weston!); daughter Jane, married James Collinson, and daughter Elizabeth married Timothy Bevan.

On August 8th 1723 David Barclay married his second wife, Priscilla, daughter of Joseph Freame, banker, of London. She was the niece of Sarah (Sally) Freame, who was the wife of his eldest son James, which complicated the relationships of the two families. (See Figure 3.) On the death of her brother John in 1766, Priscilla became sole heiress of the banking business in Lombard Street, now known as Barclays Bank. By his second wife David Barclay had six daughters, one of whom was named Catherine, who married Daniel Bell Junior of Tottenham. He also had two more sons, John and David, who both became partners in the Bank.

David of Cheapside joined the Drapers' Company as an assistant in 1729. He was fined £40 for declining to serve as Warden in 1746, and in 1756 he paid £20 to be excused serving as Master. David lived in one of the finest houses in the City, opposite the Church of St. Mary-le-Bow in Cheapside – hence his nickname. After the Great Fire of London had devastated the City in 1666, wealthy mercer Sir Edward Waldo had purchased three sites upon which he erected "a great Messuage" known by the Sign of the Boar. Owing to its situation the building commanded an excellent view of the Lord Mayor's procession, and in 1761 George 111 and his Queen were David's guests.

David Barclay of Cheapside died at his country house, Bush Hill on March 18th, 1769, and was buried in the graveyard attached to the Church Hill Quaker Meeting House. (See Plate 49.) He left Bush Hill to his second surviving son, David. It had at one time belonged to his second wife's grandfather John Freame Snr..

David of Walthamstow and Youngsbury (1729 - 1809)

David of Cheapside's second son by his second wife, Priscilla Freame, was David of Walthamstow and Youngsbury (1729 – 1809), who is captured at the start of this section. He married first Martha Hudson, and then Rachel Lloyd. For many years he was a merchant in London and became a partner in the Bank in Lombard Street in 1776. He was reputed to be one of the most influential men in the City. An interesting episode in his life was when he acted as an intermediary between Benjamin Franklin and Lord North's Ministry in negotiating for a reconciliation between Great Britain and the American Colonies in 1774-5. David purchased the Anchor Brewery in Southwark, and put his nephew Robert Barclay, son of his half brother Alexander, into the firm.

David had an estate in Jamaica where he owned many slaves, but he set them all free at considerable loss to himself. He had them instructed in trades and handicrafts before settling them in America. In later life he, like other Friends such as the Gurneys, was associated with the struggle to end the slave trade, led by William Wilberforce and his associates, Clarkson, Sharp and Buxton. It must have been gratifying, in his late 70s, to see legislation passed.

Bell's Weekly Messenger of Sunday, June 4th, 1809, contained the following notice:- "Died. On Tuesday (May 30th) at Walthamstow David Barclay Esq. in the eighty first year of his age, the last grandson of Robert Barclay of Urie, who wrote the celebrated Apology for the People called Quakers." At his death his large fortune, including his interest in the Brewery of Barclay, Perkins & Co., went to his daughter, Agatha, and her husband, Richard Gurney. David's tombstone in the Church Hill grounds was pictured on the rear cover of my 1989 *A History of Winchmore Hill.*

Katherine Barclay (1727 - 1784)

In her 1978 EHHS paper entitled *The Quakers of Tottenham 1775 – 1825* Mrs. M.A. Collie discloses that David of Cheapside's daughter Katherine, by his second wife Priscilla, married Daniel Bell Junior (1726 – 1802). They had ten children, one of whom was Catherine (1754 – 1792). She married John Gurney, and they had 11 children, one of whom was better known under her married name of Elizabeth Fry (1780 – 1845), the prison reformer portrayed on our £5 bank notes. Mrs Collie tells us that Daniel Jnr. became a coal merchant and lived at Stamford Hill with a wharf and warehouse by the River Lea, renting about 70 acres of land from the Barclay family.

John of Cambridge Heath and Lombard Street (1728 - 1787)

David of Cheapside's son John married Susannah Willett and went into the family bank. He was present when King George 111 visited his father's house in Cheapside to view the Lord Mayor's Show in 1761, when about thirty-three years of age. The King is said to have offered him a position at Court, but his Quaker father would not permit him to accept this.

At this time he appears to have been engaged in the family export business at 108 Cheapside, and after his father's death in 1769, he and his nephew Robert carried it on together for some years. This business relied heavily on exporting to America, and so declined considerably whilst the War of Independence was in progress. Following Britain's recognition of the Declaration of Independence, in 1783, it ceased to be profitable and was wound up.

The deeds of the Anchor Brewery show that John Barclay never exercised his option to become a partner in that concern, but during the last year or two of his life he devoted all his energies to the Bank in Lombard Street, though the exact date on which he became a partner in the firm is uncertain. In *The History of Barclay's Bank* the date is given as 1785, but from a 'Memorandum of Agreement' dated London, November 16th, 1781, it would appear to have been considerably earlier. At that time the business went under the name of *Barclay, Tritton and Bevan.*

John had two daughters, and three sons, named Willett, David (born in 1763), and Robert. John was buried in Winchmore Hill.

John's Descendants

Son Robert Barclay, of Clapham and Lombard Street (1758 – 1816), married Anne (the daughter of Isaac Ford of Manchester), who died in 1801. They had four sons and four daughters. Son Ford (1795 – 1859) married Esther, daughter of William Foster Reynolds of Carshalton, who died in 1889, aged 90 years. Son Abraham died unmarried in 1829. Son John of Croydon (1797 – 1838), like Ford and Esther, was buried at Winchmore Hill.

Robert's son Robert Jnr (1785 – 1853) succeeded his father in the bank. Robert married Elizabeth, daughter of Joseph Gurney, by whom he had six daughters and three sons. The sons were the unmarried Henry (1829 – 1851), Robert (1815 – 1842), who married Eliza Backhouse, and Joseph Gurney Barclay (1816 – 1898), who married twice.

The bankers in the John of Cambridge Heath and Lombard Street's lineage were John himself, his son Robert of Clapham and Lombard Street, his grandson Robert of Leyton, Higham and Lombard Street, and great grandson Joseph Gurney Barclay. Remember John's half brother James was also in the bank.

More on the Winchmore Hill Connection

We recall that on 19th August 1697 John Freame married Priscilla Gould, who was the daughter of the prominent Friend Thomas Gould. From at least 1714 John had a country house at Bush Hill. In 1733 their daughter Sarah, also known as Sally, married James Barclay, son of David Barclay of Cheapside. David's estate, at his death in 1769, included the freehold estate of Bush Hill, which he left to his second surviving son, David of Walthamstow.

In the Edmonton Enclosure land Ownership Schedule of 1801 one of the Plots John Blackburn owned, at the top of Bush Hill, was 770 'Houses, yards, gardens, & co. called Quaker's Row', the line of which is followed today by Quakers Walk. Alan Dumayne tells us that the premises were occupied by some of the Barclays, and demolished in about 1825 by that other big local landowner, Squire Mellish. We have seen that David of Walthamstow died in that locality on 30th May 1809, and was buried near his father on Church Hill. So it would seem that sometime between 1769 and 1801 David Barclay sold the freehold to the Quaker's Row house.

At Friends House in Euston Road are minutes of the local Quaker Meetings. I have copied some of these, and they bring to life the local activities of the Gould, Freame and Barclay families –

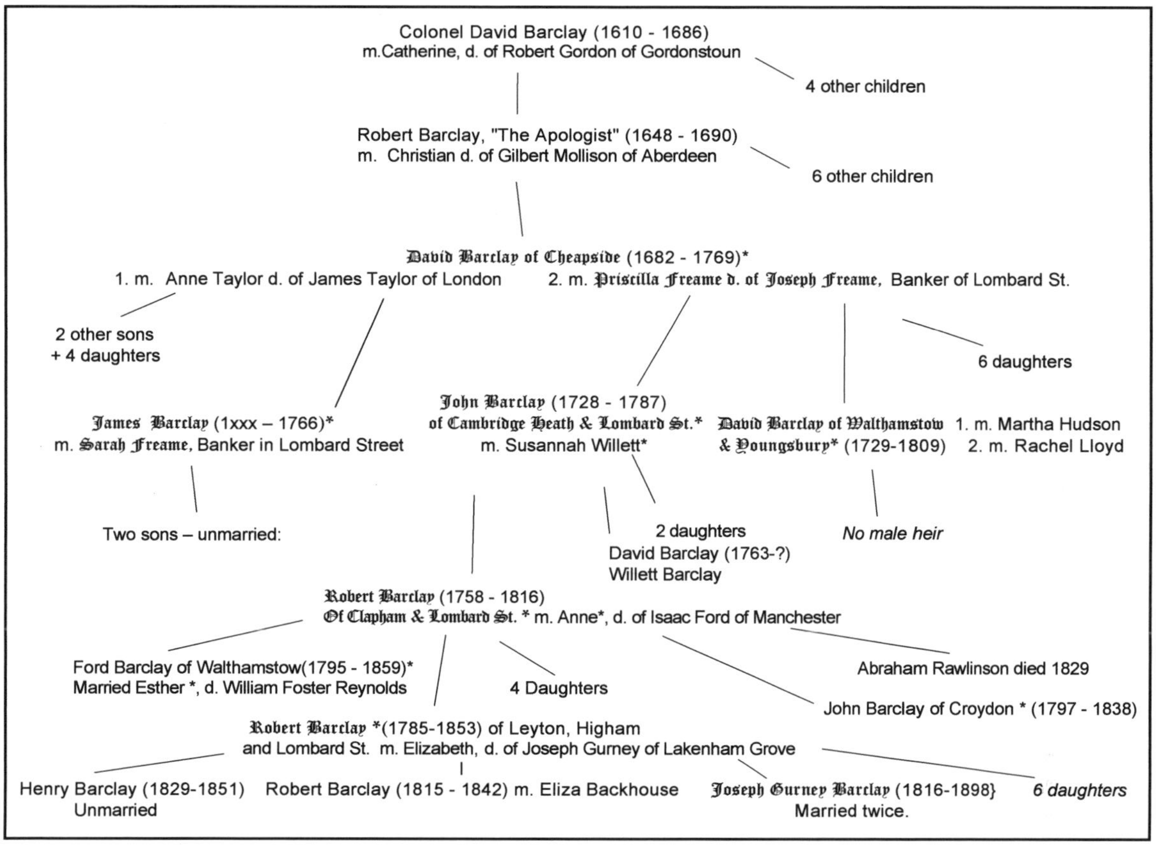

Figure 4. Barclay Family Tree.
The Barclay family relationships are complex, so I have tried to represent them diagrammatically to make the links easier to discern. As with the family tree for the Freames and the Goulds I have shown the individuals who went into the Barclays banking business in Old English *typeface. Those who are known to be buried in the burial grounds of Church Hill are marked by an asterisk.*

Meeting 24th of the third month 1710: 'John Brand is appointed to sign the paper drawn up relating to the building of a meeting house at Enfield Directed to the Quarterly meeting & give a coppy thereof to Jn Freame; Jn. Freame; Jn. Warner; Andrew Warner Jn Bennet Jn Broadgate & Jn Woodland are desired to attend the sd meeting; and as many others of this meet. as are free. The Ground that Jn. Broadgate had at Winchmore hill is let to Jn. Freame at 40 shillings per year to begin 25th 1 mo last .....'

'At a monthly meeting holden at Winchmore hill 29th 5 mo 1710. .....John Broadgate makes Report ye. poor woman of Fryan Barnet was very thankfull for what Friends sent her – whereas severall Persons have removed unto ye compass of this meeting & falling into Decay, it is left to ye Friends following to consider how to prevent it, viz. Wm. Baker John Bennet John Freame & John Warner.

Wm Collard citizen & Cheesemonger of London son of Wm Collard of Barking in ? Cheesemonger deceased and Mary Stamper Daughter of Francis Stamper citizen and watchmaker of London deceased, proposed their intention of taking each other in marriage, ye young man produced certificate of his Grandfathers consent & also a certificate from the two weeks meeting in London of his Clearness from all others, & ye young womans mother being present gave her consent; John Freame and Tho. Gould are desired to make enquiry concerning a young woman & make Report next meeting of her Clearness from all others.

This Meeting appoints the persons following or any 3 of them to draw up a paper to be presented to the next Quarterly Meeting setting forth the necessity of building a new meeting house at Enfield & desiring their Assistance therein & John Brand to sign it by order & on the behalf of this meeting viz. Wm. Crouch, John Freame, Tho. Gould, Saml. Waldenfield & John Bennet ....

.... John Brand is desired to collect all the money for the generall service & bring it in next meeting (except for Tottenham) which John Freame is desired to call for & bring in next meeting - .... Recd upon the collection for the Generall Service of Truth the severall sums following viz. From Epping £0.18s 6d; Waltham Abby. £1. 3s 6d; Winchmore hill £0.14s 0d; Barnet & Mims £0. 17s 0d; Tottenham £1. 0s. 0d; in all £4. 13s 0d. Which money is delivered to John Freame to give to the Friends that keep the Cash –

This meeting adjourns to this day 4 weeks (which is a week before its time) at Winchmore hill by reason of yearly meeting falling on that week it should be there in Course. And it is appointed for a Generall Monthly Meeting for Friends, their Children & Servants.-'

'At a Moly. Meeting at Enfield the 31st 11mo. 1710. The field at Winchmore hill (that John Freame held) is let to Wm Jones to Commence from the 2nd 12 mo at 28 shills year - Recd. of Jn Freame £40 in full to this time for rent for the ffield at Winchmore hill.'

'At a monthly meeting at Winchmore hill the 28th 1mo. 1711. No friends from Tottenham, Barnet, nor Mims - ....John Brand is appointed to give Jn. Freame a copy of a former minute concerning his visiting the Friends about Epping – John Brand is appointed to collect the burial notes & enter them against next meeting – Received of the Quarterly Collection of .... Jn. Freame £0. 5s. 0d, Tho. Gould £0. 5s 0d .....'

'At a Mo. Meeting at Winchmore hill 25:5:1711. John Freame reports that the Acct. was laid before the Quarterly Meeting, & that the Quarterly Meeting have allowed towards the charges this meeting has been at an Acct. of John Isaacs Family 8. The yearly meeting epistle received & read – John Freame is desired to receive of the 6 weeks meeting the 8th Granted by the Quarterly Meeting towards the charge this meeting have been at one acct. of John Isaac's Family –

A Bill brough in for the Nursing of Jm. Isaac's child & signed by Ann Cox amounting to £1. 15s 0d which Jn Warner is desired to pay – John Freame is desired to get a coppy of William Crowches Buriall note of Benj. Bealing ....' And there are a couple more references to John Freame in the minutes.

'At a Monthly Meeting at Winchmore Hill the 24th 7th mo. 1712. Rachel Shelley being a poor woman friend residing about Tottenham being in want, the Friends Following are desired to write to the monthly meeting of Ratclif concerning her where she does say she doth belong to take care of her and assist her in her necessity Viz. Rich Claridge & Tho. Hutson - The persons following are desired to draw up a paper to the Quarterly Meeting to know whether this meeting be a member of the six = weeks = meeting, in answer to the minute from the six = weeks = meeting, viz. Jn. Freame & Jm. Bennet – It is agreed that the words six = weeks = meeting be left out in the paper relating to Tottenham = meeting house.'

Later in these minutes is a list of, 'Received of the Quarterly Coll.' which includes subscriptions from, amongst others, 'John Freame 2 qtr. £0. 10s 0d' and 'Tho. Gould 3 qtr. £0. 15s 0d.'

'At a monthly meeting at Winchmore hill the 25th of the 6th month, 1714. This meeting having taken into consideration the paper from the Quarterly Meeting relating towards the assistance of building a meeting house at Stains this meeting agrees to pay Fourty Shillings towards the charge therof, John Freame is desired to pay the said money into meeting of Twelve – ...... The whole collection for John Isaacs Family amounts to £5 -16s - 9d whereof there is paid for the child at the workhouse £1. 7s. 8d to 25th 10 mo. 1713, and the remainder £4. 9s. 1d John Freame is desired to pay to Ann Cox in part of her ten pounds which he hath formerly disburst for John Isaacs family.'

Having looked at the Freames and Goulds early in the 18th century we now leap to the end of the century, with mention of the Barclays, 'At a Monthly Meeting held at Tottenham 11th of 8 mth. 1791. The following Report was brought in and read, from Friends appointed respecting the new Meeting House at Winchmoor hill, "We your Committee report that the rebuilding the Meeting House at Winchmoor hill is compleated; and also a Tenement for a Doorkeeper, and a considerable Addition to the Wall for the Burial Ground, the total Amount of which is £710. 2s. 6d which has been paid by the kind Subscription of Friends agreeable to Account Sent herewith. Tottenham 30th of 6 mo 1791 James Healey, John Decka, Thos Phillips, Wm. Forsters. Subscription & Expenses in rebuilding the meeting house at Winchmoorhill -......David Barclay £50 .... Joseph Osgood Freame £30 ..... Robert Barclay £10. 10s ... (Total) £710 2s 6d." '

In 1796, when Quaker Samuel Hoare was buried locally, Church Hill was described as "the Westminster Abbey of Friends in Middlesex". The same year David Barclay, Isaac Smith, Samuel Hoare, jun and Joseph Osgood, gave £100 each to be invested in a fund, the interest for which was to be applied for the upkeep of the premises. One shilling a week was to be given to the resident doorkeeper, in addition to the Monthly Meeting allowance for taking care of the building and keeping the ground in decent order. The remainder was to be used for repairs as needed.

The Barclay Clan Buried in the Church Hill Grounds

In the late 1980s the local Friends were kind enough to loan me a copy of the layout for the Church Hill Burial Grounds, where each row of gravestones was shown as logged in, I would say, probably about 1830 (given that Sarah Teshmaker, who died in 1832 is still shown as holding land to the immediate east of the grounds). The listings include the following (with surname Barclay unless otherwise indicated) –

Row F; 1. R. Barclay's Wife, Brewer 2. ditto Two Children 3. Blank 4. R. Barclay, Brewer.

This is presumably the family of Robert Barclay of Bury Hill (1751-1830) who was the grandson of David of Cheapside through his marriage to Anne Taylor.

Row G; 4. Robert, Banker. (Presumably Robert of Clapham and Lombard St. 1758-1816)

Row H; 1. John (of Cambridge Heath) 2. Susanna (his wife) 3. Two children of ditto 4 Wife of Robert Banker (Presumably 'Ann Barclay, Wife of R. Barclay, Clapham, Born 1763 Died 1801'.)

Row I; M & R wives of David 2. David Walthamstow 3. Martha 4. David Snr.

Plot 2 is clearly David of Walthamstow & Youngsbury (1729 - 1809), with

Plot 1 being occupied by his wives Martha and Rachel. David Senior at Plot 4 must be David of Cheapside (1682 - 1769).

Row K; 1. Jane 2. James 3. Sarah 4. Patience Weston 6. Joseph 7 Evan.

Row L; 1. Robert Jnr. 2 Ann Collinson 3. David 4. Priscilla 5 Thomas Weston.

Remember that at the start of this account on the Barclays we noted that as you enter the Burial Ground of The Friends Meeting House on Church Hill there are three tombstones near the pavement which are inscribed, 'David Barclay of Cheapside. Son of Apologist. Born 1682 Died 1769', 'John Barclay (Son of D. Barclay) Born 1728 Died 1787' and 'David Barclay Son of D. Barclay. Born 1729 Died 1809'.

Thomas Hood (1799 - 1845)

This account is mainly based on *Thomas Hood* by J.C. Reid, published by Rutledge in 1963, *Memorials of Thomas Hood* by his daughter Fanny (1869 edition) and a paper in the Guildhall Library on that daughter. I have also used the following websites – wansteadonline.co.uk. (in 2006), wikipedia, oldpoetry.com, readbookonline.net and poemhunter.com., mainly for the poems themselves.

In *The Story of Winchmore Hill and Southgate* of 1906, Walker Round says Hood was described by a contemporary as being, 'of middle height, slender and sickly looking, of sallow complexion and plain features, whilst being very rarely so excited as to give indication of either the pathos or humour that must ever have been working in his soul. His was indeed a countenance rather of melancholy than of mirth ... In conversation he was by no means brilliant.' He is pictured at Plate 50.

Thomas Hood was born at 31, The Poultry in the City of London on 23rd May 1799, above the bookshop of his Scottish father, also named Thomas, who was in the book publishing and selling trades. Today the area has changed beyond recognition, but the place of Hood's birth is marked by a Blue Plaque about 60 yards from Bank Tube Station, on the right as you walk towards St. Paul's along the Cheapside route. He had his first schooling in a private school in Tokenhouse Yard, from, 'two maiden ladies that were called Hogsflesh ...'.

When Thomas was eight his family moved to 5, Lower Street, Islington, later to be known as 50, Essex Road, which was to be his home for about twenty years. Very little is known is known of his childhood, but J.A. Hessey, later to employ him on *The London Magazine*, recalled him as, 'a singular child, silent and retired, with much quiet humours and apparently delicate in health'. In Islington he attended a preparatory school and he then went on to board at a 'finishing school' – Alfred House Academy at Camberwell Green, presided over by the founder Dr. Nicholas Wanostrocht, then by his great nephew Vincent.

Hood's father died on 20th August 1811 and his elder brother James died on 10th December. Upon his father's death he was withdrawn from the school and sent to a High School over a grocer's shop – which he liked. He left that school in 1813 or 1814 to work in a counting house which might well have been called Bell and Co., who specialised in imports from Russia, but his health failed and doctors advised him to leave this sedentary occupation. So it was that Hood studied engraving with his uncle, Robert Sands, and the prominent craftsmen John and Henry Le Keux. Within a year he was doing saleable work, but this equally sedentary work again brought on health problems, so in the summer of 1815 he was sent to live with his father's relatives in Dundee.

He went to stay with his aunt Jean Keay, wife of Captain Keay, owner and master of the trading brig *Hope*. He spent much time playing in the outdoors, but fell out with his aunt, and so went to live with her friend Mrs. Butterworth, who kept a boarding house in Overgate, although we don't know how he paid his way. However, he continued to spend much time walking, riding and fishing, and his health improved. He had a letter on the local Council's expenditure published in a Dundee paper, followed by a contribution to a Dundee magazine, and this seemed to spark an interest in writing.

In 1817, with his health somewhat improved by the country life, he returned to Lower Street, Islington, where he resumed his engraving to help support his mother and four sisters. He had a poor social life there, it seems, and his recreations were mainly sedentary – reading, playing chess and the flute. He also joined a short lived literary society.

In 1821 his mother Elizabeth died and he became the sole source of support for his four sisters. He had joined the staff of *The London Magazine* a few weeks before his mother's death, and aged only 22 he was able to mingle with the leading literary figures of the day. He was a proof reader cum sub editor, but he also started to contribute, with 30 of his pieces being published between July 1821 and June 1823. However, the publication went into decline, and in 1829 it was absorbed into the *New Monthly Magazine.*

Hood became friendly with two of the magazine's contributors – Charles Lamb and John Hamilton Reynolds. Lamb moved to near where Thomas was living in Islington and wrote to Bernard Barton, the Quaker poet, 'What a fertile genius (and a quiet good soul withal) is Hood ..... You'll like him much'. He met Jane Hamilton Reynolds through her brother John. She, being seven years older than Thomas, was the eldest of four sisters, and like Hood was prone to illness.

In the winter of 1823-4 Hood had a bad fever, which was almost certainly the first bout of the recurrent rheumatic fever which eventually killed him. It kept him in bed for months, and in the summer of 1824 he went to convalesce in Hastings. On 5th May 1825 he married Jane Reynolds at St. Botolph's Church, Aldersgate. J.C. Reid says that, 'The newly wed pair went for a honeymoon of some weeks at Hastings; it was the unshadowed beginning of a partnership marked by poverty, sickness and sorrow, but lighted always by a perfect love, trust and fidelity.'

In 1827 the Hoods left Lower Street in Islington for 2, Robert Street in the Adelphi. Their first child, a girl, was born in April 1827 but died immediately. That winter Thomas was again smitten by rheumatic fever, brought on by excessive work, including *The Plea of the Midsummer Fairies and Other Poems*, and *Whims and Oddities*. In 1828 Thomas edited the first edition of a new annual called *The Gem*, which proved a success. The following year, with failing health he left London for the country air of Rose Cottage, in what is now known as Vicars Moor Lane. At P52 of her *Memorials,* his daughter Frances tells us of an incident at Rose Cottage, Winchmore Hill, as follows,

'An amusing incident took place during their removal from town. A large hamper of china and glass had arrived from town by the carrier one morning, and the contents being unpacked were placed, pro tempore, on a dresser in the china closet. This wooden shelf had been only newly mortared into the wall, and when all this weight was put on it, of course it came down with an alarming crash! My father, who was within hearing, soon came to the scene of action, or rather *fraction*, and after coolly surveying the damage, very quietly sent the maid to her mistress with the message that "the china which *came up* in the morning, had *come down* in the evening!" This, to his great amusement, brought my mother, in a state of utter mystification, to the scene of the catastrophe. They were, however, both very cheerful people, and the breakage (no light one), was borne with tolerable philosophy on both sides.'

Thomas continued working hard, and in September 1829 his small volume called *The Epping Hunt* was published, with six engravings by George Cruickshank. In 1830 Frances, his second daughter, was born, and he produced his *Comic Annual*, (later merged into *Hood's Own)*, which was pioneering, in that it was in a humorous vein. The second edition, in 1831, dedicated to the Duke of Devonshire, contained 31 pieces, all by Hood, of which 20 were comic verses.

In 1832 Hood fell out with his landlord, who apparently didn't make some necessary repairs, and he moved to Lake House in Wanstead, by Epping Forest. In Edwardian times Miss Cresswell wrote of Rose Cottage, 'A part of this house is very old, and a vague tradition asserts that Henry Cromwell, son of the Lord Protector, lived here for a time ..... Tom Hood's house, a dear old place, grey fronted and bow windowed, and roofed with shingle tiles red, brown, and mossy. The house still stands, but the east front, which was its oldest part, has been altered. In those days it had long dark passages, unexpected stairs, and mysterious cupboards disguised with wallpaper. There were two enormous pollard elms by the carriage gate, and a large cherry tree in full blossom made a white mass against the after glow in the south eastern sky .....'

The bulk of the Rose Cottage that Hood lived in was destroyed by the Germans in the Second World War, as recorded in Miss Bowman's account of 1989. Today's premises at No. 59 Vicars Moor Lane bear a Blue Plaque commemorating his memory as follows, 'Thomas Hood 1799 – 1845 Poet and Humorist lived in Rose Cottage on this site'. I have not published a picture of the cottage in this volume, because I featured it at P41 of *A Look at Old Winchmore Hill*, and P172 of Winchmore Hill Village 1780-1830.

Hood later spoke regretfully of this move, especially as his new abode was dilapidated. Worse still for someone with Hood's constitution it was damp, causing periodic bouts of illness which required him to recuperate at Brighton and Ramsgate. His son Thomas was born at Wanstead on 19th January 1835, and it seems that Hood retained his impish sense of humour there. According to the Wansteadonline website his son wrote,

'I had a favourite but very ugly wooden doll, combining all the usual features of the race, a triangular nose, button mouth and inverted eyes. This lovely creature I left by some chance in the dangerous precincts of my father's study. What was my horror and amazement next morning to find her comely visage thickly studded with bright pink spots! For some hours I dared not go near her, as she lay extended on the table, being firmly persuaded she had the measles, then very prevalent in the neighbourhood. My father was, of course, the author of the mischief, and perceived the success of his plan with infinite amusement. My fears, however, were not allayed till poor dolly underwent a thorough ablution, under which her few remaining charms vanished for ever.'

It was about the time that his son was born that his finances failed, for reasons unknown. As Lake House had 80 acres of farmland attached, possibly it was simply too large for his pocket. Apparently his household expenses were treble what they had been in the more modest Rose Cottage. Anyway, whatever the reasons, he filed for bankruptcy and left for the continent. He left his affairs in the hands of Dilke and Wright, and his wife and children in the care of Dr. William Elliott of Stratford. In March 1835 he set off for Coblenz in Germany, though he doesn't seem to have taken to the locals, whilst he missed his family. On 29th March Jane set off with Tom and Fanny and Thomas met them all at Cologne.

Despite his problems Hood flung himself into his work, preparing the *Comic Annual* for 1836. His 1837 *Annual*, in which he poked fun at German doctors, was the best to date, but his poor health continued, and so, in June 1837 he left Coblenz for Ostend in Belgium, possibly to be nearer home. He found it cleaner and got on far better with the locals. He considered them civil and obliging and not, 'malicious, like the Rhinelanders'.

The 1836 collection of *Hood's Own*, and his son's subsequent collection of 1861, kept Hood's reputation alive during the Victorian era. His *Up The Rhine*, published in December 1839, was a great success, being part travel book, part novel. Ostend was cold and damp, causing Thomas's health to worsen. Jane joined him abroad, and in May they sent for their children, but they were detained pending the settlement of a Belgian debt of over £100. In July, having raised the money, he collected the children and came back to England for the sake of his health.

By May 1841 Hood's finances were so poor that he applied to the Royal Literary Fund for a grant, which led to a £50 award the following month. Later that year he was invited to edit the *New Monthly* at £300 per annum, plus fees for any articles that he might contribute. That November the last *Comic Annual* was published, not long before the family moved to a house overlooking Lords cricket ground in St. John's Wood. During this period Hood continued his friendship with Dickens, mainly by post, whilst his health, and that of his wife, fluctuated.

By September 1843, tired and unwell, he decided to holiday in Scotland, visiting his aunt Jean Keay. The fresh Scottish air again revived him, and in October he returned to London much stronger. Unfortunately, though, he fell out with the *New Monthly* and he resigned, to the detriment of his financial situation. Finding it difficult to find another editor's post he started his own periodical entitled *Hood's Monthly Magazine and Comic Miscellany*, the first edition appearing on 1st January 1844, weeks after he moved to his final home at 28, New Finchley Road and his *The Song of the Shirt* had appeared anonymously in the December issue of *Punch*.

The Song of the Shirt was immensely popular, being a powerful attack on the exploitation of workers. It was reprinted in other newspapers across Europe, including *The Times*. The poem was about a London seamstress who sold shirts that she made for the profit of her employer, and one verse given on the wikipedia website runs,

With fingers weary and worn
With eyelids heavy and red
A woman sat, in unwomanly rags
Plying her needle and thread
Stitch! stitch! stitch!
In poverty, hunger and dirt
And still with a voice of dolorous pitch
She sang the Song of the Shirt

The first edition of *Hood's Magazine* sold 1,500 copies and in the May 1844 edition he published his famous poem, *The Bridge of Sighs*. Unfortunately by then he had collapsed, but he recovered, yet again, to continue his writings. His friends and admirers could see he had little strength left, and wrote to the Government to secure a pension. He was asked to name a close female relative to benefit should he die. He named Jane, and on the 9th November he wrote to thank Robert Peel, the Prime Minister.

Hood's Magazine of March 1945 reported how seriously ill he was, whilst the April issue said he was dying. He died on 3rd May 1845, after sinking into a deep coma, and was buried at Kensal Green cemetery. A public appeal to support his widow was successful, but in December 1846 she too died, and was buried alongside him. The public subscribed to a memorial over his grave, which was unveiled on 18th July 1854.

One of Hood's most endearing and enduring poems is titled *No!,* though there are shorter versions in circulation which are called *November!* and *November in England*. It reads -

No sun, no moon, no morn, no noon
No dawn, no dusk, no proper time of day
No sky, no earthly view, no distance looking blue
No road, no street, no 't'other side this way'
No end to any Row
No indications where the Crescents go
No top to any steeple
No recognitions of familiar people
No courtesies for showing 'em!
No travelling at all – no locomotion
No inkling of the way – no notion
'No go' by land or ocean
No mail – no post
No news from any foreign coast
No Park, no Ring, no afternoon gentility
No company – no nobility
No warmth, no cheerfulness, no healthful ease
No comfortable feel in any member
No shade, no shine, no butterflies, no bees
No fruits, no flowers, no leaves, no birds
November!

It is believed that Hood had Winchmore Hill in his mind when he wrote one of his best known poems, *Our Village*, part of which runs :-

Our village, that's to say, not Miss Mitford's village, but our village of Bullock Smithy
Is come into by an avenue of trees, three oak pollards, two elders, and a withy;
And in the middle there's a green, of about not exceeding an acre and a half;
It's common to all, and fed off by nineteen cows, six ponies, three horses, five asses, two foals, seven pigs and a calf
Besides a pond in the middle, as is held by a similar sort of common-law lease,
And contains twenty ducks, six drakes, three ganders, two dead dogs, four drowned kittens, and twelve geese,
Of course the green's cropt very close, and does famous for bowling when the little village boys play at cricket;
Only some horse, or pig, or cow or great jackass, is sure to come and stand right before the wicket .....

Before leaving this account it might be as well to say something of Thomas's second daughter, referred to earlier as Fanny, since she was born in Winchmore Hill in 1830, and had some literary success herself. Her full name was Frances Freeling, being named after her father's friend Sir Francis Freeling, secretary to the GPO. On 10th September 1849 she married the Rev. John Somerville Broderip. In 1857 her *Wayside Fancies* was published, this being followed by *Funny Fables for Little Folks* in 1860, the first of a series of her works illustrated by her brother Tom Hood.

In 1860 Frances and Tom edited two volumes about their father in the previously mentioned *Memorials of Tom Hood,* and in 1869 they published the *Early Poems and Sketches* of their father. She and Tom published *The Works of T. Hood 1869 - 73* in ten volumes. Frances died at Clevedon on 3rd November 1878 aged only 49, leaving four daughters.

The Mann, Crossman and Paulin Brewing Dynasty

For this section I have used various sources, the chief being; *Winchmore Hill Cricket Club – The First Hundred Years 1880 – 1980* by Tony and Jennifer Bath, old newspaper articles, and other information gathered together in the David Hicks Archives in Enfield's Local Studies Unit.

The early years of Mann, Crossman and Paulin

The Baths tell us that the Paulin family fled southern France in the late 17th century owing to their persecution as Huguenots. They settled in Berwick - on - Tweed and appear in a marriage register for the first known time in 1697. A Paulin became master of Berwick Academy in 1800. He had three sons. One became associated with Alexander Crossman in the corn business, another became Manager of the Berwick Shipping Company in 1820, and the third son, Thomas, was introduced into the brewery business.

Thomas became associated with Robert Crossman, younger brother of Alexander, in the brewery business, and they moved south to manage Isleworth Brewery. They met James Mann at Mile End, so anticipating the start of the once famous Mann, Crossman and Paulin brewery. It seems that Thomas Paulin remained at Isleworth whilst Robert Crossman returned north to manage the Border Brewery in Berwick. He also purchased the Manor of Holy Island, which was, the Baths say, still in the hands of the Crossmans in 1980.

The Albion brewery was in Whitechapel Road, in the East End. The original version was built in 1808 near the old Mile End Turnpike by Richard Ivory, the landlord of *The Blind Beggar* pub. Access to the brewery was by a large gate at the side of the pub. For the first ten years the Albion Brewery was leased by John Hoffman, but he ran into financial difficulties, so it was put up for auction, and the lease was bought by Philip Blake and John Mann, a Lambeth brewer, in 1818. Blake retired in 1826, leaving Mann to run the business alone, so he changed the Company name to John Mann, Brewer.

It soon became clear to James Mann, who seems to have succeeded John, that if he wanted to expand the business he needed new partners and fresh capital. When James Mann died in 1844 his eldest son, of the same name, sought out Robert Crossman (d. 1883), and in 1846 they signed the first partnership deed of Mann, Crossman and Company. Later that year Crossman invited Thomas Paulin to join their partnership, which he did along with James Mann's younger brother Thomas (d. 1886). However, Paulin's name did not appear in the partnership listing until 1848. In time James Mann retired.

The Manns and their local homes

1848 saw the birth of not only Mann, Crossman and Paulin, but also the birth of two eldest sons - Thomas James Mann to Thomas Mann and William Thomas Paulin (pictured inside the back cover) to Thomas Paulin. In due course both followed their fathers into the brewing business. The Baths tell us that the Mann, Crossman and Paulin links became even stronger because Thomas Paulin's sister married Alexander Crossman's son Matthew. This Crossman line became members of the old established London firm of Solicitors Crossman Block, who were associated for some years with Winchmore Hill Cricket Club.

There seems to have been some doubt surrounding the detail of when and how the Manns came to our village, so I have tried to follow Kelly's Street Directories and Census returns for both the Manns and Paulins at Table 1.

At the London Metropolitan Archives is a document B/MMN/6/39 which states, 'E. Harvey Esq. and Thomas Mann Esq. Deed of Covenant for production of Deeds relating to a Messuage or Cottage pieces of Land and Heredits at Edmonton Middlesex. Dated 13th July 1853.' In the1801 Edmonton Land Enclosure Schedule Jacob Harvey is indicated as owning four adjoining plots of land in the vicinity of where *Roseneath* was later shown, so it is possible that Thomas Mann was involved in a transaction relating to that mansion.

At Table 1 we see that James Mann was living at *Roseneath* in 1855. We don't know whether *Roseneath* was a completely new mansion, or perhaps one that involved building upon what had existed previously. The 1859 Kelly's shows Thomas – presumably James's younger brother – living there, which is consistent with the Bath's statement that Thomas Mann is said to have come to live in the village in 1858, though they state, incorrectly I have now concluded, that at that time he lived at *Laurel Lodge* in Church Hill. The Baths say that 1858 was the year that Thomas also bought Thelveton Hall and its many acres of farmland, near Diss in Norfolk.

The 1871 Census shows Thomas Mann, Brewer, aged 46 and born in Bethnal Green, as Head of the Household at *Roseneath*, living with his wife Fanny, aged 50, who had been born in Elvington, Yorkshire. With them were their daughter Fanny, 19, born in Stoke Newington, son Edward, 17, born in Winchmore Hill, daughter Julia, 13, born in Winchmore Hill, brother - in - law Robert Spence, 84, Gentleman, born in Yorkshire. They were attended by four female servants. It looks as though Edward was born in the village before his father is known to have moved there.

An interesting entry in Table 1 is the one for Thomas James Mann – presumably Thomas's eldest son - occupying *Beaumont Lodge*, on the northern junction of Wades Hill and Vicars Moor Lane in 1880, though there appears to not yet be a *Laurel Lodge*. By the time of the 1884 Kelly's Thomas James has left *Beaumont Lodge*, and, indeed, possibly Winchmore Hill, but Edward is shown as living at the newly appeared *Laurel Lodge.*

At P52 of his *Memories of Winchmore Hill (1952)* Regnart says, 'On what is now the *Laurel Lodge* property (opposite St. Paul's in Church Hill) there was what

Miss Cresswell described as a cottage of gentility. Mr. Wright lived there. When we had been in Hill House a few months he died. About 1882 Mr. Mann bought the land and built the present house for his son who eventually became Sir Edward Mann, Baronet. He built the brick wall round the property. After his mother's death in the middle nineties, Sir Edward rebuilt his father's home, *Roseneath,* in Vicarsmoor Lane, and went to live there, but in a few years he left Winchmore Hill for good. Then Fred Barry, a son of Mr. Barry, of Bush Hill House, took *Laurel Lodge* and after a few years was followed by Mr. Charles Morgan who came from Hazelwood House in Green Lanes. He died in the house in 1909.'

At P71 of his book Regnart says of *Roseneath* that, 'It was quite a small house, about the size of Drayton Villa further down the road. His (Thomas's) son, Sir Edward Mann, built the present house in the (eighteen) nineties .... Mr. Mann had two sons and two daughters. One daughter married Mr. Paulin, and the other, Miss Julia, was totally blind. When they were small children they were playing together and her brother Edward accidentally poked a pair of scissors into one of her eyes.' The mansion is captured at Plate 52.

Walford's County Families of the United Kingdom, 1911 tells us that whilst Thomas Mann died in 1886, his wife Fanny survived until 1897, being the daughter of Robert Spence of Elvington, Yorkshire. Their youngest son Edward, was born in 1854, marrying Anna Jane, the daughter of Paul Bell of Stiffkey in Norfolk. Sir Edward, as he became, was a JP for Norfolk. He was Mayor of Stepney in 1901 and 1902 (relating to the brewery in Mile End Road), and High Sheriff for Norfolk in 1909.

The 1891 Census return for *Roseneath* shows Fanny Mann, aged 71, from Elvington in Yorkshire, and 'living on her own means', as widowed Head of Household. Her blind single daughter, Julia, aged 33, was also 'living on her own means'. They were tended by four female domestic servants and had a visitor named Helen D. Richard. The return for *The Laurels* shows the 37 year old Brewer Edward Mann as Head of Household. With him were his wife Anna, 36, from Norfolk, and their three children Edward J. (8), William (6), Francis J. (3), all of whom were born in Winchmore Hill. They were tended by five female servants. There is information on their children later in this account.

The Sentinel for Wood Green, Southgate and Friern Barnet of 3rd December 1897 reported that, 'Between ourselves Mr. Edward Mann and Mr. Paulin, of Winchmore Hill, are two of the executors under the will of the late Mr. T.J. Mann (Edward's elder brother), whose estate is put at £374,000. Nothing appears to have been left to the poor of East London, where the brewery and many of the tied houses are.'

The Sentinel for 23rd June 1899 contained the snippet, 'Roundabout Notes. The Winchmore Hill Conservative Association, of which Messrs. Mann and Paulin are the principal pillars, is not in want of money – it has a balance of £20 in hand and there's plenty more where that came from – it is more in want of "members who will support the Unionist cause". This was the lament of the chairman at the annual meeting. I hope the plentifulness of the money will not allure any men.

Messrs. Albino, Bennington, Langley, Spooner, Dunnett, Casey and Salmon were appointed canvassers. Mr. Mann (who is Conservative candidate for South Norfolk) attaches a good deal of importance to "canvassing"; he hopes it will be conducted in Winchmore Hill "in the same manner as in the past". Umph!'

The Recorder for Palmers Green, Winchmore Hill and Southgate February

1908 edition informed the public that, 'Miss (Julia) Mann has left *Rose Cottage,* and has gone to reside near Winchester, at least for two years. The "poor" miss her very much and some of them have turned to Miss Paulin for the usual help.' The April 1908 issue told us that, 'Lady Mann is the new Dame President of the (Primrose) League, succeeding Mrs. Taylor, who is going to live in Oxfordshire, where Captain Taylor has bought an estate.'

The Baths say that Edward Mann was created a baronet in 1905, and continued to live at *Roseneath* until his move to Norfolk just before the Great War. He had been a Vice President of Winchmore Hill Cricket Club for many years before resigning in 1913. *The Recorder* of April 1914 published a letter by Lady Anna J. Mann, Sir Edward's wife, on behalf of the Primrose League. She was sympathetic to the Ulster loyalists, and asked local women to sign a Covenant against the granting of Home Rule to Ireland without any reference to the electors.

An article headed 'Future of Grovelands' in *The Palmers Green and Southgate Gazette* of 12th June 1920 ran, 'The winding up meeting of the Southgate branch of the Middlesex VAO was held .... last week .... The first auxiliary hospital effort in Southgate was made in August 1914, when by the benevolence of Mr. W.T. Paulin, Miss Paulin and their friends, *Roseneath* was equipped and always remained an independent unit ....' So it would seem that when Sir Edward left the area he would have sold, or gifted, *Roseneath,* to Paulin. It was still part of Paulin's estate when he died in 1931.

The Palmers Green and Southgate Gazette of 9th January 1915 contained, 'Our Voluntary Hospital; A Visit to *Roseneath* Winchmore Hill. *Roseneath* Vicars Moor Lane, Winchmore Hill is now, as many of our readers are aware, a flourishing Voluntary Hospital, thanks mainly to the kindness of a local resident. The house has been completely equipped by the generous donor, while practically the whole of the staff give their services gratuitously ...' (See Plate 52.)

The 26th June 1915 edition of *The Gazette* told us that, 'Two ladies in Winchmore Hill have started a Pound Day for the wounded soldiers at *Roseneath.* So many are willing to help in a small way, and it has been suggested that this would be a great help to the Hospital. Below is a list from the Matron of things required. Will anyone willing to help please send a postcard to either of the addresses below, or leave the goods or order for collection at the Receiving Depot, 39, The Broadway, Winchmore Hill, where same will be collected every other Friday, starting from July 2nd .....'

The Gazette of 4th December 1915 informed the public that, 'In acceptance of the kind invitation of the St. Paul's Institute Men's Club, fifteen of the wounded soldiers from *Roseneath* visited the Club on Wednesday evening, accompanied by Messrs. Adams and Page, of the Hospital Committee. Billiards, snooker, bridge, whist, draughts and cribbage were played, resulting in a win for the soldier boys by 18 games to 16 on total played. The games were pleasantly interrupted midway by a call to supper .....' The *Domestic Servants* column of the same issue advertised, 'Wanted – A strong, clean active girl, about 18 years of age, as wardmaid. – Apply matron, *Roseneath Hospital.* Winchmore Hill'.

Returning to the Manns, *Debrett's Peerages* of 1944 tells us that Sir Edward was Chairman of Mann, Crossman and Paulin Ltd., of Brandon's Putney Brewery Ltd., and of D. Watney & Sons Ltd. *Debrett's* also tells us of Sir Edward's offspring. Edward John Mann, who became the second baronet, was born on 26th January 1886, to be educated at Marlborough College and Pembroke College, Cambridge University.

He was Captain in the Norfolk Regiment, but was wounded in the Great War. He was master in the Brewers' Company in 1921-2, and High Sheriff of Norfolk in 1939-40. His seat was listed as Thelveton Hall, Scole, Norfolk.

Sir Edward John's brother William Edgar, was born on 19th January 1885 and was also educated at Marlborough. He reached the rank of Major and earned the D.S.O., being twice wounded during the Great War. In 1913 he married Sarah Douglas Sprot, and in 1918 had a son named Edward Charles, D.S.O., who in 1944 was serving as a Major in the 12th Lancers. Sir Edward John's younger brother Charles Julian Mann was born in 1892 and killed in action in 1918, in the Great War, as a Lieutenant in the Hussars. Sir Edward John's sister, named Fanny Julia, was born in 1896.

Sir Edward John's brother Francis Thomas (1888 – 1964) was educated at Malvern and Pembroke College Cambridge. He rose to the rank of Captain in the Scots Guards, being three times wounded in the Great War, and mentioned in despatches three times. In 1916 he married Enid Agnes Tilney. The Baths tell us that he achieved some fame when he captained Middlesex and England at cricket in the 1920s, being known as 'Mighty Mann' because of his big hitting. In 1921 he brought an MCC team to play at the Paulin Ground.

In 1917 Francis Thomas had a son, Francis George, M.C., who was educated at Eton and Pembroke College, Cambridge. In 1942 he married Ann Marguerite Brockbank, and in 1943 they had a daughter named Joan Elizabeth (Lady Maclean). In 1944 he was serving as a Captain in the Scots Guards. Francis George Mann also captained Middlesex and England, and was President of Winchmore Hill Cricket Club from 1961 to 1970. In 1978 he was appointed Chairman of the Test and County Cricket Board.

The Paulins and their local homes - and staff

In my Winchmore Hill Village 1780 – 1830 I covered the early history of *Beaulieu*, which was situated in the vicinity of today's Beaulieu Gardens, and then briefly outlined its post 1830 history. The following is a precise of that account. (There is a picture of the old mansion at Page 58 of my *A Look at Old Winchmore Hill).*

In 1786 the surveyor Launcelot Dowbiggin prepared three plans and an elevation for John Gray, the brother of Walker Gray of Grovelands. John's building became known as *Beaulieu,* and the Dowbiggin work is stored today at the Sir John Soane's Museum, Lincoln's Inn Fields. Also at the Museum are two elevations for a Lodge to the main building by Soane himself, drawn in 1796. In 1796 Soane added a 'rustic gardener's house'. In 1801 the estate was over 10 acres.

John Gray sold out to a Thomas Nisbett, and in 1806 William Cass purchased the estate for £4,750, which, on his death, was handed down to his son Frederick. His son, later the Reverend Frederick Charles Cass, was born at *Beaulieu* in 1824 and moved to Little Grove, in nearby Cat Hill, with his parents in 1827. Despite this move, the Cass's retained *Beaulieu* until 1832, by which time beautiful gardens had been laid out in the grounds by John Papworth.

At the London Metropolitan Archives is document ACC/1292, which concerns Charles Johnston (1804 – 1897), third son of William and Sarah Johnston. Their second son was Edmund. The document tells us that, 'Under the term of his father's will, in 1836, Edmund received property in Holborn and was co-trustee of premises in

St. Marylebone. He did not marry and lived with his widowed mother until her death in 1851 when she bequeathed him the household effects at *Beaulieu,* Winchmore Hill, Edmonton. Here he resided until his own death in October 1864. The estate was left in trust for the children of Charles Johnston and their heirs.'

The local 1841 Census return (in which ages are rounded down to the nearest five years) shows *Beaulieu Lodge* being inhabited by the Johnston family and others. Sarah Johnston is indicated as being 75 and of Independent means, William is 60 and a Stockbroker, Edmund is 40 and Independent. Although *Beaulieu* isn't shown as such in the 1851 Census, Edward (surely meant to be Edmund) Johnson, aged 51, is listed as a fund holder, and his 87 year old mother is shown as an annuitant. They have six people working in service for them.

We earlier mentioned the birth of Thomas Paulin's eldest son William Thomas in 1848, he being one of six boys and two girls. In the 8th December 1922 edition of a paper, which I take to be *The Gazette*, the death was reported of Miss Isabel Paulin, daughter of 'the late Mr. Thomas Paulin, of Winchmore Hill'. She had been born on 16th June 1842, and her death occurred at her home *Ladykirk* on The Ridgeway on 30th November at the age of 80. Her funeral was attended by a clutch of Paulins, and Sir Edward Mann, who was then living in Norfolk.

In the Hicks Archives in the Local Studies Unit David says that John Wood Paulin moved from *Beaulieu* to rent *Rose Cottage* from the Harvey family before emigrating to New Zealand. Also in that extensive collection is a copy of a registration of the birth on 1st April 1878, in Edmonton District No. 8234B, of Alice Greta at Vicars Moor Lane (*Rose Cottage* one presumes). She was born to John Wood Paulin and Alice Paulin nee Goldring, the father being shown as a Corn and Feed Merchant. Another of David's finds is an article from what I take to be *The Democrat,* of Dunedin in New Zealand. This features John Wood Paulin, who, they say, was born in London in 1856, and attended Enfield Palace School. One presumes he is one of Thomas Paulin's six sons. He arrived in New Zealand in 1886 with some degree of expertise in meteorology. *The Democrat* said that 'his predictions regarding the weather are remarkable for their absolute correctness'.

The Baths say that in about 1864 William Thomas Paulin, aged only sixteen, became involved in the financial and legal aspects of the brewery. They say that in 1865 Thomas Paulin purchased *Beaulieu*, and moved there, presumably as direct successor to the Johnstons. The 1865 Kelly's shows Thomas Mann as living at *Roseneath*, but there is no sign, yet, of the Paulins. William Paulin is shown as residing at *Beaulieu* in the1867 Kelly's. In 1877 eldest son William Thomas married Thomas Mann's daughter Fanny at Christ Church, Southgate, and they took to farming at *Broadfields*, with a herd of Jersey cows. They had two daughters – Fanny Ina Ramsey, in January 1879, and Mary Julia Irene, in June 1882. All four family members are featured at Plate 51.

In *Winchmore Hill Lives* of 1991 Lucy Pettifer (b. 1901) says, 'Sir William lived at Broadfields, which was demolished in the 1930s. Paulin Drive of today follows the line of what, in my childhood, was Sir William's private drive from Wades Hill to his beautiful large ivy covered mansion. His coaches and horses were kept in the stables where the garage now stands in Wades Hill. The small cottage that remains in Paulin Drive next to the garage (pictured at P40 of *A Look at Old Winchmore Hill*) was the old harness room. The coachmen were an impressive sight in their top hats.'

The garage Lucy mentions was demolished in 2000 to make way for the flats on the southern corner of Paulin Drive and Wades Hill, and the 'harness room' seems to have been substantially altered. However, before that happened there was a plaque on the wall at the rear of the garage, where it adjoined the harness room, which bore the inscription 'TM 1877'. This, obviously, isn't to commemorate the work of a Paulin, but it would be consistent with the name of Thomas Mann, who perhaps built Broadfields for William and Fanny upon their marriage – a sort of 'dowry'?

Let's just follow up very briefly on the subsequent history of *Beaulieu*, before continuing with the Paulins. When the Paulins left for the newly built *Broadfields* they were followed by the Phillips family. Towards the end of the 19th century, *Beaulieu* was purchased by a Mr. Foster, who cut Elm Park Road through the estate in 1898/9, the road being developed soon after. *The Recorder for Palmers Green, Winchmore Hill and Southgate* of 5th November 1914 reported that, 'The committee in charge of the scheme for housing Belgian refugees at *Beaulieu*, Winchmore Hill, cannot be said to have wasted time, for within a week the house had been leased, the workmen put in, and everything was in full swing for the reception of the new comers. As the house had been unoccupied for four years, it goes without saying that there was much to be done.'

Following the end of hostilities *Beaulieu* struggled to find a permanent role or ownership, and the house was finally demolished in 1937, being commemorated in the name of the road that was laid over the building site - Beaulieu Gardens.

Upon the death of Thomas Mann in 1886, William Thomas Paulin became a senior partner in the brewery firm, along with Thomas James Mann and his brother Edward, (later Sir Edward). The 1891 Census return for *Broadfields* and its neighbours is to be found at Table 2. William Thomas was appointed a local JP in 1893, and became involved in benevolent work in the village. In 1895 he was elevated from Vice-President to President of Winchmore Hill Cricket Club following the death of Thomas Teshmaker Busk of Fords Grove Mansion, and continued to hold senior office until his own death in 1931.

Unfortunately William Thomas's wife Fanny died at the early age of 49 in February 1901. She was known as the Lady Bountiful of Winchmore Hill and her obituary included the line that, 'the poor had no kinder friend than she and many have lost a generous and sympathetic benefactor.' In July 1902 their daughter Ina married the Vicar, The Rev. A.J.B. Dewdney, in a service conducted by the Bishop of London. In 1903 William Thomas erected St. Paul's Institute in Station Road (Plates 57 & 58), and although this was demolished in about 1969, to make way for the current Postal Delivery Office, the foundation stone still exists in the grounds of St. Paul's Church. It reads, 'To the Glory of God and In Memory of Fanny Paulin. This building was erected by William Thomas Paulin, Ina Dewdney, Irene Paulin. 1903. Arthur J.B. Dewdney, Vicar.'

In 1904 the Reverend and his wife had a daughter. Misfortune again overtook the family in December 1907 when the Vicar contracted tuberculosis and was forced to resign his post. His health did improve apparently, but at the advice of his doctors he emigrated to Canada with his wife and daughter. *Who's Who 1941-1950* relates that Arthur John Dewdney, was educated at Jesus College, Oxford, where he obtained an MA. He was ordained in 1896 and became Curate of St. Matthew's Ponders End 1896 – 98, followed by St. Mark Dalston 1898-1900 and Edmonton 1901. He was Vicar of St. Paul's in Winchmore Hill from 1901-08 and was Chaplain to the Bishop of Calgary 1909. He was Archdeacon of Calgary 1916-26 and he died on 11th January 1946. It seems his wife predeceased him in 1939. An undated newspaper cutting in the Hicks Archives reported that 'Mrs. Saanich Dewdney wife of Archdeacon J.B. Dewdney' died in British Columbia, leaving £99,485.

The Recorder of 1st August 1912 reported that, 'The new shelter – properly speaking it is a handsome and artistic pavilion – which Mrs. Dewdney, wife of Canon Dewdney, late vicar of Winchmore Hill, and Miss Paulin, her sister, have had built for the cabmen of Winchmore Hill, was formally opened and handed over to the men by Mr. W. J. Wheeler, the designer and builder, last Tuesday week. ……. The Messrs. Martin, in reply, expressed their thanks and the thanks of their employees for what Miss Paulin had done, and said they were very pleased and would do all in their power to meet Miss Paulin's wishes in every way, as what had been done was much more than they expected. They were all very thankful.' The said cabmen's shelter was situated outside Winchmore Hill Station, where the men previously had to wait in the cold for fares. One presumes that the Martins are part of the family shown living at Broadfield Cottages in the 1891 Census return in Table 2.

In 1913 estimates totalling £2,587 were accepted and the present Vicarage for St. Paul's was built in Church Hill on land donated by William Paulin. There is an old photograph of the Vicarage, from near the Denleigh Gardens entrance, at P8 of my *A Look at Old Winchmore Hill.*

Ina's sister Irene remained unmarried through her life and assisted her father at Broadfields. Lucy Pettifer, mentioned above, says, 'The Paulins were the dominant family in the village when I was young and I worked in their kitchen and private dairy for some years. They were kind and generous people. Every two days the numerous local poor came to Broadfields and Miss Irene Paulin would fill each of their jugs with up to a quart of milk. She would also give each a can of beef tea. At Christmas Miss Irene would visit her family's tenants with two gardeners wheeling handbarrows in attendance. The barrows contained gifts of socks for the men, stockings for the women and apples and oranges for the children. Each family of tenants in Harwoods Yard also received a turkey along with pork sausages for stuffing. These items came from the Paulins' Norfolk farms.'

What I believe to be *Broadfields* is captured at Plate 53. It seems that there was a private museum at the back of the building. Lucy was, of course, not the only local to work for the Paulins at Broadfields (which was approached by what is today Paulin Drive off Wades Hill). At Plate 55 is chauffer William Martin, whose health was shattered in the trenches of the Great War. It never really recovered, and, tragically, he died in 1925 at the youthful age of 27.

At Plate 54 is a photograph of Charlotte Wragg, Miss Irene's former Lady's Maid, on 18th August 1983, aged an incredible 105. It was probably taken by the late Pauline Holstius, who gave me it for publication. Pauline did a small write up of Charlotte in *Oakleaves* bulletin No. 1 in 1987 where she told us that Charlotte was from the small Norfolk village of Litcham, her father being a blacksmith with 13 children! She left home aged 24 and a friend of her's who was companion to Miss Mann facilitated an introduction to the Paulins, who took her on.

Most of Charlotte's work was done upstairs, mending, hairdressing, and generally looking after Irene Paulin. In due course she was given a room of her own. One of her best memories of the Paulins was when she told Mr. Paulin that she had a little brother with a hare lip. He was on the Board of the London Hospital in Whitechapel and had the boy operated on, success coming at the second attempt.

Charlotte remembered the lovely rose garden, orchards and prize cattle on the *Broadfields* farm. She had two weeks annual leave, but only half a day off each week, though this didn't stop her going out for walks. She stayed with the Paulins for about twelve years until she married in 1913, when her younger sister took her place. Charlotte died at the age of 108.

The Palmers Green and Southgate Gazette of 17th September 1921 told us, 'Fete Reflections. To all moderately long residents in Winchmore Hill, one of the most pleasing aspects of the opening ceremony of last Saturday's fete in Broomfield Park was the presence of Mr. and Miss Paulin on the platform .... During the war, the acute scarcity of fodder deprived Miss Paulin of her usual driving exercise; all pleasure horses went to the war or were used solely for utility purposes. Miss Paulin at once became a hard worker on and for the Citizens' Committee, Roseneath Auxiliary War Hospital, and, when it was later established, the Southgate War Pensions Committee .....'

The Baths tell us that on 10th May 1920 an auction was held by Tuckett, Webster & Co at Winchester House, Old Broad Street, EC2, when part of the 75 acre Fords Grove Estate was put up for sale in nine Lots. Lot 2 was of interest to Winchmore Hill Cricket Club, being described as, 'Freehold building land or eminently suitable for recreation or sports ground containing 20½ acres with frontage of about 2,350 feet in Ford's Grove and Firs Lane.' Following consultation with the Cricket Club's Officers William Thomas Paulin successfully bid £8,000 including expenses. He vested the freehold with his daughter Irene.

Under an indenture dated 2nd May 1921, from 29th September 1920 Irene leased about ten acres to the Cricket club at a rent of £120 pa for 5 years. At the same time she leased a further 4.5 acres (approximately) to The Collegiate School (featured with Paul Scott's account). She also leased three sites of around an acre each to St Paul's Church Choir, Holy Trinity Church Choir and The Congregational Church Club. However, from 25th March 1929 Miss Paulin granted a five year lease for the whole 20½ acres to The Cricket Club at a yearly rent of £200, although parts of the ground were still used by the other bodies. At Plate 56 is a snap of the Paulin Ground, as it is known, in July 1986.

In the 1929 New Years Honours List William Thomas was knighted for services to The London Hospital in Whitechapel, although he was helped in his work there by his daughter Irene. An undated article of early 1929 reported the knighthood and noted that he was President of the Men's Club at St. Paul's Institute. It said,

'Sir William has always been ready to support worthy causes in the district, and the number of individual cases in which he has interested himself and given a helping hand have been legion. He has done much for St. Paul's Church for many years, and quite recently was the donor of several hundreds of pounds to purchase a house for one of the assistant clergy. Local cricketers, footballers and tennis players have much to thank him for, as he has leased them ground for their sport, which would not have been available but for his interest. Sir William has been a Justice of the Peace for Middlesex for 36 years .... For many years, however, he has not sat upon the bench, neither has he taken part in public affairs in the district.

During the summer months he resides at *Broadfields*, except when visiting Scotland, where salmon fishing provides him with recreation. Most of the winter months he stays in his London flat, and is there at present. He will return to *Broadfields* when the weather is more congenial, and when he can enjoy the beautiful gardens and take an interest in the poultry and dairy which are part of the estate which preserves the rural atmosphere of a large area, which is now practically surrounded by the extension of suburbia ....'.

Another, unidentified, article of the era reported that, 'Sir William was unable to attend Wednesday's investiture owing to illness. He is 82, and is a director of Mann, Crossman and Paulin Limited. His knighthood was granted for services to the London Hospital, of which he has been a life governor over half a century. He has been a member of the committee since 1893 and honorary treasurer since 1913. Until his illness he visited the hospital almost daily, and he is one of the most familiar figures at that institution.' He is pictured in 1930 inside the back cover.

In a letter to me of 10th January 1990 the then Tower Hamlets Health Authority Archivist, R.J. Evans, wrote that, 'Sir William Paulin, brewer, did indeed have a close connection with the hospital, being a Governor in 1857, and later Hospital Treasurer, a post he filled until his death in 1930 (stet). As Treasurer, he was instrumental in raising large sums of money, upwards of six million pounds, which was raised under Lord Knutsford's Chairmanship of the hospital, through a series of appeals to the public. During Lord Knutsford's time as Chairman (1896 – 1931) the hospital underwent a very considerable re-building programme, but the inference that Sir William Paulin provided much of the money for this out of his own pocket is mistaken.'

Sir William passed away in February 1931. The following quotation seems to sum up his approach to life, 'I shall pass through this world but once: any good thing, therefore, I can do or any kindness that I can show to any human being, let me do it now, let me not defer it or neglect it, for I shall not pass this way again.' He did not, apparently, seek plaudits for his kindness, many of his donations for worthwhile causes being anonymous in his lifetime.

The Daily Telegraph of 11th June 1931 reported that, 'Sir William Thomas Paulin, of *Broadfields,* Winchmore-hill, N., vice-chairman of Mann, Crossman and Paulin Ltd., a past Master of the Brewers' Company, for over fifty years a life Governor of the London Hospital, and for many years hon. treasurer, left estate of the gross value of £617,667 with net personalty £535,500. The death duties will amount to over £175,000. ...... After bequests to relatives and servants the residue of the property is left on trust to his daughters, Irene and Ina.'

Enfield's Local Studies Unit houses a comprehensive set of papers relating to the sale of Paulin's local estates by Alfred Savill & Sons, in conjunction with E.J. Westoby, on 24th September 1931, at 155, Queen Victoria Street, EC4. To try and reproduce even a fraction of these here would be excessive, so I hope the reader will accept this brief summary. The prices quoted are taken from a *Wood Green Herald* article of 21st October 1931.

The largest Paulin holding was *Broadfields Estate*, consisting of about 14¼ acres. This fetched what, even in those days, was the rather unremarkable price of £7,750. *The Roseneath Estate* and two nearby cottages (one being *Rose* or *Hood's*), constituting about 14 acres, sold for £14,250, only for the mansion to be demolished in 1936. Five cottages in Station Road sold for £2,000. Nos. 2-6 (inc.) Burleigh Terrace in Wades Hill fetched £1,910, whilst the nearby four Broadfield Cottages (one of which was owner - occupied by Pauline Holstius at the time she gave me her account) attracted £1,035. The ten cottages in Harwoods Yard, which would today no doubt command a fortune, sold for only £2,375. Building land of 1¾ acres on Green Lanes went for £2,000.

The Wood Green Herald said that, 'We understand parts of the Estate were purchased by members of the Ingram family, well-known builders who have erected hundreds of houses here and elsewhere.'

Elsewhere in this book is an account for Mr. A.A.E. Westoby, which contains, 'In 1931 Arthur Ingram Senior bought Broadfields, putting in the roads Paulin Drive, Broadfields Avenue and Cresswell Way. He then sold off plots to other builders, and it was Readers of Chingford who put in the attractive houses in Broadfields Avenue. So it would seem that a small detail on Page 100 of my *A History of Winchmore Hill* is slightly in error if Mr. Westoby is correct'.

The Palmers Green and Southgate Gazette of 2nd October 1931 contained the snippet that, 'The Rev. G.H. Lancaster has been invited to be curator of a magnificent collection of British birds which Miss Paulin has presented to the Institute at St. Paul's Church, Winchmore Hill. Many of these birds were shot by Sir William Paulin, and were inhabitants of the Winchmore Hill district in the days when the locality was open country.'

Irene Paulin accepted the Presidency of Winchmore Hill Cricket Club upon the death of her father, and in 1934 renewed the lease of the ground to The Cricket Club for 14 years, committing it to being a permanently open space. She reduced the rent by a half during the Second World War, and offered a new lease for 35 years from March 1947, later extending this by six years to 1988. In respect for all the help the family had given, the Cricket Club decided to name its home The Paulin Ground in 1948.

Miss Irene passed away on 30th June 1960, her latter years being lived at Thorpe Abbotts Place, Diss in Norfolk. In her Will she granted the Club a 99 year lease from the 25th December after her death at the yearly rent of one shilling. She also made provision that the land should remain a recreation area in perpetuity.

The end of Mann, Crossman and Paulin

In 1959 Mann, Crossman and Paulin merged with Watney, Combe, Reid & Co. to form Watney Mann, but in 1972 the company was bought out by Grand Metropolitan, who closed the East End Albion Brewery in 1979. In the 1990s the entrance was converted into flats, and the site of The Brewery became a Sainsbury's.

Table 1
Beaumont, Roseneath, Laurel Lodge, Beaulieu and Broadfields occupancy through the years.

	Beaumont Lodge	*Roseneath*	*Laurel Lodge*	*Beaulieu*	*Broadfields*
1841 Census	----	----	----	Sarah Johnston	----
1851 Census	John Wade	----	----	Edward Johnston	----
1855 Kelly's	John Wade	James Mann	----	Edmund Johnstone	----
1859 Kelly's	John Wade	Thomas Mann	----	Edmund Johnston	----
1860 Kelly's	John Wade	Thomas Mann	----	Edmund Johnstone	----
1865 Kelly's	John Wade	Thomas Mann	----	?	----
1867 Kelly's	Robert John Chappell	Thomas Mann	----	Thomas Paulin	----
1871 Census	Robert John Chappell	Thomas Mann	----	Thomas Paulin	----
1872 Kelly's	Robert John Chappell	Thomas Mann	----	Thomas Paulin	----
1880 Kelly's	Thomas James Mann	Thomas Mann	----	Lewis Phillips	Mrs. Paulin
1884 Kelly's	Edwin Clarke	Thomas Mann	Edward Mann	Lewis Phillips	William T. Paulin

	Beaumont Lodge	*Roseneath*	*Laurel Lodge*	*Beaulieu*	*Broadfields*
1888 Kelly's	Edwin Clarke	Mrs. Mann	Edward Mann	Lewis Phillips	William T. Paulin
1891 Census	Lewis Phillips	Fanny Mann	Edward Mann	Lewis Phillips	William T. Paulin
1892 Kelly's	?	Mrs. Mann	Edward Mann	?	William T. Paulin
1899 – 1900 K's	Avondale Ladies' Sch.	Edward Mann	Frdk. C. Barry	Nothing	William T. Paulin J.P.
1903-4 Kelly's	Avondale Ladies' Sch.	Edward Mann	Charles Morgan	Nothing	William T. Paulin J.P.
1909-10 Kelly's	Avondale Ladies'Coll.	Sir Edward Mann bart.J.P..	Mrs. C. Morgan	Miss Martin	William T. Paulin J.P.
1916 Kelly's	Avondale College for Girls	Nothing	Jsph. B. Stennett	Nothing	William T. Paulin J.P.
1928 Kelly's	Avondale College for Girls	Roseneath Nursing Home	Jsph. B. Stennett	Edward Holsworth	William T. Paulin J.P.
1930 Kelly's	Nothing	Roseneath Nursing Home	Joseph. Stennett	Edward Holsworth	Sir William Paulin J.P.
1931 Kelly's	Nothing	Roseneath Nursing Home	Joseph. Stennett	Edward Holsworth	Sir William Paulin J.P
1932 Kelly's	Nothing	Roseneath Nursing Home	Joseph. Stennett	Mrs. Holsworth	Nothing
1935 Kelly's	Nothing	Roseneath Nursing Home	Joseph. Stennett	Mrs. Holsworth	Broadfields Garages

Additional Notes:

Laurel Lodge (later known as *The Laurels*) is not to be confused with *Laurel Cottage*, which was at the top of Church Hill.

Although I could not find John Wade or Beaumont Lodge in the 1841 Census return, he is shown in the 1840 Pigot's Street Directory, although no property of residence is shown. Though the 1845 Kelly's Directory doesn't list any mansions, John Wade and Edmund Johnson (stet) are both shown.

The 1851 Census does not specifically show *Beaumont Lodge*, but where one would expect it to be, just west of the Udalls and Beadles on Vicars Moor Lane, is the Wade family. Head of Household is John Wade, 67, Retired Woollen Draper, and his wife Fanny, 52. They have unmarried daughters Elizabeth, 29, and Sarah, 26, who were both born at Holborn, living with them, along with two female servants.

The 1872 Kelly's shows Thomas Mann jun. listed below Thomas Mann of *Roseneath,* but he is not shown against any property. Presumably he too was at *Roseneath.* The 1899-1900 Kelly's has Edward Mann at *Roseneath,* with Miss J. Mann across the road at *Elvington.* The 1903-4 Kelly's shows Edward Mann at *Roseneath,* but now Miss J. Mann is his next (easterly) door neighbour at *Rose Cottage*. The 1909 – 1910 Kelly's lists Sir Edward Mann bart. J.P. at *Roseneath*, but now a Frederick William Drake is at neighbouring *Rose Cottage.* The last five Kelly's shown indicate that Miss E.V. Monk was matron of Roseneath Nursing Home.

Table 2. 1891 Census Return for Broadfields & Broadfield Cottages (Since renumbered)

26 Wades Hill - Broadfield Cottages - House occupied, but no one slept there on the 5th, the occupants being in London.

27 Wades Hill - Broadfield Cottages

Charles Bennington – Head of Household – Married – aged 44 – Gardener (Domestic) – born Earith, Kent ;
Sabina Bennington – Wife – aged 46 yrs. – born Earith, Kent
Charles Bennington – Son – Single – aged 21 – Coachman Domestic – b. Earith, Kent
Harry Bennington – Son – 16 yrs. - Single – Telegraph Boy – b. Herts ., Waltham Cross
Albert Bennington - Son – 13 yrs. – Scholar – b. Middlesex, Winchmore Hill
Annie Bennington – 11 yrs.; Nelly Bennington - 9 yrs.; Flory Bennington - 6 yrs. –

all shown as Daughters; Cecil Bennington – Son – 2 yrs.
Annie, Nelly & Flory are all shown as being Scholars. They and Cecil are all shown as being born in Middlesex, Winchmore Hill.

28 Wades Hill - Broadfield Cottages

Alfred Atkins – Head of Household – Married - aged 48 yrs. Gardener Domestic – born Herts. Market Oak.
Harriet Atkins – Wife – Married - 49 – b. Herts, St. Albans
Rosa Atkins - Daughter – Single – 21 – Servant out of employment – b. Herts. St. Albans
Arthur Atkins – Son – Single – 18 years – Gardener – b. Middlesex, Winchmore Hill
Ethel E. Atkins – Daughter – 7 yrs. – Scholar – b. Middlesex, Winchmore Hill.
In more recent years I believe this cottage was occupied by Pauline Holstius.

29 Wades Hill - Broadfield Cottages

Amos Martin – Head of Household – Married – aged 55 – Coachman, domestic – Employed – Born Preston
Ann Martin – Wife – Married – aged 56 – Born Farnborough
George Martin - Son – Single – aged 24 yrs. – Coachman, domestic – Employed – Born Middlesex, Winchmore Hill.
Willie Martin – Son – Single – aged 22 yrs. - Groom domestic – Employed - Born Middlesex, Winchmore Hill.

30 Wades Hill - Broadfields

William T. Paulin - Head of Household – Married – aged 42 yrs. – Brewer – Employer – Born Middlesex, Bethnal Green
Fanny Paulin – Wife – Married – aged 39 yrs. – b. Middlesex, Stoke Newington
Fanny I. R. Paulin – Daughter – aged 12 yrs. born Middx, Winchmore Hill;
Mary J.I. Paulin - Daughter - aged 8 yrs. – b. Middx, Winchmore Hill
Isabel Paulin – William's Sister – Single – 48 yrs. – b. Middlesex, Thand on the Green
George – William's Brother – Single – 38 years - Underwriter – born Middlesex, Stoke Newington
Emma Honey – Servant – Single - aged 39 years – Cook (Domestic Servant) – b. ?,, Crawley Moor
Charlotte Lyne – Servant - Single - aged 27 yrs. - Parlour Maid (Domestic Servant) – b. Huntingdon, Ellington
Elizabeth H. Bavestock – Servant - Single – aged 24 yrs. – House Maid (Domestic Servant) – b. Middlesex, St. Pancras
Emma Champkens – Servant – Single - 30 – Nurse (Domestic Servant) – b. Bedfordshire, Henlow
Ada M. Cressee – Servant – Single – 22 – Nurse (Domestic Servant) – b, Surrey, Brixton.
Ellen Pretty – Servant – Single – 20 – Kitchen maid (Domestic Servant) – b. Suffolk, Northam.

Norris Mc Whirter - Revisited

Winchmore Hill Lives (A Collection of Recollections) featured the following account by one of the area's more illustrious sons, Norris Mc Whirter. It was submitted by letter in March 1990, and I have included it in this section, as I feel that Norris's achievements were such as to place him firmly in the category of 'the great and the good'.

Born: 12 August, 1925, 10, Branscombe Gardens, N21.

My father William married my mother Margaret ('Bunty') Williamson in Giffnock Church on the southern edge of their native Glasgow on 10 September, 1922. They had purchased a new house in Branscombe Gardens and, understandably, named it "Giffnock". Unfortunately the house was not ready for occupation immediately and so the *Sunday Pictorial*, of which my father had been appointed editor, temporarily accommodated the couple in the Savoy Hotel – a different era indeed!

The house in Branscombe Gardens was one of the first built in what was one of the first roads constructed over the slowly developed Winchmore Hill Wood. (See Figure 1) It was on the junction with Denleigh Gardens and was available for occupation in early 1923. It had a quite capacious rear garden which boasted a tennis court although this has now been replaced by a further house. It was in 1923 that my brilliant elder brother Kennedy was born, my twin brother Ross and I following on in 1925. We are pictured together in our garden at Plate 59.

My father, his future brother-in-law Jim Williamson, Harry Muir (later a long time resident of The Mall) and 'Bud' Grant (who later succeeded my father as editor of the *Sunday Pictorial*) had made a pact that they would stay together in the ranks during the Great War. They joined the Ross Mounted Battery in the Fourth Highland Brigade and served in Egypt, Greece and Mesopotamia, entering and rigorously staying as private soldiers.

After the war my father employed his old NCO, Sergeant West, as family chauffer. (See Plate 60.) West always referred to his employer as 'The General'. Some of the local tradesmen, such as Miss Tidey's newspaper shop and Aldridge's greengrocers on The Green actually elevated him through at least the twelve ranks necessary, addressing their weekly bills to General Mc Whirter! My mother rapidly disillusioned them.

West drove our brown and highly polished Darracq car wearing a brown uniform, a cap and gleaming leather leggings. When dispatched to meet a train at King's Cross or Euston (both parents possessing first class London-Glasgow season tickets) he would give an unsolicited running commentary on the route home. He particularly relished pointing out Hilldrop Crescent, Holloway, where 'the late Dr. Crippen did foully murder his wife by carving her up and putting the pieces under the kitchen floorboards'.

My parents joined the Bounds Green Lawn Tennis Club and my father turned out in goal for Broomfield Football Club until the burdens of Fleet Street robbed him of almost all his leisure.

My mother, as was the norm in those days, stayed at home to tend to domestic matters despite her own potential in the journalistic field. She was of a kind disposition and built up a queue to our kitchen of tramps and door-to door salesmen temporarily unemployed.

It is probably hard for some of your readers to comprehend the degree of poverty that once existed in the now prosperous area but I know that others of your older contributors also bear witness on this point. In those days, of course, there was no Welfare State safety net. Anyway my father discovered that chalk signs had been put on our gateposts by some altruistic member of my mother's clientele to indicate to others of the down-and-out fraternity that the mistress of the house was a soft touch. My father arranged that henceforward there would be some selectivity to thin the throng.

Nonetheless, it was not until Britain's much belated rearmament got under way that the situation began to ease with lessening unemployment.

In 1929, my father, who by this time was establishing the chain of eleven new provincial papers known as Northcliffe Newspapers, decided to move home to a larger establishment in the shape of a house called *Aberfoyle* (now renamed *Grovelands*), only just over a quarter of a mile away in the adjoining but then unmade road of Broad Walk.

Aberfoyle had been built for his own use by a local builder named Still in 1920. It was thus of very solid construction and stood in one and a half acres of wooded garden. Beyond the back garden was the lovely Grovelands Park. The house contained seven bedrooms, four public rooms and three bathrooms. The staff, numbering eight, consisted of the cook Doris Cotton (who later married the milkman Frank Smith), two living-in maids (sisters Polly and Bertha Cable), nurse Edith Merlane, the 15 stone laundress Mrs. Burrows, the daily Queenie Smith, a chauffer named Stevens and the gardener Mr. Gosden of Wilson Street.

Like Ross and Kennedy, I was educated at Marlborough College and Oxford University. Kennedy took an M.Sc. at Manchester University and went on to gain recognition for his excellence as a geneticist in the form of his Professorial appointment at the University of Alberta. Unfortunately he passed away in 1989 when completing the index of a book on ancient languages.

Ross and I followed a different path to Kennedy's. We both became sports journalists in 1950 and in 1951 published a history of athletics entitled *Get To Your Marks*. In that same year we established an agency to provide facts, figures and features to Fleet Street. It was in 1954 that we were invited by the Guinness brewery to compile a book on records and extremes in various fields. The resulting *The Guinness Book of Records* became, of course, a world famous multi million seller. Unfortunately the success was clouded when after twenty one years of co-editing the book with me Ross was murdered by the IRA in nearby Enfield on 27 November, 1975.

I'm sure that if my brothers were still with us today they would verify that we all looked with affection on the Winchmore Hill of our formative years.

More on Norris

On the evening of Monday 19th April 2004 Norris fell ill whilst playing tennis at his home in Wiltshire and died of a heart attack, aged 78. The news was reported in all the national papers. *The Enfield Gazette* also published an obituary. I think that these articles reveal Mr. Mc Whirter to have been somewhat modest in his original account, and so I now add the following about him, as kindly co - drafted through the post by his widow Tessa, and son Alasdair.

As a young athlete Norris had represented Scotland and Britain and was a timekeeper and the announcer when Roger Bannister broke the four minute mile barrier on 6th May 1954. In 2004 *The Daily Mail* ran a feature which explained that in April 1954 the BBC had launched its programme *Sportsview* and Norris had called on one of its main producers, named Paul Fox, to persuade him to send a camera to Iffley Road track in Oxford to cover the event. Fortunately the BBC sent a team and it was preserved for posterity on film. Norris was the man who announced the new record to the crowd.

Norris later became a sports journalist and was athletics correspondent to the London *Evening Star* and *The Observer* before joining the BBC as a sports commentator. He covered the 1956 Olympic Games in Melbourne and the subsequent ones in Rome, Tokyo, Mexico City and Munich.

1954 was the year that he and his twin Ross started the *Guinness Book of Records*, though the first edition did not appear until 1955. He edited the book until 1986. It had been commissioned by the Guinness brewery and until 1997 it was published from an office in London Road, Enfield. Only a few months before his death, Mr. Mc Whirter had hosted a London reception to celebrate the sale of 100 million copies of the *Guinness Book.*

In 1960 Norris married his first wife Carole, who died in 1987, by whom he had a son named Alasdair and a daughter named Jane. In 1964 he stood unsuccessfully as a Conservative candidate in Orpington, Kent. In the same year Ross stood as Conservative candidate in Edmonton, also unsuccessfully, at a time when the tide was turning in Labour's favour. Ross, in 1967, famously issued a writ against Enfield Council to try and prevent it making all its Secondary Schools Comprehensive. In 1972 Mr. Mc Whirter started a 23-year stint on the BBC children's show *Record Breakers*, hosted by Roy Castle, in which he answered questions from the audience on records.

Ross was shot dead by the IRA in November 1975, in his Village Road home, after he and Norris had formed the right wing lobby group called *The Freedom Association*, which promoted the free market, individual freedom and limited government and opposed the EEC. On the advice of the police, Ross had been buried in an unmarked grave in an unspecified north London cemetery. I remember feeling particularly shocked by Ross's death at the time, not to mention a little frightened, because I was living only a stone's throw away in Radcliffe Road.

Norris was awarded the CBE in 1980 and in 1991 married his second wife, Tessa.

Not long after the 1991 *Winchmore Hill Lives* was published, Norris kindly treated Yasmin and myself to a meal at La Fondue restaurant on the Green, to discuss the book and wish me well with it. We both found him a very pleasant man.

In 1994 Norris co-wrote a book which criticised the European Union for undermining the British Constitution. He was also an honorary Member of the British Weights and Measures Association (BWMA), which opposes the EU related compulsory programme of metrication in the UK. I attended a talk he gave to one of that society's AGMs a few years ago. He looked in good health and drew out his unhappiness at some of the constitutional aspects associated with the programme, and his belief that it was allied to the creation of a European superstate.

Upon his death Tessa and his two children issued a statement which said, 'Norris cared passionately about Great Britain, democracy and the rule of law and was always active in politics but usually behind the scenes. Apart from his family, his great loves were visiting the 1,049 offshore British islands and having a good game of tennis.' His friend of 60 years, Sir Roger Bannister, said that he had 'kept his courage' through personal tragedies and 'never lost his total conviction in the greatness of Britain .... He was a human dynamo.'

Despite a life of outstanding achievement, the death of his twin was a particularly heavy blow and he once said that 15 minutes never went by without thinking of Ross. He was also at great odds with the direction the UK was going in relation to the

EU. However, Tessa ensured that the final fourteen years were some of his happiest.

Sir Hugh Myddelton (c. 1560 - 1631) & The New River

Running north – south through the length of Winchmore Hill is the man made New River. In 1606 Parliament granted power to the Corporation of London 'for the bringing in a fresh Stream of Running Water to the North parts of the City of London.' The Act provided powers to construct a 'New River for bringing water to London from Chadwell and Amwell in Hertfordshire.' The City gave this task to merchant adventurer Hugh Myddelton, and he started the work on 21st April 1609 at Chadwell Spring. (See Plate 61.)

The course of the River was constructed along the 100-foot contour for a total distance of nearly 40 miles to its, then, final distribution point by Saddlers Wells in Islington. Its fall over this distance was, incredibly, a mere 18 feet. The New River was opened on 29th September, 1613, by the Lord Mayor of London, Sir John Swinnerton, in the presence of the Lord Mayor elect, Sir Thomas Myddelton - Hugh's brother.

At Bush Hill, Salmons Brook was originally spanned by a bridge and an aqueduct. In 1682 the bridge was replaced by an arch named after the Earl of Clarendon. It was rebuilt in 1725, and is now a Grade 11 listed structure. The wooden aqueduct was exactly a furlong (1/8th mile) in length. It carried the New River in a 6' wide, 5' deep lead lined trough. The wooden arches were 24' above Salmons Brook, and locally the New River was, apparently, referred to as 'Myddelton's boarded river'. The old 'Frame' was replaced by the present clay embankment in 1786.

Over the years the route of the River has been altered somewhat, and today the river's southern termination is at Stoke Newington. But it still rises near the River Lea, and a spring, nearly 160 feet across, known locally as 'the banjo', can yield up to a million gallons of water a day.

So who was the mastermind behind this remarkable piece of engineering? The following is mainly based on JW Gough's *Sir Hugh Myddelton, Entrepreneur & Engineer,* published by Oxford University Press in 1964.

In spite of their English surname the Myddeltons of Denbighshire were an old Welsh family, who claimed descent from Rhirid Flaidd, one of the nobility of medieval North Wales. The original spelling seems to have been different, when, in the 14th century, one of them married the daughter of Sir Alexander Middleton, of Middleton near Chirbury, in Shropshire.

In the 16th century the main line of the Denbigh Myddeltons was established at Gwaenynog, a couple of miles west of the town. Richard was the first member sent by Denbigh to Parliament in 1542, and he was Governor of Denbigh Castle at the start of Elizabeth's reign in 1558. He married Jane Dryhurst, and had his home at Galch Hill, now a farm between the town and Gwaenynog.

Hugh Myddelton was the sixth of Richard's nine sons, though the exact date of his birth is uncertain. It is usually taken to have been in, or around, 1560. He went up to London in 1576, and on 2nd April he was apprenticed to Thomas Hartop (also spelt Hartopp or Hartoppe) of the Goldsmiths' Company. As a goldsmith he learned and practised the craft of making and testing articles of gold and silver, but goldsmiths also dealt extensively in precious metals, coined money, and carried out many of the money changing and lending functions currently carried out by banks. In these early days he is believed to have set up shop in Cheapside. Hugh's name first appears as a liveryman of the Goldsmiths' Company in 1592.

He visited the Netherlands in 1585, and soon after his return he married Anne, daughter of Richard Collins of Lichfield. In 1589 the brothers Hugh, Thomas and Foulk participated in the Goldsmiths' Voyage against Spain. Unfortunately Anne died childless on 11th January 1597, aged only 54, being buried in St. Matthew's, Friday Street, where her husband worshiped for many years, and where he was church warden in 1598 - 9 and 1599 - 1600.

In 1598 Elizabeth Olmstead became Hugh's second wife, by about which time it is thought he had moved to Wood Street. Hugh's first engineering project, in about 1600, was the, 'seeking of coale for the town of Denbighe', but this proved a failure. He represented Denbigh in Parliament from 1603 to 1628. In 1604, and again in 1605, he was made a Warden of the Goldsmiths' Company, and in 1610 he was made Prime Warden, achieving this office once more in 1624. On 9th May 1611 James 1 went to the Star Chamber to have his gold and silver tested by a Jury of 16 Goldsmiths, headed by Hugh Myddelton.

Hugh, it will be recalled, was a member of James 1's Parliament, as were his brothers Sir Thomas and Robert, who was MP for Weymouth. All three sat on the Committee concerned with bringing water to the City. Hugh's brother, Sir Thomas, was Lord Mayor of London in 1614.

During the building of The New River Hugh lived just north of Winchmore Hill at a mansion on the site of Bush Hill House (more recently known, before its demise in 1993, as 'Halliwick'). Whilst there he became a trustee of the then recently founded Latymer School. 'Halliwick' has now gone, but on its former site there is a Blue Plaque to Hugh's residency from 1609 – 13, captured at P178 of **Winchmore Hill Village 1780 – 1830.**

On 21st June 1619 a charter of incorporation was granted to 'The Governor and Company of the New River brought from Chadwell and Amwell to London'. Hugh was named as the first Governor, and the constitution of the company was unusual. Although he was not involved in the running of the company, the King held a half share in it (a moiety as it was called), yet he was not supposed to be able to incorporate himself!

James 1 created a new title of baronet, which was offered to any knight or esquire with land worth £1,000 p.a. who was prepared to pay £1,080 in three annual instalments. Sir Hugh was made a baronet on 19th October 1622, being titled Sir Hugh 'of Ruthin in the county of Denbigh', but he was exempt from the normal fee, as it was intended as an honour in return for three acts of distinction. These were the creation of the New River, reclaiming land at Brading Haven on the Isle of Wight, and finding silver in Cardiganshire.

James discouraged competition, but in 1625 Charles 1 succeeded him, and he was happy for competitors to the New River Company to spring up. In the changed circumstances the new King gave his moiety (half share in the business) to Sir Hugh in return for a guarantee from him personally, with no claim on the company, of an annuity of £500 p.a. from Michaelmas 1630. This came to be known as the Crown Clog, or King's Clog.

In 1631 brother Thomas died on 12th August, aged about 81, Sir Hugh following on 7th December. On 10th December he was buried near his first wife at St. Matthew's, Friday Street. He left Bush Hill House, including its content, to Lady Myddelton, where she spent the rest of her widowed life. She died on 19th July 1643, aged 63, and was buried at Edmonton All Saint's Church. She had borne her husband seven sons and eight daughters, though not all survived infancy.

In 1845 a statue of Sir Hugh by Samuel Joseph was placed in a niche on the north side of the newly rebuilt Royal Exchange, and in 1862 a marble statue by John Thomas, together with a drinking fountain, was erected in Islington Green, being inaugurated by the then Chancellor, William Gladstone. This is pictured at Plate 62. Sir Hugh's name lives on in Winchmore Hill in the street name of Myddelton Gardens, and his memory is also commemorated in other street names in north London. Quite an achievement for someone who, apparently, had no mathematical or technical training!

We Don't Want No New River

At The Green Dragon ale house this lunch hour
A real fine dandy walked in
He spoke with the brogue of a Welshman
And to me what came forth was a sin

He said that he planned a new river
To run near Tilebarrow Field
Or was it the strong ale talking
'Cos the idea it didn't seem real

I say we don't need no new river
Flooding our fine stacks of hay
A danger to all of our children
If they should trip out at play

This Myddelton spoke of great progress
How the river would benefit all
Bringing spring water to London
To me it's just arrogant gall

It's true there'll be work for my brother
And the water might help in a drought
But it will cut through the edge of our village
And ruin the ale houses no doubt

I dare not broadcast my feelings
Or I might be out of a job
Who cares for the views of a poor man?
Afeared to lose his weekly few bob

I've heard of the many fine galleons
That navigate over the seas
But man don't alter the oceans
There ain't no felling of trees!

I tell you it can't be natural
It must be offensive to God
To try and construct a new river
Over land where man's always trod

I say we don't need no new river
Flooding our fields of fine grain
I'm sure the good Lord is frowning
And he'll send down gallons of rain

We don't want no new river
No, we don't need no new river

© Stuart Delvin 9th February 2011

Humphry Repton (1752 - 1818)

According to the *National Trust Magazine* for Autumn 2002 Repton vies with 'Capability' Brown for the title of English landscape gardening's most prolific designer, although they were contrasting characters. Brown, who was bluff and unpretentious, rose from humble origins as a working gardener to acquire an estate of 13,000 acres and dine with King George 111. Repton, on the other hand, had the affected foppish airs of a gentleman, despite the fact that he didn't grow wealthy! It is estimated that Repton took 400 commissions between the ages of 36, when he took up landscape gardening, and 65, when he died.

The Trust's garden historian, Katie Fretwell, said that, 'Repton revived the idea of creating a garden by the house for the enjoyment of the family, with the landscaped park beyond it.' He made homely touches like kitchen gardens and terraces fashionable once more whereas Brown, in striving for a natural setting, tended to strand his houses in a sea of pasture.

A small softback on Humphry Repton by Kay N. Sanecki for Shire Books in 1974 (ISBN 0 85263 273 8} tells us that Humphrey Repton was born at Bury St. Edmunds, Suffolk, on 21st April 1752, the second child of John and Martha Repton. During Humphry's schooldays his family moved to Norwich and, having begun his education at Bury St. Edmunds Grammar school, he continued it at the grammar school in Norwich until he was twelve years of age. In 1764 he was sent to continue his education in the Netherlands.

At 16 he returned home to Norwich and took up an apprenticeship in the textile trade. In May 1773 he married Mary Clarke, upon his turning 21. They had 16 children, seven of whom survived into adulthood. About this time his father set him up in business as a general merchant in Norwich. He did quite well at this, but on inheriting his parents' wealth in 1778, he retired to the countryside to live the life of a Squire. He moved to the village of Sustead, north of Norwich, but in 1783 the family moved to humbler accommodation in Harestreet, Essex. With a growing family he decided that, in an effort to earn more money, he would become a landscape gardener, earning his first commission in 1788.

From the beginning Repton applied his skill as a water colourist and writer in explaining his proposals to his clients. This he did in the form of a 'Red Book' about 12 by 9 inches in size, handsomely bound in red Moroccan leather. He used a revolutionary overlay system for his landscape illustrations, which included the final revelation of the envisaged end state.

In 1794-5 Repton entered into a partnership with John Nash, which only lasted until 1799. During this time Repton improved the grounds of the Brighton Pavilion and landscaped the grounds around John Nash's Grovelands Mansion of 1797-8. We can still see the essence of Repton's work preserved in Grovelands Park, explaining why his name is commemorated in the flats overlooking the Upper Green – and his brief inclusion in this book!

Humphry sustained a bad spinal injury in a carriage accident on 29th January 1811, from which he never properly recovered, and he died on 24th March 1818 at his Harestreet home.

Cliff and a Shadow

The Local Studies Unit has an array of books on one of the most famous of the area's former inhabitants. For the following account I consulted *The Biography: Cliff Richard* by Steve Turner,1993 (ISBN 07459 2249X) and *It's Great to Be Young* by Cliff Richard,1960. In addition, I also referred to my own books on The Shadows - *The Story of The Shadows, An Autobiography with Mike Read* (ISBN 0-241-10861-6), 1983, and *Rock 'n' Roll - I Gave You the Best Years of My Life* by Bruce Welch,1989 (ISBN 0-670-82705-3).

Having drafted an account using all those, at Christmas 2010 I received *My Life, My Way* – Cliff's 2008 autobiography (ISBN 978 - 0 - 7553 - 1589 - 5), from my eldest niece, Anushka, who somehow seems to have (wrongly) interpreted my regard for The Shadows as extending to Cliff, so I have used that too.

Both of Cliff Richard's parents were of British Caucasian background, but had been born abroad. His father, Rodger, was born in Burma, his mother, Dorothy, in India, which is where they met. Cliff was born as Harry Rodger Webb in Lucknow, India on 14th October 1940, and in September 1948 the family returned to what they viewed as their homeland, even though they had never actually seen it, following India's independence.

The family moved near to Dorothy's mother, who was living in a three bed roomed semi detached house in Carshalton, Surrey. Harry enrolled at Stanley Park Road Primary School, Carshalton, where in those less tolerant times, and despite being white, he was racially abused because he had a tan and spoke with an Indian accent.

Rodger was 16 years older than his wife and, being in his forties, found getting a job difficult, though eventually he found a menial post in Essex, requiring a complicated two hour commute each way. He chose to do that, rather than take state benefits, which he looked on as charity. The family was so poor that the shoes Harry wore to school each day were worn by his mother when she worked night shifts. His father was a disciplinarian, who once caned Harry when he learned he had already been caned at school for some misdeed! In his autobiography the singer respects the discipline that he received.

In late 1949 the family moved in with Rodger's sister Dorothy, and her husband, in Hertfordshire. By now the family consisted of Rodger, Dorothy, Harry, and his sisters Donna, Jacqui and Joan, yet they were living in only one room! A neighbour who worked for the council was shocked and told her housing officer, who put the Webbs at the top of his list. So it was that on 11th April 1951 the Webbs moved into a brand new

Cheshunt Council house at 12, Hargreaves Close in Cheshunt.

Still the children slept on mattresses on the floor, finally progressing to beds made by Rodger from packing cases he bought from Atlas Lamps, who were his new employers. Atlas were a part of Thorn Electrical Industries on the Great Cambridge Road, Enfield, which also incorporated Ferguson Radio Corporation. Rodger became a blue collar worker in the credit control office, whilst mother Dorothy Marie sorted components on the assembly line.

Cliff – or Harry as he still was then – had been top boy in his last year at primary school, so it was something of a surprise and disappointment when he failed his 11 Plus in 1952. He enrolled at Cheshunt Secondary Modern School, where he again initially met racial abuse, until he proved himself a good footballer, whence it stopped. He was sufficiently talented to represent his school at Rugby and Hertfordshire Schools at soccer. His English and drama teacher Jay Norris brought out his ability to sing. One day he and his pals played truant in order to get tickets to see the new rock and roll sensation Bill Haley perform at the Regal, Edmonton, which led to him being stripped of his prefect's badge.

By now, despite his reluctance to sing in public he was besotted with the idea of becoming the new Elvis Presley, and he started practising. This distracted him from his studies, and so in 1957 when he sat his 'O' Levels he only passed in English. Rodger bought his son a £27 guitar, and through his experience as a trad jazz banjo player when young, was able to teach him about chords. In his autobiography Harry says, 'After a summer job picking tomatoes, I started at Atlas Lamps, where my father had found me a job. By day, I clocked in as a filing clerk, which bored me witless, on £4 a week; by night I played rock 'n' roll in pubs and youth clubs'.

Harry's heart was in rock 'n' roll, but a local skiffle band, led by Dick Teague, was looking for a singer, and he got the job. This allowed him to build up experience in local pubs and village halls. After a while he and drummer Terry Smart left to form their own more rock 'n' roll oriented band with Harry's former schoolmate Norman Mitham on guitar. They rehearsed every night at Harry's home, and called themselves The Drifters. Early in 1958 whilst playing *The Five Horseshoes* in Hoddesdon they met 'agent' John Foster, and agreed to meet him on the Green Line bus the following Saturday in order to audition at the 2i's coffee bar in Soho, which was then a mecca for rock 'n' roll. They passed the afternoon audition, and started a week's run that evening, playing for peanuts.

There was no overnight success, but they did meet Ian Samwell, who was to become their lead guitarist, and who was to write Harry's first hit, *Move It.* Harry Greatorex, who ran a ballroom in Ripley, Derbyshire, wanted to book them as Harry Webb and the Drifters, but Harry wanted to be known as just The Drifters. Greatorex wouldn't have this because he wanted a front man. Still Harry couldn't consent, so they went off to the pub and agreed on his new stage name Cliff Richard, which Harry felt had more star quality to it. Cliff also felt that his Teddy Boy style stage clothes were an important part of his developing persona. At one stage he performed in a talent show held at the Capitol Cinema in Winchmore Hill (now the site of the Inland Revenue offices – see Plate 64), where he sang Frankie Laine's *A Woman in Love,* which won him second place.

After a few more well received gigs Ian Samwell put the group in touch with agent George Ganjou, who introduced them to Norrie Paramour, Artiste and Repertoire

(A & R) Manager for Columbia Records. They made a £5- demo' at the HMV shop in Oxford Street. George gave it to Norrie, who played it to his teenage daughter. She thought it wonderful, and so the group were invited to No.2 studio at Abbey Road to record an American hit song called *Schoolboy Crush.* On the 'B' side was the song *Move It,* guitarist Ian 'Sammy' Samwell had written when sitting on the top of a Green Line bus between Cheshunt and Oxford Street in London!

Norrie Paramour said that one day in 1958 he received a demo' recording and, 'liked the noise on the record and sent for this youngster, who was an office boy somewhere, in Enfield I think, and he brought his group along. He (Cliff) said that Ian Samwell had written a song that might be all right to put on the back. It was called *Move It* ..... The Drifters were not quite complete in those days. I hired an extra bass player and guitarist and a vocal group I wanted to use on the other tune called *Schoolboy Crush* ....' The session musicians were Frank Clarke on double bass, and Ernie Shears, who played the riffs Samwell had devised on lead guitar. They were each paid a £6.10s session fee. Ian Samwell played rhythm guitar, with Terry Smart on drums.

On 9th August 1958 Cliff turned professional, and gave up his job at Ferguson's. The group played a short season at the Butlins at Clacton, during which time Norman Mitham decided to leave, to be replaced by Ken Pavey, a guitarist they had met there. On 13th September 1958 Cliff performed *Move It* on the TV programme *Oh Boy!,* which helped the record to achieve a No. 2 chart placing. The record was perhaps the first 'classic' British rock 'n' roll record, and Cliff has continued to regularly perform it throughout his long career. It featured strongly in the Queen's Golden Jubilee Celebrations in 2002.

The success of the so called 'B' side led agent George Ganjou to get a spot on the Kalin Twins' forthcoming tour, but Ken Pavey wasn't keen, which just left drummer Terry Smart and (by now) bass player Ian Samwell backing vocalist Cliff. Two guitarists were required and so John Foster went back to the 2is, where Bruce Welch was working. Bruce was down from Newcastle with his friend Hank Marvin, and the two 16 year olds were playing with the Chesternuts. Foster offered Hank a job, and he accepted so long as his friend could come on board too. And so it was that Bruce became Cliff's rhythm guitarist, Hank the lead guitarist.

The tour kicked off at Hanley in Staffordshire on 5th October 1958, and the group proved more popular than the headlining Kalins. Also on the package tour was bass player Jet Harris, who asked to join. As he was better on the instrument than Ian Samwell, Cliff asked John Foster to sack Ian and hire Jet – which he duly did. Cliff then invited Tony Meehan, who had also played at the 2i's, to replace the less capable Terry Smart on drums, and Terry went off to join the Merchant Navy. Jet and Tony had been with Hank in Wally Whyton's backing group called The Vipers (currently the name of a Shadows tribute band, who played at The Millfield Theatre in the Spring of 2010).

And so we arrive at the line up of Marvin, Welsh, Harris and Meehan that has consistently - obviously perversely – been referred to as 'the original line up'! Harris and Meehan did not stay many years, despite their great success. Tony Meehan died a few years ago to little publicity, but early in 2011 Jet succumbed to cancer and received a substantial write up in the national press, acknowledging his contribution to popular music.

Cliff says that after the Kalins tour things 'went crazy'. He sacked his agent George Ganjou and 'relegated' John Foster to road manager, getting in the Canadian

Franklyn Boyd as his manager. Cliff won a bit part in the film *Serious Charge*, and appeared regularly on TV's *Oh Boy!*, but his new manager felt he was too inexperienced, and so insisted on more touring. In late 1958 Cliff also appeared in a variety show at the Finsbury Park Empire. He and the band were so exhausted that Cliff could no longer even sing, and he became ill. His father made sure all his commitments were cancelled and Cliff went home to Cheshunt for two weeks total rest. Cliff says that it was at this stage that he learnt how important it is to rehearse, and to put all personal problems aside so that the only aim of an appearance is to entertain the public.

The film *Serious Charge* featured a Lionel Bart song called *Living Doll*, done as a rock 'n' roll number, which they didn't feel worked well, but they were contracted to record the song. One evening on tour Bruce came up with a more laid back country approach. The resulting arrangement sold nearly two million copies and spent six weeks at number one in 1959. The Drifters, as they still were at this time, started to release records of their own, one of which was *Feelin' Fine*. This was released in the USA, where there was already a well established vocal group called The Drifters, who threatened a legal action. So it was that, at Jet Harris's suggestion, the English Drifters became The Shadows.

Around then Cliff replaced Franklyn Boyd as his manager with Tito Burns. That arrangement lasted about two years, until Burns was replaced in turn by the Australian Frank Gormley, after The Shadows had signed for him. Incredibly, in his first year in post Gormley wouldn't take payment from Cliff, as he felt everything had already been set up by Boyd! Cliff writes glowingly of Gormley and his record producer Norrie Paramor, who performed the same key role for Cliff and The Shadows that George Martin did for The Beatles.

In January 1960 Cliff toured North America, accompanied by both of his parents. The tour in the winter cold was by poorly heated Greyhound buses, travelling vast distances at a stretch. Cliff's Dad was now in his fifties and it seems likely that the strain contributed to him becoming ill. Having been a heavy smoker, he developed a bad cough, but the doctors didn't establish what was wrong soon enough. On returning to England the Impresario Leslie Grade sent his own doctor to look at Rodger, and he rushed him to intensive care at Winchmore Hill's Highlands Hospital, where he was immediately put in an oxygen tent. Cliff is reported as saying, 'I don't know whether he knew he was dying but he was such a stubborn man. They actually caught him once undoing the oxygen tent from the inside so that he could have a smoke ...'.

It was about this time that Cliff had a clandestine affair with Carol Costa, wife of Jet Harris, who had a drink problem. His father found out about it and severely scolded Cliff, saying it was against Christian beliefs to have an affair with a married woman. Just prior to the social revolution that seemed to come in 1963, with the Beatles and the Profumo scandal, such a thing was still generally frowned upon, so any adverse publicity might ruin Cliff's career. He called the affair off, but as so often he did this through someone else, in this case by asking drummer Tony Meehan to ring Carol. The affair has resonated through the decades, and in recent years it has been cited in the national press as part of the reason why Jet wasn't invited on the band's 50th Anniversary World Tour.

In those days Cliff's record income was something like 1d per record sold, meaning he would need to sell 240 records to make £1. Even so, his records were selling so well that in May 1960, following the American tour, Cliff bought his parents their first ever owner-occupied house for £7,000 – the four bed roomed semi at the corner of Colne Road, Winchmore Hill, pictured at Plate 63. His wealth also enabled both his parents to give up work, whilst Cliff paid for little 'luxuries' such as a taxi for his Mum to have her hair done every week. Finally, on 15th May 1961 Rodger died from heart disease at Highlands Hospital, whilst still only 57. Cliff regretted that his father never saw him go on to achieve all that he did.

The loss hit Cliff particularly hard, and influenced him in his well known turn to Christianity. However, five months after Rodger passed away he and The Shadows toured Australia and New Zealand, where he was better liked than in America. Just prior to departure Bruce Welch and Tony Meehan had a blazing row, leading to Tony's departure from the band, and his replacement by local boy Brian Bennett. The tour was a great success, as were the early 1962 film and record *The Young Ones.*

In April 1962 Jet's drinking was getting to be a major problem, and he was replaced by Brian 'Licorice' Locking, upon the recommendation of Brian Bennett. It was 'Licorice' who further pushed Cliff towards Christianity because, unusually for a pop musician,he was a Jehovah's Witness. He had converted to the sect after meeting Brian Bennett's mother, Hilda, who had brought young Brian up as a Witness, only for him to resign upon departing home. Through his commitment to the religion 'Licorice' resigned from the band only 18 months after joining. (Incidentally, Hank Marvin has long been a Jehovah's Witness too.) In 1964 Cliff met Bill Latham, and became a staunch Christian, which he remains to this day.

Cliff says that he was 12 ½ stone when making the *Young Ones*, and he lost 1½ stone by the time of his successful 1963 follow up film and album *Summer Holiday.* Cliff boasts he is still that 11 stone today, which would seem to be rather on the low side for a man of 5' 10 ½".

During this period of exceptional success Cliff, it will be remembered, was living at 2, Colne Road. At one point he hired a young Irish tour manager named Mike Conlin, who they'd met at the 2i's, and he moved into the corner house with Cliff so that he was available 24 hours a day. Although the house was unglamorous it contained items that in those days weren't necessarily the norm. There was a telephone, a stereo record player, a 21 inch television (black and white only, of course), a radiogram, a leather topped bar, and wall to wall carpeting.

Cliff told reporters, 'This house and everything in it is all paid for. It will last us a lifetime.' He tried to live a normal family life there, but it proved impossible, as the house was often besieged by fans. The front gate had to be padlocked, and the garden fence was raised two feet to prevent intruders. Ten year old Sheila Teague was a friend of Cliff's youngest sister Joan, and would spend weekends at Winchmore Hill. She remembered that his room was in the roof, being accessed through a door on the landing, which looked as if it was the airing cupboard. She said,

'When you opened the door you went up this beautiful deep blue velvet carpet to Cliff's room. It was like a concealed room and I remember it being green and yellow with sheepskin rugs. We were all very poor and so seeing a taxi arrive for Cliff's Mum to take her to the hairdresser was like watching royalty. Cliff wasn't big headed though. He was very calm, very relaxed and very casual. He showed a lot of love to his sisters and he'd often spend time in the garden with his dog getting it to bite on the end of a rag and then swinging it around. He took us all out in his car sometimes but when he tried to park he would get recognised and he found he just couldn't go shopping.'

His mother was reported as saying, 'He has very faithful fans. There were four from Liverpool, four from Birmingham. They would travel anywhere. They turned up at the Palladium and would end up at my gate at Winchmore Hill, at two o'clock in the morning, maybe when Cliff came home from a party after the show, they would be waiting for him. He'd wake me and say: "Mum, can you give them a pot of tea? Give them some blankets and they can sleep downstairs." And they would do it. Often I would go out to the gate to them, and say that Cliff would not come home for a long time and they really should go. They would say that they'd go, but they never did ...'

At the end of 1963 he bought *Rookswood*, a six bed roomed Tudor style mansion set in eleven acres in Upper Nazeing, Essex, where he lived with his mother and sisters. Elsewhere in this book local 'Bobby' Bill Traigis remarks on the problems Cliff had with girls, and in his *My Life, My Way* Cliff says, 'Fans had made life difficult for us and our neighbours at the previous house in Winchmore Hill and that was part of the reason for the move. The new home gave us much more privacy but it still seemed to attract fans, who would often march down the drive and invade us.'

And with Cliff leaving Winchmore Hill, we shall leave his life story. He is remarkable in having been so successful in this country, and many others, for so long. I thought it might be interesting to list a few of the big hit singles he had in his period of residence in the suburb, with his highest chart placing in brackets according to *The Guinness Book of Hits of the 60s,* by Tim and Jo Rice, Mike Read and Paul Gambaccini:-

Please Don't Tease (1), *Nine Times Out of Ten* (3), *I Love You* (1), *Theme for a Dream* (3), *Gee Whiz It's You* (4), *A Girl Like You* (3), *The Young Ones* (1), *Do You Wanna Dance* (2), *It'll Be Me* (2), *Bachelor Boy* (1), *Summer Holiday* (1), *Lucky Lips* (4), *Don't Talk To Him* (2). These were all made with The Shadows, who went on to great success and fortune in their own right, but according to Bruce Welsh, in his autobiography, in 1959 the group were paid only £24 *between them* for playing on Cliff's first hit album.

So Cliff, one of the country's most successful singers, once lived in Winchmore Hill. The drummer on many of his early hits went to school there, and enjoyed the local cinema. Brian Bennett was born in London on 9th February 1940. After a 6 month spell as an evacuee in Worksop, Notts., he moved to rented accommodation in New Southgate with his Mum, his father serving abroad in the Army.

His father returned from the forces six years later, and the Bennett family moved to Farndale Avenue, near Barrowell Green. Brian says, 'Saturday was the big night out for us: after my face had been scrubbed to make me a cherubic pink colour, and I'd made exaggerated sound effects in the bathroom to give the impression that I was cleaning my teeth, I'd be off to the Capitol Cinema at Winchmore Hill. As with most picture houses in those days, there was a fantastic restaurant where you'd order up expensive looking cakes, toast and tea cakes and be served by waitresses in smart hats and black and white uniforms. Then with your tummy almost busting through your blazor buttons, you'd be plunged into the subdued lighting of the cinema, to the strains of an old boy pounding away like the Phantom of the Opera on the theatre organ. They were magic, those nights at Winchmore Hill!' The Capitol is shown at Plate 64.

Brian was by then attending Hazelwood Lane School and his father was establishing his printing company Arnos Press. He failed his eleven plus and ended up at Winchmore Hill School, Highfield Road, where, surrounded by fellow music enthusiasts, he procured a drum kit and joined the school orchestra as drummer. In order to find the money to enhance his drum kit he took on a paper round, which included the house Cliff would move to eight years later!

Brian left school without any qualifications at the age of 14 and formed his own music trio. In 1956 he joined a skiffle group that had a season in Ramsgate, Kent. Nothing came of that, and a while later he entered a talent contest in Edmonton, where rivals included Hank Marvin and Bruce Welsh of The Railroaders. There was still no 'break though', and in 1959 Brian joined the Wildcats, who backed Mart Wilde, with another future Shadow, Brian 'Licorice' Locking, on bass. Their version of *A Teenager In Love* got to No.2 whilst Cliff and The Drifters (soon to be renamed The Shadows) were at No. 1 with *Living Doll.* Marty and The Wildcats had two further big hits that year, and in December Brian married Margaret, who he had met at the 2i's. The reception was held at The Palm Court Restaurant, Palmers Green.

Brian earned an apparently decent, but relatively anonymous, living in the music industry in the succeeding months, but this all changed when Tony Meehan left The Shadows. Bruce Welsh invited Brian in as his replacement, and in October 1961 Brian Bennett started his career as part of one of the most distinctive and successful musical acts this country has seen. His first appearance on a Shadows record was on *Stars Fell On Stockton*, the 'B' Side of *Wonderful Land*, which topped the charts for eight consecutive weeks in the Spring of 1962.

A catalogue of The Shadows' career is not appropriate to this book, even though I have been a lifelong fan of theirs. Before those other favourites of mine, The Beatles, were known nationally, The Shadows pioneered the now well worn line up of bass, rhythm and lead guitars with drums, and wrote hit songs. They inspired me to pester my father for a £6 acoustic on which I learnt the same three chords as Status Quo, though with somewhat less success. They also inspired more gifted youngsters who were later to pay tribute to Hank and colleagues, including Mark Knopler, Peter Green, Brian May, Pete Townsend and Eric Clapton. The Shadows helped establish the iconic Fender Stratocaster as one of rock's most favoured guitars. You can read more about them in the books I cited at the start of this account.

In *My Life, My Way* Cliff says, 'Brian Bennett now writes scores for television programmes and is very successful. He has a house in Portugal near mine and we see each other from time to time. His son, Jonathan, a tennis pro, comes across and coaches me when I'm there.' His son Warren Bennett is a professional musician and joined his father and Sir Cliff Richard on stage during their sell out 50th Anniversary Tour.

Paul Scott

Scott only resided in what I would consider Winchmore Hill for a short while, but attended school there, thus justifying his inclusion here. For this section I rely principally on *Paul Scott's Raj* by Robin Moore, published by Heinemann in 1990 (ISBN 0-434-47588-2).

Paul Mark Scott was born on the 25th March 1920 in an upstairs bedroom at 130, Fox Lane, Palmers Green. His father had been born in Leeds in 1871, his mother Frances Mark had been born in London in 1886. The three of them, along with Paul's older brother Peter, stayed at this rented semi detached until 1933. In 1936 the family moved to 15, Cannon Road in Southgate.

When he was six years old Paul was sent to The College, in Fox Lane, which was the preparatory part of the Collegiate School, to which he progressed in 1929 together with Peter. This school, at the top of Farm Road, i.e. near The Broadway (Plate 65), was intended for 'the sons of gentlemen', though Paul's father could barely afford it. In her *Paul Scott: A Life,* Hilary Spurling tells us a little about his days at the school.

Hilary says that Paul was remembered as something of 'an outsider'. He was inseparable from brother Peter, but otherwise he was quiet, and kept to himself, excepting their friendship with Geoffrey Ridehalgh, in Geoffrey's last year of 1930-1. The basis of their relationship with him was probably that he too didn't like team games. Geoffrey remembered Paul as a good story teller and mimic, with a great interest in film making. Given his lack of talent at football, it is perhaps surprising that Paul was very good at the individual athletic events of the high jump, 100 yards, and 220 yards. In studies he was, 'always a shinning light in class', and could memorise any passage after only a single reading. By the time he was fourteen he was writing 12 page essays, which would clearly amuse the class if he read them aloud.

Unfortunately, because of his family's financial problems Paul had to leave school at fifteen without qualifications, and so found it difficult to get a job. In due course he was taken on by the accountant C.T. Payne at Regent's Arcade House in Regents Street where he worked, apart from the war years, for the next 25 years.

In 1937 he won the Royal Society of Accountant's Silver Medal for advanced accounts. He was also reading widely, and writing poems, plays and a novel. Apparently he led a merry social life, which involved attendance at the Proms and Saddlers Wells. His first published works were letters of film criticism in the *Picturegoer.* In June 1939 he moved with his family to his last pre war home at 63, Bourne Hill – on the fringes of our suburb. Here his neighbours Ruth and Clive Sansom encouraged his literary efforts.

In 1940, after toying with the idea of becoming a conscientious objector, he joined the army. On 17th July he enlisted as a volunteer private in the Royal East Kent Regiment at Slough, rising to brigade intelligence sergeant. On 23rd October 1941 he married nurse Nancy Edith Avery in a little church in Torquay, Devon.

In late 1942 he volunteered for India and became an officer cadet at Wrotham. He sailed for Bombay, as Mumbai was then called, in February 1943, with about a hundred other cadets, and spent several weeks at a camp in Cape Province, soon being based at Belgaum, where he learnt basic Urdu. He spent six months there, sharing quarters with his friend Robert Mason. Moore alleges that Scott and his writer friend James Leasor, cheated at exams by standing in for each other. It seems that Scott hated Belgaum, perhaps because he contracted jaundice whilst there, and because he was afraid of the locals, who were following Gandhi's 'Quit India' campaign. Fortunately, though, he got on with his brother officers.

He was subsequently posted to Bengal, and other places, meeting a variety of people who gave him ideas for characters in his books. In the summer of 1945 Scott's division was posted to Malaya. He arrived in Singapore just after the surrender to the Japanese. By then he realised that he had fallen in love with India, and he obtained a posting back there until his demob. He deplored the 'continued arrogance, extravagance and domination of the white Raj', and this influenced his later writings.

On 18th June 1946 the Permanent Under Secretary of State for India wrote to Scott to thank him for his services to his country and to grant him release with the honorary rank of captain. He arrived home with a cheque for £98. 5s to cover his service, including forty months as sergeant and thirty months as a commissioned officer. This was not enough, as one would well imagine, to enable him to easily start a life in literature , especially as his wife was newly pregnant. He turned down a job at £6 a week with Brown Shipley, and another in the accounts department of the RAF Malcolm Club in Belgravia. He was hired as a bookkeeper by an officer who had published his poems in a wartime broadsheet. His name was Captain Peter Baker, founder and chairman of a London publishing firm, Falcon Press.

Paul resumed his accountancy studies, and though he never qualified he became secretary of Baker's four associated publishing companies. He resigned in 1950 and wrote *Lines of Communication,* set in India, which was accepted by the BBC and broadcast on radio in February 1951. He began then, also, a career as a literary agent to such authors as Muriel Spark. During the 1950s Eyre and Spottiswoode published his *Johnnie Sahib, The Alien Sky, A Male Child, The Mark of the Warrior* and *The Chinese Love Pavilion.*

By the late 1950s Scott was feeling disillusioned with Britain, and wasn't helped, Moore says, by, 'his self image of "the Fat Boy of Dean Street", carrying two extra stone of agent's fat.' Scott therefore jumped at an offer by American publisher William Morrow in 1959 to guarantee him an income of £1,800 per annum over three years, to be set against any literary earnings during the period, establishing him as a full time author. When the agreement took effect in March 1960 he resigned his partnership with David Higham Associates. He was now living in Hampstead Garden Suburb.

Scott wrote *The Birds of Paradise,* published in 1962, which was his first novel set in a civilian Indian background. He declined Muriel Spark's suggestion that he move to Macmillan, but in 1962 he signed to Secker and Warburg, publishing *Bender* in 1963, and *Corrida* in 1964, the year that he moved to Secker's parent company, William Heinemann. It was in February of that year that he went out to India again, and was appalled at the way that the British residents lived parallel lives (as we would now say) to the indigenous peoples. He thought that race relations were worse than under the Raj, and in April he left, feeling that he now had enough raw material to underpin his *Raj Quartet.*

He began research for *Jewel in the Crown,* the first of the quartet, in June 1964, and set the book in India during and after the Great War. The central character was named Ronal Merrick. In October 1964 he was an active constituency worker for the Liberal Party during the General Election, putting in a twenty one hour stint on polling day.

The second of the quartet was entitled, *The Day of the Scorpion,* which he completed in December 1967. It had been intended to take the reader to India's Independence Day of 1947, but he ran out of space before even reaching the end of the Second World War! Scott's theme was that the Raj did not really manage to unify or unite the country, which fell into a religiously based civil war upon achieving independence.

Unfortunately 1968 was proving to be a nightmare for him, with his mother, wife, and younger daughter all suffering severe illness. He was also beset by household repairs, whilst he was struggling with the construction of *The Towers of Silence,* the third book in what had originally been intended as a trilogy, ending with the independence of 1947. When completed in December 1970 the book was quite different to what he had originally intended, and took a look at the way that the British in India differed from their brethren at home. The hardback edition sold only 5,000 copies in Great Britain.

Scott visited India again in 1972, but it was another year that must have strained his nerves. The day before he left for the sub continent his daughter miscarried in the psychiatric ward of the Middlesex Hospital, whilst he had to resign from the Society of Authors as he couldn't afford the subscription. He was now working on the final book of the Raj Quartet - *A Division of Spoils.* This last title appears in two books of different sizes. The first is set in 1946, the second in the period June to August 1947. Sales in Britain and America were disappointing.

As no British University ever approached him, Scott sold his manuscripts to the University of Texas, and he did a three week lecture tour of the USA which earned him a mere $583 net. Scott returned to live unobtrusively, rarely leaving his house in Hampstead Garden Suburb. In February 1975 he temporarily set *Mango Rain* aside, and started *Staying On,* which he described as, 'a comic novel which I think of as an Indian version of *The Bender* ..... set in 1972, in a place where the last of the stayers – on from the old Raj are fading rapidly away ....' It was published in 1977, and in November of that year it won him the Booker Prize.

Despite this late recognition of his talents it seems that Paul's life was far from ideal. His youngest daughter's illness was a worry from 1968, whilst relations with his wife were often strained, perhaps exacerbated by his heavy drinking. His financial situation seems to have been constantly strained. For the period 1965 – 75 his highest annual taxable income was £3,032, his lowest £1,999. As late as 1975-6 his total pre tax income was only £3,324. Of that, £1,164 was earned by reviewing, £360 from lecturing in the USA. The pre tax income from his twelve novels, all still in print, was a mere £1,800!

It is probably no surprise to learn that in mid July 1976, just before embarking on a lecture tour of the USA, to earn some money, that his wife of 36 years left him. In October 1977, whilst on another American tour, he went into hospital to have surgery for cancer. He was reunited with his wife on his homecoming, but died in Middlesex Hospital on 1st March 1978.

None of the *Raj Quartet* novels sold more than 10,000 hardbacks in Paul's lifetime, but when Granada screened their adaptation in early 1984 they attracted up to eight million viewers, and Scott's reputation was secured. As Scott's inclusion in this book is primarily due to his attendance at The Collegiate School in Winchmore Hill, let us now take a look at that institution.

The Collegiate School, Winchmore Hill

This account is based on *All Our Yesterdays – A History of the Winchmore Hill Collegiate Schools 1906 – 1963* by Roger Mansfield (1995). The School is pictured at Plate 65 in an era when the road and pavement were merged into one.

The school was founded by the New River in 1906 by John Stephen Temblett – Wood, and his wife Jessie Louise, on what would become the junction of Farm Road and Queens Avenue. They had arrived in the district in 1901 after he had served as a Senior Tutor at Archbishop Tennyson's School in Leicester Square. It was one of several private schools started in London about this time with the object of producing well rounded individuals, who would be well behaved, mannered and spoken. In a nutshell, 'little gentlemen'. The school motto was *Conjuntis Viribus,* meaning "all pull together".

The School Prospectus for 1908 boasts that,

'The Winchmore Hill Collegiate Schools provide a high school education for 150 boys and 100 girls from 5 – 18 years of age. The school premises are specially built, are modern in every respect, and consist of two main classrooms, cloak rooms, lavatories, cycle stores, asphalted playground, and sports grounds of three acres. The boys' schoolroom is built over the girls' schoolroom, and each classroom subdivides by use of revolving shutters and glass partitions into smaller classrooms. Each main schoolroom is supplied with proper, efficient and up to date cloak rooms and lavatories, and the ventilating arrangements are perfect.

The Headmaster's house adjoins the school buildings, and in it special accommodation has been made for weekly and termly boarders. There is a boys' dormitory and a girls' dormitory on separate floors. Details of the staff, premises, work (courses and subjects), hours, regulations, fees, etc. can be had upon application, or a personal interview (with inspection of the premises) given by the secretary at any time. Admission cannot be guaranteed for any particular term until the result of the candidate's entrance examination is known.'

Clearly there were girls as well as boys to begin with, but Mansfield's researches led him to conclude that the last of these in the senior school probably attended in the early 1920s. The boys at this time wore grey school blazers, grey shorts, and striped red, white and black school ties. They wore the black school cap with its red piping, and school badge on the front, and even had swimming trunks in the school colours for their visits to the Barrowell Green swimming baths every Friday morning in the summer term. Except for prefects pupils wore Eaton collars until the early 1920s.

Mansfield says that the ethos of the school can be gauged from the fact that one boy was expelled for telling lies to one of the senior masters. Team spirit was encouraged by games such as cricket, football, and hockey, whilst arguments could be settled under supervision in the boxing ring. The following is an extract from the school prospectus sent out in the 1930s, 'The school teaches the need for serving the community and sacrificing personal interests for the common good, but at the same time it accepts the modern theory of education and begins at training and understanding the individual ...' In that decade there was a Meccano Club at the school.

During the war John Churchin, a former pupil from Old Park Ridings, lost his life as a Spitfire pilot in the Battle of Britain, whilst Ramsey Aitken, whose parents ran *The Woodman,* joined the Black Watch, and was killed in action. One pupil living in Farm Road remembered that one morning he woke up to find his kitchen windows blown in, this being perhaps a lucky near miss, because there were craters in the playing fields of Highfield Road School where bombs had landed. Clifford Goodall recalled the ceiling plaster on the school desks following the blast from the bombs, and the boys throwing it at each other.

There was a Royal Observer Post on top of the Capitol cinema, which would trigger an air raid siren at the police station near The Broadway if enemy planes were presenting a danger. There was an air raid shelter in the Paulin Ground, and in 1949 some of the boys decided to destroy this 'eye sore', with partial success.

Roger Mansfield recounts a prank from the late 1950s or early 1960s which he swears to be true. It seems that one boy managed to string several bangers together, served by one continuous fuse, and put them under the window sills of the NatWest Bank that used to be situated on the corner of Fords Grove and Green Lanes.

He lit the fuse and then, using a megaphone from the opposite bank of the New River, shouted 'This is a hold up, come out of the bank with your hands up! I repeat, this is a hold up!' The Bank Manager and all his staff, obviously alarmed at the sound of the exploding fireworks, came out of the front door with their hands up, exactly as requested, only to find thin air. After a short interval they sheepishly lowered their hands and went back inside. The prankster had forewarned his schoolmates, and some of them enjoyed the stunt from a nearby viewing point.

It is clear from this episode, and the tone of Mr. Mansfield's book, that the school by this late stage had declined in ethos and academic reputation, with the staff even burning the school records in the final week in 1963. A sad end for a school that was started to help groom local boys 'to be gentlemen'.

Leslie Smith

I can remember delivering a copy of my *A Look at Old Winchmore Hill* to Leslie Smith on Broad Walk, in response to an order from him, though I didn't know until his death was announced in the papers, a few years later, what he had achieved. The following is based on articles in;- *The Enfield Gazette* of 14th May 1992; *The Gazette* for Thursday 9th June 2005; *The Enfield Independent* of 27th July 2005; The Daily Telegraph of 10th June 2005, and *Matchbox Toys* by Bruce and Diane Stoneback (Apple Press 1993 ISBN 1-85076-441-7).

Leslie Smith was born in Enfield as the son of a carpenter and jobbing builder on 6th March 1918, being brought up in Palace Gardens, and he remained within the area all his life. Like so many of that era he left school at 14 and worked as an office boy in the accounts department of J.R. Wilson and & Co., a London confirming house which specialised in shipping items to Australia, New Zealand and the Far East. Smith attended night school to study book keeping and moved on to the buying department, where he learnt about factory operations, and began travelling. He joined the Royal Navy as a signals rating in 1940, his first posting being to the converted trawler *Phineas Beard,* which he left a week before it was bombed and sunk. After being commissioned at HMS King Alfred, Brighton, he commanded a motor torpedo boat on the Dieppe Raid. He subsequently served in landing craft at Sicily and Salerno, before commanding a minesweeper off Gold Beach on D-Day.

In January 1947, further to his return from service in the Royal Navy, he and childhood friend Rodney Smith – no relation – invested their combined service gratuities of £600 in a die-casting company which they set up in a bombed out public house called *The Rifleman's Arms* in Edmonton, where they were charged £2 a week rent. They bought their first die casting machine from Rodney's former employer and named the company Lesney after combining the first and last part of their first names. The company used zinc to make car engine parts until the government commandeered all of the metal for the Korean War, whence Rodney emigrated to Australia. But they had been joined by an engineer name Jack Odell, who loved model making, having made his first miniature vehicle for his daughter when she was told she couldn't bring any toy into her school unless it fitted into a matchbox!

They soon started producing models of steamrollers, tractors, dumpers and cement mixers, before moving on to a model for the Queen's Coronation Coach in 1953. They miniaturised these early models, thus launching the famous Matchbox series. The popularity of the expanding range meant production was extended to factories around the South East, which brought Lesney a fortune. However, Mr. Smith remained concerned for the welfare of his employees and organized buses for women on his Staff so that they could pick up their children from school. The Company was floated on the stock exchange in 1960, and continued to expand until 1968, the year that Leslie and Jack Odell each got an OBE. Their company was now worth £120 million – about a third of the value of British Leyland.

That seems to have been about the high point of their success. In 1969 the American company Mattel made 'Hot Wheels' in Hong Kong, and with its low friction wheels changed the market almost overnight, especially in the USA, where Matchbox Toys held 40% market share. Leslie considered moving production to Hong Kong, but declined to do so for fear of inferior workmanship and out of loyalty to his employees in their Hackney factory. During the following year Lesney automated their production, which enabled them to compete, and the company prospered, whilst Smith and Odell reduced their own salaries from £100,000 to £25,000 each.

The company expanded its range to include Superfast cars, Tomcat fighter aircraft and dolls. By 1980 Lesney employed more than 10,000 people worldwide, operating from buildings with a total square footage equivalent to 30 football pitches, supplying 138 markets in the world. The company won the Queen's Award for Export on five occasions. Unfortunately the company experienced the Trade Union militancy that had wreaked havoc in British industry in the 1970s, whilst there were financial problems. The banks would not continue to support the business, and in 1982 it was sold to Universal Toys of Hong Kong. Matchbox toys continue to be manufactured by the American company Mattel, in the Far East. Speaking to the Southgate Rotarians in 1992 Leslie complained of Government policies which had led to greatly fluctuating exchange rates.

Leslie retired, but his son Andrew said that he was nearly as active in retirement as he was when working! He was a keen yachtsman, and developed a successful marina at Poole in Dorset. He tended his two acre garden in Broad Walk, and was seemingly a great one for helping people. He opened up the swimming pool attached to his house to children from local schools and Scout Clubs from across the Borough. He Chaired the Board of Governors at a school in the poor East London area of Brick Lane, and also served as a Governor at St. Paul's School in Ringwood Way, helping to steer them out of debt. He also used to help out at St. Paul's Church.

It was fitting that Leslie's funeral, following his death from cancer, aged 87, on 26th May 2005, was held at St. Paul's. His wife Nancy predeceased him in 1969. The Daily Telegraph records that in later life he had to buy each of his two sons and his daughter a set of Matchbox models from a dealer because he had never bothered to collect them himself!

Stevie Smith

In September 2005, along with dozens of others, I attended the unveiling of an English Heritage plaque to Stevie Smith at 1, Avondale Road. (See Plate 66.) The plaque was unveiled by the then Poet Laureate, Andrew Motion, and reads, 'English Heritage. Stevie Smith 1902 – 1971 Poet lived here 1906 – 1971'. Although Avondale Road is post coded N13, I have always considered it to be within the bounds of the old village, whose southern boundary seems to lie naturally at The Bourne/Bourne Hill. I therefore feel it is appropriate to include the famous poet in this book. For the following I have relied mainly on *Stevie Smith: A Critical Biography* by Frances Spalding, published by Faber & Faber Ltd. in 1988 (ISBN 0-571-15207-4). (I have refrained from quoting from Stevie's work for fear of infringing copyright.)

Stevie's mother, Ethel Spear, was aged 22 when she married Charles Ward Smith on 1st September 1898. Stevie was born with the name Florence Margaret Smith in Hull on 20th September 1902, and was not known as Stevie until the 1920s, when, riding over a London Common, some boys called out, 'Come on, Steve,' alluding to the then well known jockey Steve Donaghue, whose fringe stood on end when he rode.

It seems that the marriage between Ethel and Charles broke down, and he left for a life at sea, initially with the White Star Line as a pantry boy. Ethel's sister Margaret (Madge) came to live with her, and they came south to 1, Avondale Road in 1906, when Stevie was just three years of age. The area was, of course, then still very rural.

At the age of five Stevie developed a rare form of tuberculosis and was sent to a sanatorium at Broadstairs in Kent, where she stayed for three years, returning home, it is said, only in the summer holidays. At the age of nine, having left Broadstairs, she entered Palmers Green High School, known locally as 'Miss Hum's'. It had opened in 1905 with twelve pupils in a small private house on the corner of Osborne Road and Green Lanes, soon over spilling to the house next door. Stevie was considered to be one of the brighter pupils, and showed a penchant for drawing. She took part in many plays, and generally her home life was apparently happy, despite financial strains, and her mother's poor health.

St. John's Church (see Plate 67), around the corner in Green Lanes, played a leading role in Stevie's young life, both spiritually and socially. She also enjoyed playing in the nearby Winchmore Hill Wood and she said 'paradise' was, 'that part of the wood which lay just behind the railway cutting, an open pleasant place it was with a little stream, all open and sunny as the day itself. But behind that again lay the dark wood, with the trees growing close together, the dark holly trees, the tall beeches and the mighty oak trees.'

Stevie generally liked life in the area and was always grateful that the local Council bought land from the Taylor family and preserved it as Grovelands (opened on 12th April 1913). She particularly liked walking in it when the weather was poor, writing, 'When the wind blows east and ruffles the water of the lake, driving the rain before it, the Egyptian geese rise with a squawk, and the rhododendron trees, shaken by the gusts, drip the raindrops from the blades of their green-black leaves. The empty park, in the winter rain, has a staunch and inviolate melancholy that is refreshing. For are not sometimes the brightness and busyness of suburbs, the common life and the chatter, the kiddy cars on the pavements and the dogs, intolerable?'

Stevie got top marks in the Oxford Local Examinations for the Enfield area in the summer of 1916, and the following year won a school prize for literature. In September 1917 she followed her sister Molly to North London Collegiate, Camden, but she didn't do well there. During her time there the family received occasional visits from three soldiers who were convalescing at Grovelands Hospital. (See Plate 94.) One of these was Sydney Scheckell, a Lieutenant in the Lincolnshire Regiment who had been wounded in the Battle of the Somme. After his death in 1968 she wrote a poem about him entitled, *A Soldier Dear To Us.*

Stevie's mother Ethel died on 6th February 1918, at about the same time as she had re-established a relationship with her father, though it seems she didn't like him. She and her sister left North London Collegiate in July 1920, whence Stevie trained at Mrs. Hoster's Secretarial Academy. Her first job was with an engineering firm for a year, followed by an appointment as Secretary to Sir Neville Pearson of Pearson's Publishing, later amalgamated with Newnes. She remained there for 30 years!

By the late 1920s Stevie had a range of acquaintances. Amongst them was Rosemary Cooper, a young woman who worked on magazines and was to become editor in chief of the Commonwealth editions of *Vogue.* She lived with her parents at 110, Woodberry Avenue and first met Stevie at a dance held by the *Sixteen Plus* social club run by St. Paul's Church in Winchmore Hill. Miss Cooper was quite scathing about Stevie, saying that at first sight she was, 'a drab looking little person who didn't appear to have much character and at a dance was almost invisible,' and, 'a rather pathetic little creature' who was not enjoying herself. However, their relationship obviously improved later on, because when Stevie's Aunt Margaret became severely invalided and Stevie was away, Rosemary would look in on her.

In 1924 Stevie joined the Choral Society and its conductor Maurice Jacobson, along with his wife Suzannah, soon numbered amongst these early acquaintances. To begin with they lived in Aylesbury, but then moved to London and invited Stevie to their parties. Maurice had been a child prodigy, playing all of Bach's 48 Preludes and Fugues, and all of Beethoven's sonatas, from memory by the age of sixteen. Among those he discovered was Kathleen Ferrier, who he accompanied at her first London recital.

When Maurice and Suzannah read her *Novel On Yellow Paper* they instantly recognised themselves as Herman and Rosa, and were astonished by the negative portrayals. They also objected to Pompey's (i.e. Stevie's) moment of elation at the start of the book when she noticed that she was the only non Jew at a party and observed, 'Hurrah to be a goy. A clever goy is cleverer than a clever Jew.' The Jewish Jacobsons had nothing to do with Stevie for more than thirty years.

Another Jewish friend, Ionee Massada, also broke with Stevie. Perhaps Stevie had foreseen these reactions, because she had begun her book with, 'Goodbye to all my friends, my beautiful and lovely friends ....' Frances Spalding says that although Stevie owned a copy of an anti Semitic tract by Hilaire Belloc, 'she never displayed anti Semitic tendencies in her life.'

In the summer of 1927 Stevie went on holiday with her sister and aunt to Cornwall, where she met a woman named Joan Prideaux, as well as her parents and cousins. Joan and Stevie found that they worked in the same area of London, and so agreed to keep in touch. Over the next ten years they did just this, sometimes at lunchtime, sometimes in the evening. Surprisingly, Joan said that Stevie never talked about poetry, and reported that, 'Her job suited her well. She liked and got on quite well with Neville Pearson, it was not too demanding, and left time for her to do her own work, and for those days, was reasonably well paid and her means of support.'

It was during this period that Stevie apparently turned her back on Christianity, and declared herself to be an agnostic. She became friendly with a German called Karl Eckinger, who is the Karl in *Novel on Yellow Paper.* On 13th September 1929 she posted a card to Molly from Berlin, and visited Germany again two years later. The economic crisis in the winter of 1929-30 had allowed a surge in power for the Nazis, and anti Semitism was now evident. She was therefore now uncomfortable with Eckinger's idolization of German culture, and by the time she wrote *Novel on Yellow Paper,* five years later, she realised the culture had been hijacked by fascism.

She became friendly with the local Mitchell family, including the brothers Charles and David. The former became an art historian, and David a philosophy don. Through them she met the Flower family, who she regularly visited at their home in Ullswater Road, Southgate. In her novel *Over the Frontier* Charles Mitchell is cruelly characterised as 'young professor Dryasdust', whose cleverness is entirely derived from books. This was quite cruel, but clearly typical of the authoress.

Her best documented admirer appears to be Frederick Hyde Armitage, also confusingly known as Eric, the son of a Palmers Green solicitor. The family was associated with St. John's Church, which might have been where the couple met. 'Eric' spent his entire working life with the insurance giant Guardian Royal Exchange. He was, apparently, tall and good looking, with a neat conservative appearance. Doreen Diamant remembered her surprise when Stevie said, 'What do you think – I'm engaged!'. Joan Prideaux thought that he was the last sort of man she would want to marry. Whilst the engagement lasted sister Molly made her disapproval public. Frederick/Eric appears rather obviously in *Novel on Yellow Paper* as 'Freddy'. Frances Spalding says the substance of his character was diminished by, 'Stevie's light, mocking style'.

In about 1935 'Eric' took a more suitable woman as his wife, and they moved to Potters Bar, though he and Stevie never completely lost touch, and she remained in contact with his sister Dora, who married Winchmore Hill solicitor Frank Vanderpump. She would occasionally call on them on Sunday mornings for sherry, and though they enjoyed her company, they never took her poetry seriously.

After Karl and 'Eric' ceased to be central to her life Stevie depended more on her female friends. The two closest to her in the latter part of the 1930s were Inez Holden and Olivia Manning. According to Sally Chilver, Inez was 'a very brave and remarkable person' with whom Stevie enjoyed an 'easy and humorously argumentative friendship'. Stevie's friendships with both these women appear to have been marred by professional jealousy.

In the autumn of 1935 the *New Statesman and Nation* accepted six of Stevie's poems. Meanwhile she had begun *Novel on Yellow Paper,* and almost certainly finished it before Christmas. When the book appeared in September 1936 it won instant acclaim. It was only after this success that Stevie's poems were in demand. With help from Rupert Hart-Davis and Hamish Miles she eventually selected 76 compositions for her first book of poems, entitled *A Good Time Was Had By All*, which was published in the spring of 1937. Her next novel, *Over the Frontier*, hit the bookshelves in January 1938. Meanwhile she had poems published in a variety of outlets such as *The London Mercury.*

During this period Stevie became friendly with G.W. Stonier, of *The New Statesman* magazine. He was an Australian who had been educated at Winchester and Oxford, and he set tongues wagging by visiting Stevie at Avondale Road whilst her aunt was away, though subsequent visits were made whilst the aunt was at home. Her life, at the time, was very much based around parties, and her staid home life with her aunt gave a counterbalance. It seems aunt was particularly conservative in her tastes as she wouldn't have a wireless in the house because of the noise that it made, nor did she care much for the male sex.

The person that Stevie was seemingly most friendly with in the war years of 1939 – 1945 was Inez Holden, and it was probably through her that she met George Orwell and his wife Eileen. Her relationship with George has also prompted speculation, and the characters Basil and Tom in her book *The Holiday* are reputed to be partly based on him. No doubt there were further spicy rumours when the Indian novelist Mulk Raj Anand visited her at 1, Avondale Road. It was during the war that Stevie became friendly with the writer Cecily Mackworth, who commented on how sparsely she furnished her bedroom, which lacked even a bedside lamp. Meanwhile she assembled her next anthology of poems entitled, *Mother, What Is Man?*

Stevie was still taking walks in Grovelands Park, where she watched the Home Guard practise bringing in the wounded. In the mornings the air was sometimes filled with dust from bomb damaged buildings. She continued to make new friends, one of whom was Kay Dick, who was living with the novelist Kathleen Farrell, who also, therefore, became a friend. She became friendly with Norah Smallwood, who worked at the publishers Chatto and Windus, and Sally Chilver. When visiting Sally at Maida Vale her husband Richard encouraged her agnosticism. When Sally visited Stevie at Avondale Road her aunt took to her, as the pitch of her voice was amenable to her failing hearing. Stevie also fire watched in Central London.

According to Frances Spalding, soon after the War, whilst revising the manuscript to her last novel, *The Holiday*, Stevie had a brief affair with a woman who resided in Fitzroy Street, whom she had met through Inez Holden, though the real name of this flame is not disclosed. The affair lasted less than a year and was, it seems, ended by Stevie.

By the late 1940s Stevie was broadcasting on BBC radio. She produced *Syler's Green* on 5th August 1947, which is thought to be about her local childhood, and this was repeated on 26th December 1959. She read her story *Sunday at Home* on 20th March 1949, and then did three programmes entitled *Poems and Drawings*. She became friendly with the producer Anna Kallin, but they fell out and Stevie never did a programme of her own poems again until 1956.

Most of Stevie's eleven short stories were written in the 1940s. The late 1940s and early 1950s were an exasperating time for her, as she had so little of her poetry published, though in 1950 Chapman and Hall published her collection entitled *Harold's Leap*. Her novel *The Holiday* was published in 1949, and in it she abandons Pompey's world of publishing, to be the central character Celia Phoze, who works in a government ministry. Celia (i.e. Stevie) experiences a nervous breakdown and attempts suicide. *The Holiday* became a Book Society recommendation and sold well, but Stevie never produced another novel.

At Newnes Publishing her workmates Kay Dick and Barbara Vise moved on, leaving Stevie as something of a misfit. She often sat alone in the canteen. However, her close relationship with her aunt continued. She attended many parties and at one of these she met a senior Civil Servant named Ronald Orr-Ewing, who occasionally visited her in Avondale Road. She, in turn, occasionally visited him in Kensington Square. She also became friendly with the composer Elisabeth Lutyens, daughter of the famous architect Sir Edwin Lutyens, who set nine of Stevie's poems to music. Other friends at this time were Barbara and Alan Clutton – Brock of Chastleton House in Oxfordshire, and the Brownes and Buxtons on the Norfolk coast.

On 1st July 1953 Stevie appears to have attempted suicide by cutting one of her wrists. She had a breakdown and stayed in bed for three weeks. She recovered, but Newnes would not let her return to work, although they paid her until 31st December 1953, whence they paid her a pension of £5. 10s. 0d a week, rising by £2. 2s. 6d when she reached 60. So it was that Stevie retired to write in her dinning room, from where she made regular visits to the newsagents for cigarettes.

My 2004 *More Winchmore Hill Lives* featured Dorothy 'Babs' Collins, who was born in 1916 into the Fentum family that kept a newsagent by *The Dog and Duck*. 'Babs' says of Stevie in her account, 'She walked round every evening for her paper. I remember, she tended to dress in an unglamorous way and had an absent minded air, sometimes wandering past the shop door, deep in thought, before realising what she had done and retracing her steps.' Elsewhere in this volume is the account given by the Holstius sisters, where Joan (b. 1921) comments on Stevie's, 'slightly eccentric appearance'.

Frances Spalding reports that Stevie read George Gissing's *New Grub Street*, 'on the advice of her dentist, Wallace Finkel,' who was, I might mention, my dentist until his tragic death after, I was told, a wall collapsed on him. By 1955 her friendships with Olivia Manning and Sally Chilver were over.

The health of Stevie's aunt was declining, with arthritis afflicting her hips. However, professionally things were beginning to look up, because in 1955 David Wright took over as editor of *Nimbus* and published 14 of her poems in one issue. Her collection *Waving Not Drowning* was published in 1957, and the title piece is now so well known that Prime Minister David Cameron used it in one of his Parliamentary jousts with Ed Miliband in the autumn of 2010.

She was slowly becoming a public figure, and on 12th April 1956 she did a short broadcast of her poetry, followed later in the year by another titled, *Too Tired For Words*. In May 1959 she featured in the radio play *A Turn Outside,* and she even appeared on *The Brains Trust.* Her objection to religion did not always endear her to people, though. 1959 was the year of what she considered her least satisfactory publication, entitled *Cats in Colour.*

By now her GP Dr. James Curley, whose own recollections of the area are recorded in my *More Winchmore Hill Lives* of 2004, had become a personal friend. In January 1961 Stevie entered Wood Green and Southgate Hospital to have one of her knee caps removed, but in April she still had mobility problems. By 1962 her Aunt's health had deteriorated so much that she had to stay upstairs, and Stevie had to take her food to her. Despite her affection for her aunt, who was now in her 90s, the latter's immobility, deafness and other problems must have made life very difficult for Stevie, although she did have the help of a district nurse and a kindly neighbour named Mrs. Martin.

Stevie's *Selected Poems* appeared in the autumn of 1962, and for the remainder of the 1960s her work was extensively published in various magazines such as *The New Statesman, Listener* and *Times Literary Supplement.* By now, under the cumulative weight of all her efforts over the years, she had become a national public figure, and did many readings of her work up and down the country.

However, with her star rising in the public domain, it was sinking in the private one. In 1963 her sister Molly had a stroke at her home in Devon, where Stevie visited her from time to time. By 1964 she had become so tired from her efforts with her family that she was referred to a specialist at Guy's, who couldn't find any medical cause at the root of this. With hindsight it seems her tiredness might have been caused by a developing brain tumour.

Molly visited Avondale Road in February 1966 for their Aunt's 94th birthday, by which time Stevie herself was beginning to look aged. In February 1968 her Aunt had a stroke, and on 11th March died in hospital. To commemorate her life Stevie and Molly donated a small oak lectern to St. John's Church. Madge Spear made Stevie the sole Executor of her estate, which after tax amounted to £3,698.18s. 0d. Stevie was Madge's sole beneficiary. That same March Stevie did a ten minute interview for BBC TV's *Monitor*. She still didn't own a televison, and so went to see it on the Rev. Doyle's set, whence he told her she looked very ill.

Stevie worked on another radio programme titled *Poems and Conversations* with Douglas Cleverdon, which was broadcast on 3rd September 1968, repeated in a revised form that November. She produced a children's annual called *Allsorts.* In that book she says, 'In one of those parks which is called Grovelands, I spend a great deal of my present time. It has a very large deep lake with an island in the middle. Often I take a boat out and have a picnic lunch, first tying my boat up carefully to one of the trees that drop into the water from the lake's island, which is also where the swans have their house. In winters, if we have a hard winter, the lake will be frozen right across ....

......Our suburb is now a very much alive sort of place; there are clubs and societies for everything.....There are a great many Chinese, Indian and African people who have come to live here, and that makes it very much nicer, because there is so much variety in everybody's looks and interests, and all of it going on at the same time.

I do not know many people in Palmers Green very intimately, but I like living here and I like the people to talk to, in the shops and streets, and that is how *they* like it too. There is this politeness I notice. Everybody smiles and is friendly, but it is a sweet distant smile on our faces that we have. In trouble or difficulties we help each other a great deal, and then, when it is over, smile again this sweet distant smile. Sometimes I feel rather peculiar, as if I were looking out through a beautiful window at a distance that is full of amiability, but has cast a spell. I do not mind this; in fact rather like it.'

I moved to Radcliffe Road, Winchmore Hill in November 1972, not long after Stevie's demise. There was a small Cypriot community in Palmers Green, but Winchmore Hill was still inhabited overwhelmingly by Caucasian English speakers. When Yasmin joined me in Fernleigh Road, upon marriage in December 1981, there were still not many other Black or Asian people in Winchmore Hill, or indeed Palmers Green. So I would question Stevie's portrayal of the area in her time as being multicultural.

In May 1969 Molly had another stroke, which initially caused paralysis down her left hand side, and left her unable to speak, so Stevie spent much time in Devon with her. Molly slowly recovered her speech, and was able to walk with the aid of a three pronged stick, but her left arm remained permanently paralysed.

On 21st November 1969 Stevie went to Buckingham Palace to receive the Queen's Gold Medal for Poetry from Her Majesty, and this brought her considerable further publicity. She spent much of the summer of 1970 at Buckfast, Devon to be near her ailing sister, though she was far from a physically fit woman herself, with a mental disposition that required anti depressants.

In December 1970 whilst still at Buckfast she almost passed out, and then she could not speak properly or finish her sentences. On 27th December she wrote to Dr. Curley of her verbal problems and almost permanent exhaustion. The frequency of her fits soon increased and on the 6th January 1971 she was taken to Torbay Hospital in Torquay. She was subsequently taken to a hospital in Plymouth, where tests revealed a brain tumour too advanced for surgery. She was moved to the cottage hospital at Ashburton and died on 7th March 1971.

A play on her life called *Stevie,* was staged in London, and in 1979 this was made into a film starring Glenda Jackson. Stevie has been remembered locally long after her death, and in September 2002 there was a ten day festival to celebrate her life and works.

Note from the Author

Thank you for buying this book. I hope you enjoyed it's contents. If so, please consider the other publications available by post listed inside the front cover.